Perspectives on India's National Security Challenges

External and Internal Dimensions

Perspectives on India's National Security Challenges

External and Internal Dimensions

Editors

Shivendra Shahi

Amar Singh

PENTAGON PRESS

Perspectives on India's National Security Challenges: External and Internal Dimensions
Editors: Shivendra Shahi and Amar Singh

First Published in 2016

ISBN 978-81-8274-924-5

Disclaimer: The views expressed in this volume are of individual contributors and do not represent the viewpoint of the editors.

Published by
PENTAGON PRESS
206, Peacock Lane, Shahpur Jat,
New Delhi-110049
Phones: 011-64706243, 26491568
Telefax: 011-26490600
email: rajan@pentagonpress.in
website: www.pentagonpress.in

Printed at Aegean Offset Printers, Greater Noida

Contents

SECTION II
INTERNAL DIMENSIONS

Preface

India's peculiar position among its neighbours makes the question of its national security quite interesting. A declared nuclear power itself, India shares its borders with two other nuclear powers with whom it has fought wars in the past, i.e., Pakistan and China. Despite having a regional association for cooperation with its South Asian neighbours, India's relations with Pakistan and Bangladesh (erstwhile East Pakistan) have seen various ups and downs in the past. The Indian Diaspora in Nepal and Sri Lanka, i.e., *Madhesis* and *Tamils,* respectively, have been crucial in determining the terms between these countries, and the country has already lost one of its ex-prime ministers to the terrorism that came as a counter reaction to Indian intervention into the ethnic problem of Sri Lanka. India's preponderant size, relative to its neighbours, is one of the main causes of the stalemate in relationship.

The South Asian region is also known as a playground of the global powers. In its backyard, 'global war on terror' has been fought by US and its NATO allies. After 13 long years of war, the US is withdrawing its forces from Afghanistan. However, Afghanistan is still facing stiff challenges from the Taliban and Al Qaeda. Pakistan is not able to control its own homegrown terrorist groups like TPP (Tehrik-i-Taliban Pakistan) due to which its own stability is at stake. Both Pakistan and Afghanistan are countries very close to being called failed states. Ethnic problems have been troubling South Asian countries for decades. After eliminating LTTE, Sri Lanka is still not able to address the Tamil people's aspirations. A different problem has been witnessed in Nepal. The problem is promulgation of a new Constitution wherein *Madhesis* have not got a fair representation. Both Sri Lanka and Nepal continue to cope with the post conflict challenges of peace building. Bangladesh is more concerned with religious fundamentalism which affects the security of South Asia. Liberal voices are crushed. The so called peaceful rise of China and its One Belt One Road strategy is undermining India's role in South Asia and the Indian Ocean region.

The idea of bringing out a book on this subject originated from the fact that in the contemporary strategic environment, new security threats and challenges are emerging, both traditional and non-traditional ones.

Perceptions have a direct bearing in discussing security challenges. The interesting part of perceptions is the striking contrast between realism and idealism. The manner in which policies are projected and interpreted by States demonstrates a positive relationship between civil society, the political State and system of governance. India has been a victim of misperceptions in the past. The book is focused on the cooperative and competitive efforts of non-state actors in disturbing the conditions of peace, because of the gravity of the existing security dilemma and defence dilemma of nation states.

The contributors of the book have examined different dimensions of these problem areas and, therefore, the book has broadly been divided into two sections: (I) external dimensions; and (II) internal dimensions.

The present change in international perception about India, due to its rise as an emerging power, raises certain questions. It is the answer to these questions which form the focal theme of this book.

Shivendra Shahi

Amar Singh

Acknowledgements

We wish to extend our sincerest gratitude to all the contributors who have come together and laboured to examine the many facets of India's relations with its neighbours. We must acknowledge our heartfelt gratitude to Prof. Shekhar Adhikari and Prof. Sanjeev Bhadauria for their constant encouragement and support. Our appreciation is also due to Prof. R.N. Swarup, Prof. P.L. Dash, Prof. Rajendra Prasad, Prof. Savita Pandey, Prof. M.N. Varma, Prof. P. Agarwal, Prof. Rajesh Kharat, Dr. Shyam Kumar Singh, Dr. Manish Sri and Dr. Sanjay Jha for their kind support.

Our learning and this book could not have been completed without the help and support of our friends and colleagues especially Colonel Mohinder Pal Singh, Brigadier Narender Kumar (Retd.), Dr. Sharid Jamal Ansari, Dr. Sanchita Bhattacharya and Mr. Chirantan Kumar. A special thanks to Mr. Rajan Arya, Pentagon Press for publishing the book. His feedback and invaluable comments enhanced the quality of this work. Last, but not the least, we are grateful to our family members for showing great patience while the book was being completed.

Contributors

1. Amar Singh is a Researcher, Centre for South Asian Studies, School of International Relations, JNU, New Delhi.
2. Prashant Kumar is a Research Scholar, Centre for South Asian Studies, School of International Relations, JNU, New Delhi.
3. Awkash Kumar is a Research Scholar, School of International Studies, Central University of Gujarat, Gandhinagar.
4. Shivendra Shahi is a Post Doctoral Fellow, Department of Defence and Strategic Studies, University of Allahabad, Allahabad.
5. Shekhar Adhikari is a Professor and former Head, Department of Defence and Strategic Studies, University of Allahabad, Allahabad.
6. Atul Mishra is a Guest Faculty, I.S.D.C., University of Allahabad, Allahabad.
7. T. C. Karthikheyan is an Assistant Professor, School of Politics and Public Administration, Tamil Nadu Open University, Chennai.
8. Mohinder Pal Singh is an Army serving officer and Research Scholar at University of Allahabad, Allahabad.
9. B. C. Upreti is a Professor and Former Director, Centre for South Asian Studies, University of Rajasthan, Jaipur, Rajasthan.
10. Shreesh K. Pathak is an Assistant Professor, Galgotia University, Noida.
11. Sanchita Bhattacharya is a Post Doctoral Fellow, School of International Studies, JNU, and Visiting Fellow, Institute for Conflict Management, New Delhi.
12. Ravindra Prasad is a Research Fellow, Department of Defence and Strategic Studies, University of Allahabad, Allahabad.

13. Raghvendra Pratap Singh is a Research Fellow, Department of Defence and Strategic Studies, University of Allahabad, Allahabad.
14. Narender Kumar is a Senior Fellow, Centre for Land Warfare Studies (CLAWS), New Delhi.
15. Mayur Dumania is a Research Fellow, Centre for Studies in International Politics, School of International Studies, Central University of Gujarat, Gandhinagar.
16. Saurabh Sharma is an Assistant Professor, Centre for Studies in International Politics, School of International Studies, Central University of Gujarat, Gandhinagar.
17. Sanjeev Kumar Shrivastav is a Research Associate, Institute for Defence Studies and Analysis (IDSA), New Delhi.
18. P. L. Dash is a Visiting Professor, MEA Central Asia Program, CRRID, Chandigarh, India.
19. Rajendra Prasad is a Professor and Vice Chancellor, Allahabad State University, Allahabad.
20. Uddipan Mukherjee is a Researcher and presently an IOFS Officer, working under the Ordnance Factory Board, Ministry of Defence, Government of India.
21. T.K. Singh is an Assistant Professor, Department of National Security Studies, Central University of Jammu, Jammu.
22. Nanda Kishor MS is an Assistant Professor, Department of Geopolitical and International Relations, Manipal University and Post Doctoral Fellow (Erasmus Mundus) of Leiden Institute of Area Studies, Leiden University, Netherlands.

SECTION I

External Dimensions

1

India's Policy towards Afghanistan: Post-2014 US Withdrawal

Amar Singh

India and Afghanistan have a strong relationship based on historical and cultural links. India has played a significant role in the reconstruction and rehabilitation of Afghanistan. It is believed that democracy and development are the key instruments to ensure that Afghanistan becomes a source of regional stability. This has been reflected in the Strategic Partnership Agreement, signed between Afghanistan and India in October 2011, which reinforced the strong, vibrant and multi-faceted relations between the two countries and at the same time formalized a framework for cooperation in various areas between the two countries: political and security cooperation; trade and economic cooperation; capacity development and education; social, cultural, civil society and people-to-people relations. This agreement is a strong signal of India's abiding commitment to peace, stability and prosperity in Afghanistan during this critical period of security and governance transition. The commitment is also reflected in India's extensive developmental assistance programme, making India the 5th largest bilateral donor in Afghanistan after the US, UK, Japan and Germany. This, by any reckoning, is a substantial amount for a non-traditional donor like India.[1] India is showing some prioritization in its foreign policy matters. There is a new dynamism in neighbourhood ties as India is putting renewed emphasis on revitalizing its regional profile. India's neighbours, barring Pakistan, are certainly looking at

India with a new sense of expectation. New Delhi now has to operationalize the aspirations that have been articulated. Recognizing that the implementation phase has always been a problem for Indian credibility, the Indian government is focusing on completing projects in its neighbourhood that are already in the pipeline rather than announcing new ones. Afghanistan is now a critical challenge with the departure of Western forces. India will have to articulate its own role more cogently. India has immense goodwill in Afghanistan that it can leverage but that would mean stepping up its security role. Can the present government go beyond what the previous government has done on the security front? This will be critical as India's reputation as a regional security provider will be under scrutiny.[2]

Introduction

India's influence over Afghanistan, and vice versa, can be traced back to the Indus Valley Civilization. More recently, since the rise of Taliban, India has taken the stance of a friend who wants to help Afghanistan rise to its feet again. India did not recognize the Taliban led government to be a legitimate government. India's policy in Afghanistan is to prevent it from going back to the Taliban era while Pakistan favours Taliban (including its proxies) rule to have strategic depth inside Afghanistan. Pakistan feels threatened that if a pro-India government comes to power in Kabul then it could be strangulated from both sides. India favours democracy in Afghanistan as Taliban rule would mean another safe haven for Kashmiri terrorists. India enjoys cordial relations with Afghanistan. India wishes to see a stable government installed in Kabul that is independent of any external interference. India's role in rebuilding Afghanistan may go unnoticed in the international media but it creates a lot of goodwill for India among Afghans. A 2009 BBC/ABC News/ARD poll found that although only 8 percent of Afghans held a favourable view of Pakistan, 74 percent of Afghans viewed India favourably. Similarly, although 86 percent thought that Pakistan had a negative influence in Afghanistan (with only 5 percent saying Pakistan made positive contributions), India's impact was seen as positive by 41 percent of Afghans and negative by only 10 percent.[3]

Afghanistan's Strategic Importance for India

- Afghanistan's location at the strategic crossroads between South Asia and Central Asia, and South Asia and the Middle East makes the country extremely important for India.[4]

- Alexander Thier, an expert on Afghanistan at the United States Institute of Peace (USIP), says that Afghanistan looks to India as a 'potential counterweight in its relationship with Pakistan.' India's influence in Afghanistan waned in the 1990s after Pakistan-backed Taliban rose to power. By helping rebuild a new Afghanistan, India strives for greater regional stability, but also hopes to counter Pakistan's influence in Kabul. 'Indian officials strongly resist the idea that Pakistan should have veto power over its regional role,' said Alyssa Ayres, former US Deputy Assistant Secretary of State for South Asia.
- Afghanistan is a potential route for access to energy resources of Central Asian. India now, as a member in the Shanghai Cooperation Organization, has been pursuing better relations with Central Asian states for energy cooperation.
- 'Afghanistan has been a prize that Pakistan and India have fought over directly and indirectly for decades.' Pakistan supported the anti-Soviet mujahideen and then the Taliban 'to ensure that in the event of conflict with India, Afghanistan would provide Pakistan with support and use of its land and air space if needed. Pakistani military planners refer to this as the quest for "strategic depth." Pakistan's military establishment has always approached the various wars in and around Afghanistan as a function of its main institutional and national security interests:' first and foremost, balancing India.'[5]

US withdrawal from Afghanistan

In 2011, US President Barack Obama had approved plans to drawdown 10,000 US troops from Afghanistan during 2011 and another 23,000 in 2012. The withdrawal of the remaining combat troops was to be completed by December 2014. It was apprehended that NATO-ISAF withdrawal is likely to leave a security deficit in Afghanistan and there is a possibility of the situation deteriorating into a civil war. The fledgling Afghan National Army (ANA) and the Afghan National Police (ANP), which have now assumed full responsibility for security from the ISAF, are not yet equal to the task. Their numbers are small (352,000); they lack experience; they are inadequately trained and equipped. Hence, they are not yet capable of undertaking counter-insurgency operations autonomously and need more time to settle down as cohesive infantry battalions. While the ISAF forces control most of the large towns, the Taliban, together with the Al-Qaeda, control large swathes of the countryside, particularly at night. Governance is virtually non-existent outside Kabul.[6] Taking this into account, President Barack Obama reversing the policy on Afghanistan announced that he will prolong the 14-year-old US military engagement. Calling it a 'modest but meaningful' adjustment to winding down the American presence in Afghanistan, US will maintain a force of 9,800 through most of 2016. Under the new plan, troops will be drawn down to 5,500 starting sometime in 2017 and will be based at four locations—Kabul, Bagram, Jalalabad and Kandahar.[7] 'The bottom line is in key areas of the country, the security situation is still very fragile and in some places there is risk of deterioration, Afghan forces are still not as strong as they need to be ... meanwhile the Taliban has made gains.'[8]

Afghanistan's security situation has deteriorated as 92,000 innocent Afghans are believed to have been killed since 2001, while nearly 100,000 others have been wounded. Just recently, the number of conflict-related civilian casualties (deaths plus injuries) has almost doubled from 5,968 in 2009 to 10,548 in 2014, according to data compiled by United Nations Assistance Mission in Afghanistan (UNAMA). After the withdrawal, Afghan security forces are currently struggling to maintain a stalemate with insurgents after enduring a lethal Talibani spring offensive. Last year (in 2015) has already seen an increase of more than 50 percent in deaths of Afghan security forces as compared to the first six months of 2014, according to data accessed by The New York Times.[9]

Mapping Indian Engagement in Afghanistan

India has played a major role in the development and reconstruction of Afghanistan over the past decade. India is the fifth largest bilateral donor after the US, UK, Japan, and Germany. Not a donor country by tradition, it has provided Afghanistan aid mainly for projects in power, roads, agriculture, and education. India has provided thousands of scholarships to Afghan students and training grants for Afghan civil servants over the past few years, most of whom have returned to Afghanistan and are an important part of the current critical mass in the country. Afghanistan's new Rs 710-crore Parliament building, financed and constructed by India—part of a $2 billion (Rs 12,800 crore) aid package—is symbolic of India's support for strife-torn Afghanistan, as it struggles to transition into a stable democracy. India has given nearly Rs 2,000 crore ($300 million) in aid to Afghanistan over the past four years, after signing a Strategic Partnership Agreement in 2011. India has also funded the construction of other projects, including a Rs 1,500-crore dam in the Herat province in western Afghanistan. The dam will generate 42 mega watts (MW) for Afghanistan. The Indian government has spent Rs 476 crore between 2011-12 and 2014-15 to provide 250,000 metric tonnes of wheat to Afghanistan to overcome food shortages. India's Border Roads Organisation is building a 218 km, Rs 600 crore road from Zaranj to Delaram in south-western Afghanistan. This is a key link to Iran's Chahbahar Port via Afghanistan's garland highway, linking the Afghan cities of Herat, Kandahar, Kabul and Mazar-e-Sharif. It will also allow access to the landlocked Central Asian countries that border Afghanistan.[10]

Afghanistan is crucial to India's energy security as a pipeline from Turkmenistan to India, the TAPI project, will pass through the country (and Pakistan). Afghanistan also represents investment potential for Indian companies in several sectors. The country is home to resource deposits worth one trillion dollars, according to the US Geological Survey. A consortium of six Indian companies led by public-sector Steel Authority of India won a 2011 bid to mine steel in the province of Bamiyan; it will invest around $10.8 billion (Rs 69,120 crore). A consortium of Indian public and private companies has invested to develop the Hajigak iron ore mine in Afghanistan. India has also undertaken a range of small-scale development projects.[11] Some of them are:

- Funding for the Afghan Ministry of Health to build and maintain medical clinics,
- The construction of cold storage food warehouses in Kandahar,
- Construction on the Habibia School,
- Renovation of the Indira Gandhi hospital,
- Establishing an agricultural university and a mining school,
- Restoring the Stor Palace,
- 1,300 annual college scholarships and training grants for civil servants (a further 200 scholarships for agricultural degrees were provided from 2010),
- 20 Indian technical advisors in Afghan ministries under a trilateral agreement with the UNDP, and Capacity building for Afghan ministers.

A key focus for Indian engagement is the security relationship. India has agreed to increase training for Afghan soldiers and police within India following the strategic partnership agreed in October 2011. The agreement does not include the deployment of Indian combat troops in Afghanistan. In July 2013 it was reported that India had increased its training for Afghan troops from 574 in 2012 to more than 1,000 in 2013. India is aware that the situation in Afghanistan could deteriorate markedly. The withdrawal of most Western troops coupled with questions over the 2014 election both give grounds for concern. While India is investing heavily in measures to support the central government of Afghanistan, its response to the worst case scenario, the collapse of central government authority and return to full-scale conflict, is relatively easy to gauge. India's is already taking steps to reinvigorate its relationship by boosting its government-to-government relations with Central Asia and Iran.[12]

India's engagement with Afghanistan has made it a terror target. India's embassy in Kabul has been attacked in 2008 and 2009, as were the consulates in Herat (2014), Jalalabad (2013) and Jalalabad Consulate (January, 2016). India has accused Pakistan of being behind these attacks. But India will press ahead because Afghanistan is strategically important.[13] India has trained personnel of the Afghan National Army in Indian military institutions such as the Indian Military Academy. While India has provided military hardware such as trucks, jeeps and helicopters, it remains reluctant to provide 'lethal' weapons such as tanks and artillery guns, fearing they could fall into the hands of the Taliban.[14] But with the US withdrawing its forces from Afghanistan in a recent deal with Moscow, India has agreed to pay for military equipment sourced from Russia to Afghanistan. The equipment will include artillery, helicopters, tanks, and armoured vehicles. India will also pay to repair old Soviet hardware left behind after the Russian withdrawal in 1989. The scale and exact composition of the deal have yet to be announced, but it is known that the first order has already been placed. The reason behind that rethink is fairly simple, the winds of change that are blowing last year in Afghanistan. The ISAF is winding down its presence. Transitions have prompted Afghanistan's neighbours to accelerate their thinking about the future of the region. India has frequently expressed a desire to see the emergence of a strong, stable and independent Afghanistan. With foreign forces no longer taking the lead role, the only way to ensure stability in Afghanistan, and by extension in the region, is to help increase the capabilities of its young army. Other interests are also at stake. Any economic assistance provided by India to Afghanistan would be stripped of meaning if the latter was not strong enough to defend the products of the assistance. Moreover, India needs Afghanistan to be able to defend itself and not fall again to the Taliban.[15]

Regional Players in Afghanistan: Options Post US Withdrawal

India as a Responsible Regional Stakeholder

India's approach to its neighbourhood has swung in recent years. In the mid-1990s a policy of no reciprocity, the 'Gujral doctrine', reflected an understanding that India, as the dominant regional power, had a duty to support and accommodate its neighbours without necessarily expecting to receive reciprocal benefits. This policy stalled from the late-1990s as the government led by the Bharatiya Janata Party prioritized India's global rather than its regional importance. Since the change to a Congress Party-led government in 2004, India has generally shown renewed commitment towards its regional role and its Afghan policy is frequently justified in these terms. India frames its active role in Afghanistan on the grounds that social and economic development in Afghanistan is crucial to regional stability. The dynamics of the trilateral relationship between Afghanistan, India and Pakistan are complex and overlap other geopolitical rivalries and tensions. Initially, the US was concerned about Indian involvement in Afghanistan, largely reflecting Pakistani concerns. Now it wants more active Indian involvement, although with the caveat that the US recognizes Pakistan's likely concern at an Indian military presence in Afghanistan. India is highly unlikely to commit troops to a security role following the withdrawal of most Western troops and does not wish to take a unilateral security role in Afghanistan. This stems from long-standing memories of the ill-fated peace-keeping mission to Sri Lanka in 1987-90, and the recognition that this would raise tension with Pakistan. However, it has announced steps to upscale training for Afghan security forces. India remains somewhat sceptical that the West's long-term commitment to Afghanistan is genuine. C. Raja Mohan notes that 'the initial widespread concern in Delhi has now been replaced by a stoic resignation and determination to pursue its enduring interests in Afghanistan on its own steam.' While there is concern about a possible Taliban resurgence, for now there is a recognition that the West will continue to support the Afghan National Army. Furthermore, Pakistan's military will not be able to support the Taliban as it did in the 1990s.[16]

Iran and India in Afghanistan

Stabilising Afghanistan has long been a shared objective of India and Iran. It has become even more salient after the US ended its combat role at the end of last year. Kabul is finding it increasingly hard to cope with the vigorous military offensive by the Taliban.[17] Both Delhi and Tehran value the Chabahar port as a means to improve their geopolitical leverage vis-a-vis Pakistan and pursue their common interest in providing Afghanistan and Central Asia alternative routes to the Indian Ocean. The NDA government has sanctioned nearly $85 million for the construction of two berths at Chabahar and the development of a container terminal. India, which long chafed at Pakistan's refusal to provide overland access to Afghanistan, viewed the Chabahar port as a credible alternative to gaining physical access to Afghanistan. Land-locked Kabul, whose only route to the sea is through Pakistan, welcomed the project as a way to ease its strategic dependence on Islamabad.[18]

China

'China's footprint to our west will continue to grow bigger as it seeks access to the waters of the Arabian Sea through Pakistan, the energy resources of Iran and the mineral resources of Afghanistan,' said Vikram Sood, former head of RAW.[19] China's interests in Afghanistan are tied to its economic investments in the country and concerns that instability in Afghanistan will embolden separatists in its western Xinjiang province. Some evidence suggests that the Uighur-separatist group the East Turkestan Independence Movement (ETIM) has been trained, armed, and sheltered by Al-Qaeda and the TTP. As China pursues an enhanced economic presence in Afghanistan, it is concerned about a simultaneous increase in attempts by these terrorists to sabotage Chinese investments. Likewise, China has signalled concerns that ETIM terrorists could traverse the mountainous Sino–Afghan border to launch attacks in Xinjiang and elsewhere. Therefore, China's economic development strategy is directly linked to stability in Afghanistan. China, however, has been reluctant to play a military role in Afghanistan despite requests by NATO countries. Nevertheless, Beijing may have to rethink strategies to safeguard its own interests as American forces withdrawing from the region.[20] China has concerns over the security of its western regions and the possibility of spillover from Afghanistan to Xinjiang. China is trying to bridge Afghanistan-Pakistan relations and it has also been in contact with the Taliban in recent years. With the unstable security situation in Khyber Pakhtunkhwa, China also faces difficulties in transporting copper from Afghanistan. However, China is not willing to build a railway from northern Afghanistan to Aynak and the Torkham border with Pakistan despite it being part of the Aynak contract.[21]

The Chinese President Xi Jinping reciprocated by hailing Ghani as an old friend of the Chinese people with whom China is prepared to work towards 'a new era of co-operation' and 'to take development to a new depth.' Despite China's concerns that a deteriorating security situation could threaten greater investment, it agreed to give Afghanistan $327 million in aid over the next three years – $81.8 million in 2014 and the remaining sum between 2015 and 2017. More significantly, China also agreed to act as a mediator between Afghanistan and Pakistan while Ghani pledged to help China fight its own Islamic militants. Both Beijing and Kabul recognize each other's importance. Providing assistance to Afghanistan may form a part of Xi's wider plan to establish a 6,437 km 'Silk Road' economic belt to connect China's western regions with Europe by way of Central Asia. Security concerns have prevented Chinese investments in Afghanistan from getting off the ground. China is interested in playing a larger role in Afghanistan, long seen as primarily a US responsibility after its 2001 invasion. China's Afghan policy is now feeling the pressure emanating from the withdrawal of western troops and Taliban surge threatening to give a boost to Islamist militancy in China's western Xinjiang region. Much like the rest of the region, China remains worried about the withdrawal of western forces from Afghanistan as it fears a broader destabilization of the region post-2014.[22]

Pakistan's Security and Economic Interests in Afghanistan

Pakistan's policies toward both militant groups and Afghanistan are determined as much by incompetence, inertia, and a lack of capacity as by calibrated duplicitous manipulation. Pakistan's geostrategic outlook and the limitations of its selective counterterrorism policies have not resolutely changed. Crucially, Pakistan's willingness to accommodate Afghanistan-oriented militant groups is motivated by a fear of provoking militants to incite violence in Punjab and threaten the core of the Pakistani state instead of focusing externally. This paralyzing fear persists despite Pakistan's desire to defeat Tehrik-i-Taliban Pakistan.[23] Over the last few months, President Ghani, the newly elected president of Afghanistan, endeavoured to maintain closer contacts and ties with Pakistan's military establishment. Sending Afghan cadets for military training to Pakistan, allowing Pakistani intelligence officers to interrogate detainees in Afghan detention facilities, conducting military operations on Afghan soil at the request of Pakistan's military, are but a few examples. According to Pakistan's interior minister and local sources in Afghanistan, Kabul has also allowed Pakistani security forces to conduct 'joint military operations' in the eastern parts of Afghanistan (Nangharhar, Kunar), which Kabul and Islamabad both later rejected.[24]

Afghanistan's landlocked status means it relies on neighbours to facilitate the transit of its trade with the broader global economy. The two countries initially signed the Afghanistan Pakistan Transit Trade Agreement (APTTA) in 1965. It was redesigned in 2010 to allow the transit of Afghan exports through Pakistan to the Wagah border with India, and to the seaport cities of Karachi and Gwadar. Pakistani trucks in turn are allowed to move products to all regions of Afghanistan.[25] Despite past agreements, continued tensions have prevented the full realization of Afghanistan and Pakistan's bilateral trade potential, and the row over Indian goods has jeopardised the deals, with India and Pakistan locked in a decades-old standoff. 'If you put India on the table, then the whole thing stops,' said a Pakistani official, speaking on condition of anonymity.[26]

Pakistan welcomed the formation of the new unity government in Afghanistan and the signing of the 'Bilateral Security Agreement' (BSA) with the United States. However, Pakistan remains cautious about the implications of the BSA for its own security given the long-term presence of US forces in Afghanistan (even in a non-combat mode), and joint US–Afghan counter-terrorism operations. Counter-terrorism training and operations against Al-Qaeda and the Taliban in the coming years will demand extensive intelligence sharing between the United States, Afghanistan, and Pakistan with probably continued US reliance on drone warfare inside Pakistan's tribal belt. Pakistan itself has been pursing domestic counter-terrorism operations since June 2014 through Operation Zarb-e-Azb to combat local and foreign Taliban forces operating from North Waziristan. For decades, Pakistan viewed Afghanistan as an important part of its sphere of influence, shaping its intrusive foreign policy towards Afghanistan. However, a 'strategic shift' in Pakistan's policy towards Afghanistan in recent years is driven by three considerations. These are, 'the rise of domestic instability and terrorism, which is now its top priority; its longstanding rivalry with, and suspicion of, India; and its desire to avoid a surge in Pashtun nationalism among its own large Pashtun population.' Pakistan's attitude towards Indian presence in Afghanistan has also changed in recent years from that of insecurity to reconciliation. However, it remains cautious such that Afghanistan 'does not provide India the space to pursue security-driven agendas against Pakistan.'[27]

Peace talks with Taliban

In early July 2014, Pakistan hosted the first round of peace talks between the Afghan government and the Taliban in the resort town of Murree, adjacent to Islamabad. The Murree meeting followed a series of unofficial interactions between the Afghan government and the Taliban representatives in recent months in China, Norway and Qatar. The admission by the Taliban that its leader Mullah Mohammed Omar had in fact died two years ago has caused a serious rift within the Taliban, with a hardline faction clearly opposed to any peace negotiations with Kabul. The new leader, Mullah Akhtar Mohammad Mansour has promised to continue fighting. The ISI is in the process of freeing one hundred Taliban, whom it had earlier jailed, to renew their contacts and discuss peace with Taliban. In the meanwhile, Taliban has opened 'offices' in Doha and Qatar. As reconciliation negotiations are going on, it would be premature to expect too much headway to be made. Afghan government will find it difficult to negotiate with guns being held to their heads, even though the US is eager and willing. Unless reconciliation talks are Afghan-led and Afghan-owned, any agreement that might be reached will not last long. Also, the Taliban could be playing for time and the talks could be a ploy to rest, recoup and refit. It is hard to see them being serious about negotiations when they are on the verge of achieving a moral victory with the impending withdrawal of US forces.[28] However, India is being frozen out of the talks. The official stand of the Government of India is that it is 'supportive of the peace process' provided 'it brings genuine peace and internationally accepted red lines.' However, officials in Delhi and Kabul feel that India is far from comfortable with the 'direction the talks are taking,' saying that 'all red lines have been violated so far.' In 2010, former Afghan President Hamid Karzai had listed these 'red lines' as an acceptance of the Afghan constitution; peace or a ceasefire as a pre-condition for talks; and following an 'Afghan-owned, Afghan-led' process, which had been endorsed by the Indian government.[29] With Islamabad and Beijing taking centre stage in the Taliban-Afghan talks, New Delhi has felt entirely excluded from any say in the future of a country with which it has close ties, and regards as strategically vital to its interests. It has rankled that President Ghani has played an important role in marginalizing New Delhi.[30] Afghanistan is very important for both India and China. Stability in both countries is dependent on the situation in Afghanistan. The rich natural resources of Afghanistan are a good reason for more cooperation.

The Way Forward

Given the potential future direction of the regional environment, some risks could be addressed by robust engagement by the regional stakeholders (i.e., India, Pakistan, and China) facilitated by the United States. This idea comprises our key recommendations for policymakers, which are presented as follows:

- Encouraging a trilateral counter-terrorism mechanism with bilateral negotiations on the side, e.g., US–China, China–Pakistan, India–Pakistan, and China–India, where the US plays mostly the role of the facilitator. While the trilateral mechanism would permit the three stakeholders to engage together, their bilateral differences could prove to be stumbling blocks. As a result, an additional bilateral mechanism would be necessary for the resolution of frequent India-Pakistan, China-India, and China-Pakistan disagreements on terrorism. In order to prevent this mechanism becoming another regional 'talk fest,' attempts should be made to incorporate: a) innovative dialogue structures, b) extended period of participation, and c) non-official but establishment-friendly partners as starting points.[31]
- Beijing and New Delhi must become important stakeholders in Afghan stability through increased joint Sino-Indian civilian projects. In order to ensure that Sino-Indian civilian cooperation does not worry Islamabad, a second track of Sino-Pakistani civilian cooperation ought to be encouraged.[32]
- The United States must continue to encourage the Afghan reconciliation process with the regional stakeholders, as it has been doing.[33]

Conclusion

Afghanistan and India have a full agenda of shared objectives to execute. The framework, within which bilateral aid programs and projects should be implemented, is the Strategic Partnership Agreement (SPA), which Afghanistan signed with India in 2011. Over the long run, the multi-dimensional Indo-Afghan relationship will only grow, in line with the two nations' historic ties and converging interests, which they share with China and Russia. Like Afghanistan, India, China, and Russia have been targets of terrorist attacks, and remain concerned about the growing threats of terrorism, radicalism and criminality that primarily destabilize Afghanistan but also undermine regional peace and stability. To avoid an Iraq like situation happing in Afghanistan, especially in light of the rising presence of ISIS in Afghanistan, President Ghani called on the key regional players to join in a 'forceful and coherent action' against any threats that undermine the security and stability of the region.[34] Afghanistan's peaceful future depends to a great extent on an auspicious regional environment, with Pakistan at its core. Vice versa, an unstable Afghanistan will complicate Pakistan's ability to refurbish its weak state and economy, and suppress dangerous internal militancy.[35]

India has major concerns regarding the future of peace and security and Afghanistan. A weak government in Afghanistan is a threat to Indian interests. It may result in fragmented control of the government over the country, with parts of the country, especially the South and East under the Taliban influence. In the absence of US-led troops in the country, an unrelenting Pakistan and a resurgent Taliban, it could become a major concern for India, not only for its assets in the country, but also its spillover effect on Indian Territory. A political and security vacuum would thus constitute a direct threat to India.[36] Social and economic development of Afghanistan is the key to its stability and India is committed to maintaining close and friendly relations with Afghanistan as its historic friend and partner. President Ghani should emphasize that Afghanistan will never accommodate Pakistan's wish to control Afghanistan's foreign policy, especially in regard to India. For its part, India should consider Afghanistan as its strategic priority and build upon the solid foundation of its bilateral relations with Afghanistan laid and strengthened under President Ghani's predecessor, President Hamid Karzai. Afghanistan doesn't need more of the 'great game' being played on its soil.[37] India as a responsible regional power should heal the Afghan wounds and not let Pakistan feast on the blood that oozes out of them.

NOTES

1. GOI (2012), "India-Afghanistan Relations", Ministry of External Affairs, New Delhi, [Online: web], Accessed 5 Sept. 2015, http://mea.gov.in/Portal/ForeignRelation/afghanistan-aug-2012.pdf
2. Pant, Harsh V.(2014), "Out With Non-Alignment, In With a 'Modi Doctrine'", *The Diplomat,* [Online: web] Accessed 25 August 2015, http://thediplomat.com/2014/11/out-with-non-alignment-in-with-a-modi-doctrine/
3. Hanauer, Larry and Peter Chalk (2012), "India's and Pakistan's Strategies in Afghanistan: Implications for the United States and the Region", Occasional Paper, Center For Asia Pacific Policy, International Programs at RAND, [Online: web] Accessed 2 Nov. 2015, http://www.rand.org/content/dam/rand/pubs/occasional_papers/2012/RAND_OP387.pdf

4. Kanwal, Gurmeet (2013), "Post-2014 Transition in Afghanistan: Options for India", CLAWS Journal l: Winter, [Online: web] Accessed 25 August 2015, http://www.claws.in/images/journals_doc/1656439390_GurmeetKanwal.pdf
5. Bajoria, Jayshree (2009), "India-Afghanistan Relations", [Online: web] Accessed 12 August 2015, http://www.cfr.org/india/india-afghanistan-relations/p17474
6. Kanwal, Gurmeet (2013), "Post-2014 Transition in Afghanistan: Options for India", CLAWS Journal l: Winter, [Online: web] Accessed 25 August 2015, http://www.claws.in/images/journals_doc/1656439390_GurmeetKanwal.pdf
7. Rampton, Roberta And Jeff Mason (2015), "Citing 'very fragile' security in Afghanistan, Obama slows pace of U.S. troop withdrawal", *Reuters,* Washington, 16 Oct 2015, [Online: web] Accessed 25 August 2015, http://www.reuters.com/article/2015/10/16/us-afghanistan-usa-idUSKCN0S910M20151016
8. Roberts, Dan and Spencer Ackerman and Sune Engel Rasmussen(2015), "Barack Obama delays withdrawal of US troops from Afghanistan" *The Guardian,*15 October 2015, [Online: web] Accessed 25 August 2015, http://www.theguardian.com/world/2015/oct/15/obama-delay-withdrawal-us-troops-afghanistan
9. Sethi, Abheet Singh (2015), "Why India aids Afghanistan, and why it matters", [Online: web] Accessed 2 August 2015,http://scroll.in/article/745257/why-india-aids-afghanistan-and-why-it-matters
10. Price, Gareth(2013), "India's Policy towards Afghanistan", Chatham House, London, [Online: web] Accessed 11 August 2015, https://www.chathamhouse.org/sites/files/chathamhouse/public/Research/Asia/0813pp_indiaafghanistan.pdf
11. See http://eoi.gov.in/kabul/?0707?000 for details
12. Ibid.
13. Sethi, Abheet Singh (2015), "Why India aids Afghanistan, and why it matters", [Online: web] Accessed 2 August 2015, http://scroll.in/article/745257/why-india-aids-afghanistan-and-why-it-matters
14. Ibid.
15. Betkerur, Niharika(2014), "India Stepping Up to the Plate in Afghanistan: A deal with Moscow makes clear that India has no plans to abandon Afghanistan post 2014", *The Diplomat,* 07 May 2014, [Online: web] Accessed 2 August 2015, http://thediplomat.com/2014/05/india-stepping-up-to-the-plate-in-afghanistan/
16. Price, Gareth (2013), "India's Policy towards Afghanistan", Chatham House, London, [Online: web] Accessed 15 August 2015, https://www.chathamhouse.org/sites/files/chathamhouse/public/Research/Asia/0813pp_indiaafghanistan.pdf
17. Mohan, C. Raja (2015), "The Great Game Folio: Iran Opportunity", *The Indianexpress,*16 June 2015, [Online: web] Accessed 25 August 2015, http://indianexpress.com/article/opinion/columns/the-great-game-folio-40/
18. Mohan, C. Raja (2014), "Iran and India's Road to Afghanistan", *The Indianexpress,* 20 October 2014, [Online: web] Accessed 2 August 2015, http://indianexpress.com/article/opinion/columns/iran-and-indias-road-to-afghanistan/
19. Miglani, Sanjeev (2015), "India to host Afghan leader, seeks to regain ground lost to China, Pakistan", *Reuters,* New Delhi, 24 April 2015, [Online: web] Accessed 25 August 2015, http://in.reuters.com/article/2015/04/23/india-afghanistan-idINKBN0NE2SF20150423
20. Akhtar, Rabia and Jayita Sarkar(2015), "Pakistan, India, and china after the U.S. Drawdown from Afghanista", Stimson Center, Washington DC, [Online: web] Accessed 25 August 2015, http://www.stimson.org/images/uploads/research-pdfs/pakistan-india-china-after-us-afghanistan.pdf

21. Baheen, Sultan Ahmed (2015), "Afghanistan: A Platform for Cooperation between India and China?", The Royal United Services Institute commentary, [Online: web] Accessed 2 Dec. 2015, https://www.rusi.org/analysis/commentary/ref:C558A9E4E8A696/#.ViLUW34rJD9
22. Pant, Harsh V. (2015), "Can India and China Both Court Afghanistan?", *The Diplomat*,4 May 2015, [Online: web] Accessed 25 August 2015, http://thediplomat.com/2015/05/can-india-and-china-both-court-afghanistan/
23. See http://www.brookings.edu/research/papers/2015/05/14-pakistan-afghanistan-regional-politics-felbabbrown for details
24. Faizi, Aimal (2015), "Has India lost Afghanistan to Pakistan?", 26 April, [Online: web] Accessed 25 August 2015, http://www.aljazeera.com/indepth/opinion/2015/04/india-lost-afghanistan-pakistan-150426051958020.html
25. Husain, ishrat and Muhammad Ather Elahi (2015), "The Future of Afghanistan-Pakistan Trade Relations", United States Institute of Peace, August, [Online: web] Accessed 25 August 2015, http://www.usip.org/sites/default/files/PB191-The-Future-of-Afghanistan-Pakistan-Trade-Relations.pdf
26. Ibnlive (2015), "Afghanistan stalls intelligence sharing on Taliban, trade deals as Pakistan unwilling to include trade from India", 17 September, [Online: web] Accessed 1 Nov 2015, http://www.ibnlive.com/news/world/afghanistan-stalls-intelligence-sharing-on-taliban-trade-deals-as-pakistan-unwilling-to-include-trade-from-india-1100721.html
27. Akhtar, Rabia and Jayita Sarkar (2015), "Pakistan, India, and China after the U.S. Drawdown from Afghanista", Stimson Center, Washington DC, [Online: web] Accessed 25 August 2015, http://www.stimson.org/images/uploads/research-pdfs/pakistan-india-china-after-us-afghanistan.pdf
28. Kanwal, Gurmeet (2013), "Post-2014 Transition in Afghanistan: Options for India", CLAWS Journal l: Winter 2013, [Online: web] Accessed 25 August 2015, http://www.claws.in/images/journals_doc/1656439390_GurmeetKanwal.pdf
29. Haidar, Suhasini (2015), "India ignored as Pak. takes charge of Afghan-Taliban talks," The Hindu, 28 July 2015, [Online: web] Accessed 25 August 2015, http://www.thehindu.com/news/national/afghantaliban-talks/article7470910.ece
30. Subramanian, Nirupama (2015), "Life after Mullah Omar: For Taliban, Afghanistan, and the peace talks", *The Indian express,* 31 July 2015, [Online: web] Accessed 25 August 2015, http://indianexpress.com/article/explained/life-after-mullah-omar-for-taliban-afghanistan-and-the-peace-talks-2/#sthash.OkNhyZtW.dpuf
31. See http://www.stimson.org/sites/default/files/file-attachments/pakistan-india-china-after-us -afghanistan.pdf
32. Ibid.
33. Akhtar, Rabia and Jayita Sarkar (2015), "Pakistan, India, and china after the U.S. Drawdown from Afghanista", Stimson Center, Washington DC, [Online: web] Accessed 25 August 2015, http://www.stimson.org/images/uploads/research-pdfs/pakistan-india-china-after-us-afghanistan.pdf
34. Haidari, M. Ashraf (2015), "India and Afghanistan: A Growing Partnership", *The Diplomat,* September 16, [Online: web] Accessed 21 Sept. 2015, http://thediplomat.com/2015/09/india-and-afghanistan-a-growing-partnership/
35. Felbab-Brown, Vanda (2015), "Pakistan's relations with Afghanistan and implications for regional politics", [Online: web] Accessed 25 August 2015, http://www.brookings.edu/research/papers/2015/05/14-pakistan-afghanistan-regional-politics-felbabbrown

36. Agarwal, Rajeev(2015), "Post-2014 Afghanistan: Policy Options for India and Iran", The Institute of Peace and Conflict Studies, New Delhi, [Online: web] Accessed 8 August 2015, http://www.ipcs.org/issue-brief/iran/post-2014-afghanistan-policy-options-for-india-and-iran-247.html
37. Bhadrakumar, M.K. (2015), "India's Modi faces tough Afghan choices", Asia Times News & Features, 17 August 2015, [Online: web] Accessed 11 Sep. 2015, http://atimes.com/2015/08/indias-modi-faces-tough-afghan-choices/

2

Islam in India-Bangladesh Relations

Prashant Kumar

Islam acts as an influencing factor on the foreign policy and diplomacy of most of the Muslim countries. The degree of its role on the foreign policy may vary from country to country depending on the state ideology. Islamic factor acts independently as a determinant on the foreign policy and diplomacy of Bangladesh. Bangladesh has developed close relationship with the Islamic countries, the process of which was started during the Mujib period. Ideologically, BNP is very close to Pakistan as religion is the core part of its external and internal politics; but the generations having the memories of atrocities and rapes committed by Pakistan in 1971 are still alive and, except among a few there, the image of Pakistan in the public domain is poor. So it creates a dilemma for BNP while dealing with Pakistan. The dilemma for the Awami League happens when it deals with India. BNP always accused the Awami League to sell out its interest to India. Political and religious factors lend a very paradoxical image of India in the eyes of Bangladesh. Various aspects of these paradoxes while dealing with to these two countries would be accessed in this chapter.

Changing Ideology and Changing Perception in Indo-Bangladesh Relation

India and Bangladesh share cultural, linguistic, racial affinity and a historical legacy which is strengthened by geographical proximity, but the religious factor always plays a more dominant role in Bangladesh-India relations. Since its inception, in general, in the post-Mujib period particularly, Islam has been playing a critical role in Bangladesh in dealing with India and this trend intensified as religion starts affecting the relations between the two to a larger extent in the time when the growth of religious revivalist parties emerged in both in India and Bangladesh. Historically, the 'Hindu phobia' of Bengali Muslims, a legacy of the British colonial days, transforming into 'Indophobia' during the Pakistani period remained embedded in the psyche of the average Bengali Muslims, even though India had acted as the midwife in the birth of the new nation.

This legacy has been fostered by Bangladeshi political giants for their political legitimacy and to gain their ends from time to time. The secular measures of the Mujib government, such as the constitutional ban on religious parties and neutrality of the state in matters of faith, were seen as attempts to please the rulers in Delhi. 'Bengali nationalist sentiment', according to an observer, 'as too strong to tolerate a high level of Indian influence in Bangladesh affairs...'[1] Religious difference, political dominance and the physical size of India have continued to evoke a sense of uneasiness towards India. Apart from this, the military size and trade imbalance increased this notion of dichotomy.[2]

We know that the present is the outcome of much socio-economic historical process which has been spurred by geopolitical necessity. So, to get a holistic picture of it we must go through the socio-religious formation of this country. As Richard Eton considers that the area, which now constitutes Bangladesh, was historically peripheral in the Indian subcontinent. This location of the geopolitical backyard meant comparative neglect and dissonant evolutionary processes. Earlier, Buddhism as a way of life prevailed in the eastern part of Bengal, now Bangladesh. Over the years, Buddhism was supplanted by rulers and another wave of Brahmanism took place during the early medieval period. This was the time when the Bengali language started taking shape in its modern form. What is noteworthy is that this aryanisation or Hindu culture was already present in the western part of Bengal which is now West Bengal in India. So, social formation in the eastern part of Bengal and the western part of Bengal took shape differently. In the medieval period, the local rulers of this region were very liberal in terms of religious practices so the environment of syncretism had emerged. The process of Islamisation which happened in the early 13th century was faster and more intense than in other parts of the Indian subcontinent. As Eton suggests, it happened due to conversion of the native people into peasantry class. Since the river Ganges had changed the course which was followed by emergence of fertile land, the native people started agriculture and Sufi saints influenced them by providing money and spiritual guidance. Nevertheless, there are many theories like the sword theory, social relies theory, etc., which try to explain this conversion process. However, the converting to Islam did not result in refutation of the Bengali language and culture, which continued to be a vital force.

Akbar (1556-1605), was the first ruler who controlled and took this part of east Bengal under the direct control of the Mughal Empire in 1576. Earlier this area was known for political disunity and was an ignored area because of scattered human settlements. Bengal had emerged as the large centre of trade and commerce with the related benefits of *Monsoon Islam*. Monsoon Islam denotes the Islam adopted and practiced by Bengali Muslims, mostly influenced by their language and culture, because thier social formation took place differently. Due to the distance from the centre, the central and West Asian influence was too narrow in this part of the country. Conditions became worse in the period of the British East India Company. Since British got this part after the Buxar War in 1765 as a Zamidari and their prime motive was only to fulfil their economic greed, so they adopted a very suppressive and discriminatory economic policy. This again caused extremely asymmetrical and dissimilar evolutionary processes between East Bengal and West Bengal and was in favour of the latter. So the nature of elitism, local culture and political discourse differed from the western part. It was, therefore, not unexpected that a large populace in East Bengal favoured the partition of Bengal in 1905 (annulled in 1911) and it is not a coincidence that here (in Dhaka) in 1906 that the first meeting of the All India Muslim League was held. So religion and culture both co-existed at the same time. One other thing is worthy of mention that since the medieval period there had also been divergence in interest of the landlords and the peasantry class who constituted the majority. The landlord class had adopted the *Bhadralok* culture, which was elitist in nature and duplicated the ruling class. For instance, they spoke Urdu and Persian, which were court languages at that time, and were strict followers of Islam as it was practiced by the rulers the in Delhi, whereas Bengali was spoken by the native people and local festivals and local culture were being practiced by the local peasants. However, the Muslim League was formed in 1906 by the Urdu speaking Muslims to safeguard their political and economic interest. After partition in 1947, Bangladesh (then East Pakistan) faced a serious negligence and discriminatory treatment in each and every area including the armed forces. The dichotomy between East Pakistan and West Pakistan resulted in their separation in 1971 due to events that spiralled beyond control of the Pakistani rulers.[3]

The creation of Bangladesh earned for India a paradoxical image. On the one hand it was seen as active supporter of the Liberation War and on the other as an unprincipled self keeper. Behaviour of Indian soldiers and behaviour of Indian bureaucrats are discussed and exaggerated many times and in many ways. The close proximity of the nationalists with New Delhi became a political liability for the Mujib government, so much so that its failure to deliver was attributed to interference and pressure of India. The secular measures of the new government such as the constitutional ban on religious parties and neutrality of the state in matters of faith were seen as attempts to please the rulers in Delhi. 'Bengali nationalist sentiment', according to an observer, was 'too strong to tolerate a high level of Indian influence in Bangladesh affairs...'[4] The traditional social divisions in Bangladesh are heavily influenced by the spirit of nationalism based on religion and culture. In other words, either of the one is evoked to mobilize the masses whenever the people have felt threatened from outside.[5] When the Mujib government came down heavily against the collaborators during the first few years of its rule, pro-Islamic people, who were otherwise known as devout Muslims, were brought under the state's surveillance and the reaction went deep down to the grass-root level having a corroding effect. The propaganda that it was all done against the 'believers' at the instigation of Hindu India was taken to be true by a large section of the rural population. Maulana Bhashani, the old man of Bangladesh politics, talked of the necessity of Islamic Socialism and was part of the anti-Mujib campaign.

Bhashani in his public speeches was rhetorical about the greedy *Marwari* traders and their economic manipulative activities in Bengal. Small Bengali traders felt that the secular policies of the Awami League would motivate the wily Hindu businessmen to return and reclaim their abandoned property.[6] Rise of communal tensions between Hindus and Muslims in the latter half of 19th century was due to the similar perceived economic and social competition between the two main communities.[7]

Inevitably the Islamic fundamentalist forces in Bangladesh which had, for tactical reasons, endorsed the Indian intervention received in the spring of 1972, were active during the Hindu religious festivals reportedly causing communal violence in several part of Bangladesh. The activists of Muslim

Bangla had started to threaten Bangladeshi Hindus and Indian diplomats with anonymous letter and advising them to escape to India. Later they became more vocal and slogans like 'we shall not allow Sikkim to be repeated in Bangladesh' started appearing on the walls of Dhaka. The so-called Muslim Bangla Movement was launched in summer of 1973 by right-winged Islamic forces, to resist political secularism of Awami League. The Muslim Bangla Movement had opened its centres in London and Mecca and tried to collect funds to raise a guerrilla army to promote the objectives of movement. A magazine titled *Sangram* was published. Leftist Parties utilized the growing anti-India and communal sentiment to fulfil their interests. According to Maniruzzaman, Islamic identity became the centre of resistances against India's pre dominance in Bangladesh politics.[8] When the Mujib government came down heavily against the collaborators during the first few years of its rule, pro-Islamic people, who were otherwise known to be devout Muslims, were brought under the state's surveillance and 'the reaction went deep down' to the grass-root level having a corroding effect. The propaganda that it was all done against the 'believers' at the instigation of Hindu India was taken to be true by a large section of the rural population. This also led to the thought of establishing a Muslim Bengal from then on, consciously or unconsciously.[9]

The most controversial issue in the aftermath of the Liberation War was the 1972 Treaty. This treaty was considered as a price that Bangladesh paid to India for its contribution in 1971. The anti-India sentiments found its favourite flogging horse in the Indo-Bangladesh Friendship Treaty signed by the Indian Prime Minister Indira Gandhi and Mujibur Rahman on March 19, 1972. The treaty claimed to be 'inspired by common deals of peace, secularism, democracy, socialism and nationalism.' Some Bangladeshi analysts argue that this treaty compromised Bangladesh's sovereignty. The entire propaganda mills created an India phobia. The fear of being dubbed an Indian agent was great among political parties and even mainstream parties. This explains why the Awami League chose to maintain silence in the face of various criticism and clarifications on renewing the Indo-Bangladesh Friendship Treaty.

Finally, the Bangladesh economy faced greater challenges and the nationalist fervour triggered during the Liberation War was not enough to wish away problems of hunger, famine and rehabilitation. India along with numerous other countries provided assistance, but the vilifying campaign did not stop. The increased smuggling between India and Bangladesh made India look like a country with hegemonistic designs, out to dominate the economy of the smaller neighbours.[10] The obsession of Bangladesh with the Indian state strengthened the Islamists and led towards ideological polarisation within the country. In a show of open defiance towards India, the junta rulers, after the 1975 coup, undertook corrective measures to set all that had gone *wrong during* Mujib's tenure.

After the assassination of Mujib, the Bengali nationalism which is based on linguistic territorial-secular nationalist line turned into Bangladeshi nationalism that is basically linguistic-territorial-Islamic nationalism. The elements of 1947 were working very sharply. Ziaur Rahman was known for his anti-Indian, pro-west and pro-Islamic attitude. Bangladesh improved its relations with China and Pakistan. Bangladesh endeavoured to consolidate, preserve and strengthen fraternal relation among Muslim countries, based on the Islamic solidarity.[11]

Zia secured the support of Islamic revivalist section for getting the legitimacy at home. During the 1979 election, many candidates from the Muslim League contested the election under the banner of BNP with the slogan 'Defeat Awami League and keep Islam safe in the hands of President Zia.' There were other symbolic efforts which includes showing Quaranik verses and the Prophet's advice in public places and public institutions. Apart from flying of Eid Mubarak festoon with the national flag on Eid festival, propagating the values of *Shariyat* through the radio and so on, Zia began to preface his public speeches with *Bismmilah ar Rahman ar Rahim* at the social level.[12] The tension over the Border dispute and sharing the Ganga water created the worst image of India at that time. Zia tried to internationalize these issues. He took the Farrakka issues to OIC Foreign Ministers Conference in Istanbul in 1976. In the tenure of General H.M. Ershad, anti-India sentiments remained in politics. Ershad declared Islam as the state religion. During his regime the water sharing issue continued to make the image of India bad in the eyes of Bangladesh.

The restoration of democracy in 1991 brought in its own dynamics to the Indian image in the Bangladeshi view. Relations and Image became the flavour of internal politics and it has been extended to international relations. Political mobilization made India a crucial factor in domestic politics during the election campaign. For instance, the Awami League manifesto that talked of secularism and return to the 1972 constitution was attacked by BNP as selling the country to India. Since Awami League is perceived as pro-Indian, Anti-Indianism is a major tool for BNP. Awami league led by Sheikh Hasina represents Bengali nationalism while the BNP led by Khalida Zia represents the Bangladeshi nationalism.[13] The Jamaat-e-Islami, Islami Oikyo Jote are very Islamic in nature, they are always very critical of India. Bengali nationalism and its supporters tand for the good image of India. The Bangladeshi nationalism that represents the ethos of 1947 has a clear tilt towards Pakistan and Saudi Arabia. In ideological front the Awami League and BNP differ fundamentally in their interpretation of the historical emergence of Bangladesh. Unlike Awami League, BNP acknowledges that history begins not from 1971 or 1947 but from establishment of Muslim rule in Bengal. In the BNP eyes, the creation of Bangladesh did not invalidate the basis of Pakistan's *Two-Nation Theory*. Awami League is seen by many as a stooge of India and obstacle to the development of an independent identity for the people of Bangladesh. Under the BNP government, the history of the Liberation War was being rewritten that it was Ziaur Rahman who was the real hero of Liberation War and not Mujib ur Raman, because it was the former who first gave the call for independence of Bangladesh on 26 March 1971.[14] But due to growing Islamisation in the country and within society, the Awami League is unable to retain its secular image to take any benefit in elections, and the party started speaking against India and also uses Islamic symbols and gestures during the election campaign. It also mentions 'Allah is great' as a slogan in their banners.

The Babri Masjid demolition in India and the riots that followed in Bangladesh show how deep-rooted this factor is in the minds of the people in Bangladesh. Khaleda Zia, the then Prime Minister of Bangladesh, proclaimed, 'The situation arising out of the demolition of the Babri mosque is fraught with a possibility of an adverse impact on Indo-Bangladeshi relations' and Matiur Rahman Nizami, the secretary of Jamaat-e-Islami, called upon the Muslim world to boycott India economically unless the Babri Mosque was rebuilt.[15] The Jamaat-e-Islami observed that the Babri Masjid incident showed that India could not accept the existence of an independent Bangladesh. India wanted to see Bangladesh as subservient to it. According to these extremists, only Islamic values could help their independence and sovereignty. Godhra riots took place in India in the year, 2002. The growth of religious tension in India had a spillover effect and Bangladesh witnessed a major outbreak of communal violence.

Therefore, fundamentalist outfits in Pakistan and Bangladesh have called for a renewed jihad against India. Khaleda Zia has turned to the Organization of Islamic Conference and the US to take 'strong action against India.' In 2004, the pro-Islam section was demanding to change the Nation Anthem that was written by R.N. Tagore as well as the National Flag. The growing number of Madrassas in the Bangladesh is ever controversial as the funds come from the Jeddah based Islamic Development Bank.[16] There are several Islamic militant outfits operating in Bangladesh; most important are Harakat-Ul-Jehad, Islami-Chhatro-Shibir, Samjukta-Islamic Organization and the Islamic-Markaz-Party which aim at the wiping out all enemies of Islam including the United State and India.[17]

Implications for India

Bangladesh is Safe Haven to Insurgents of North–East India

Except for Myanmar, with which Bangladesh shares a 193 km long land boundary, its remaining land boundary of 4096 km is shared with India. The biggest strategic gain that accrued to India from the creation of Bangladesh was that Pakistan lost a naval presence in the Bay of Bengal, i.e., in the vicinity of India's eastern seaboard and thereby also ceased to have a geographical interface with Southeast Asia.

The big brother syndrome with respect to India looms very large on Bangladesh's security horizon. The India-fear has also led Bangladesh to forge close relationship with China and Pakistan, the two countries, which it perceives India is disconcerted with. Bangladesh is conscious of the fact that it is not capable of undertaking any offensive against India, given the huge mismatch in the size and military capabilities of the two countries. It has, therefore, adopted a wholly defensive strategy.[18]

Sanctuary to Indian Insurgent Groups

Since inception, Pakistan has been promoting and patronizing different northeast insurgent groups to create turmoil in the region. In his book 'Myth of Independence', the then Pakistani Prime Minister Zulfikar Ali Bhutto wrote claiming Assam to be part of Pakistan (East) and came up with some suggestions that some areas of India's northeast must be integrated in Pakistan.[19]

There are sufficient indications that this policy was played out successfully. In 1956, Naga National Council leader A.Z. Phizo, who was leading the Naga insurgent group, fled to Dhaka and from there, he went to London on a forged passport, managed and provided by Pakistan. There are many evidences to prove that these Naga insurgents had been getting weaponry and training till 1971. Similarly, Mizo insurgents were also being provided a helpful hand by East Pakistan. When the Mizo National Front (MNF) were unsuccessful to win the district council in 1963, its chief Laldenga and his supporters reached out to Pakistan for weapons and training.[20]

The ascendancy in religious fundamentalism in Bangladesh affects India-Bangladesh relations in two ways. On the one hand, it forced the Indian Hindus to feel sympathetic towards their Bangladeshi brethren. If they are instigated by fanatic Hindus, then it could lead to communal conflicts in India. On the other hand, Islamic fanaticism in Bangladesh is closely associated to the phenomenon of Islamic terrorism.

In 2001, in the aftermath of the elections, the anti-Hindu atrocities in Bangladesh were very high, and the people of West Bengal had protested against these atrocities. The other controversy has been the increasing number of Madrassas in the districts bordering Bangladesh. Even Buddhadeb Bhattacharjee, the then Chief Minister of West Bengal and, the Tripura Chief Minister Manik Sarkar, had alleged that these madrassas were the sanctuary of ISI activity. It was proved by media reports in June 2001, which highlighted the presence of a number of camps in Bangladesh being operated by the National Liberation Front of Tripura (NLFT), United Liberation Front of Assam (ULFA) and National Democratic Front of Bodoland (NDFB).[21] It is said that the ULFA, particularly, and other insurgent groups have several profitable income generating projects in Bangladesh for sustaining their insurgency activities in India. The NLFT, which has spearheaded the anti-Bengali agitation in Tripura, has bases in the Sajek range of the Chittagong Hill Tracts. Another insurgent group, Kamtapur Liberation Organization (KLO), maintained very close links with other militant groups in the north east as well as with the ISI.

However, the present government of Sheikh Hasina is more committed to curb the terrorist outfits operating from its soil. The Khaleda Zia Government, before October 2002, refused to acknowledge the terrorist activities on its soil and avoided any strong action against these outfits. However, the government continued to pay only lip-service to Bangladesh's support to the war against international terrorism.[22] ISI and Bangladesh's Directorate General of Force Intelligence (DGFI) had been playing a very active role in fomenting Islamic militancy in India's northeastern region and that is a major concern for Indian intelligence.[23] The region, in general, is a central ground of various insurgent groups, at least 100, many of which have their hideouts and training camps in Bangladesh and Myanmar.

Bangladesh and Pakistan's Proxy War against India

Bangladesh's policies toward India have been always getting overtaken by Islamic fundamentalist parties, which never want that there should be good relations with India. It is in this outlook that has to be observe the apparent contours of Pakistan has been exploiting Bangladesh and its territory along with India as an substitute base for continuance of its proxy war against India.

Pakistan governments have used Bangladesh as an alternative base for its Proxy War against India. Bangladesh's internal factors provided a force-multiplier effect in the sense of Bangladesh's ability to be an alternative place for Pakistan's proxy war. Pakistan's ISI and its Islamic Jehadi organizations had enjoyed pan-Islamic linkages with fundamentalists in Bangladesh and Bangladesh's Armed Forces during BNP government.[24] 'Islamic Madrassas' under the costume of religious teaching schools provide a nucleus network for Islamic Jehadi and that are used by ISI in the proxy war against India.[25]

Bangladesh's territory, geographically porous and difficult to keep under close surveillance, provides lSI with multiple ingress routes to these sensitive Indian states. Bangladesh territory sits astride squarely on India's "strategic Siliguri Corridor" through which narrow corridors run India's slender communication links with its seven North Eastern states. Pakistan's ISI can play havoc against this corridor from Bangladesh territory.

Cox's Bazar in Bangladesh has emerged as a vital part for supply of illegal arms and ammunition worth crores of rupees to the insurgent outfits of the region. One of the important routes has for years, been the see route, with arms originating in South-East Asia, passing through Thailand and reaching at Cox's Bazar in Bangladesh. Bangladesh's prominent militant's outfits, the Harkat-ul-Jihad-al-Islami (HuJI), was established in 1992. It is said that it was formed with financial support from Osama Bin Laden himself.[26]

Assam state assembly was informed on April 6, 2000 by Prafulla Kumar Mahanta about ISI network in Bangladesh. According to the report, on the pretext of *jihad* youth were misled and caused fundamentalism and communal tensions in Bangladesh. The report also illustrated the relation between the ULFA leaders and Pakistan High Commission in Dhaka.[27] In Bangladesh, ULFA is said to be trained and helped by Pakistan's ISI and even Al-Qaeda.

The Awami League and the BNP have different stands and approaches on the support to Indian insurgents. During the Awami League rule, Bangladesh is more sympathetic towards India and during the BNP tenure the responses have been somewhat different over the support to Indian insurgents. ULFA leader Anup Chetia was arrested in December 1997 when he tried to illegally enter into Bangladesh. Even though Chetiya had not been extradited to India, despite India's persuasion, Bangladesh rejected his request for asylum and sentenced Chetiya to a six year prison term. Sanjeev Deb Berman, who was a senior ATTF member, had been illegally staying in Bangladesh since 1993 was arrested in 1998 by the Sheikh Hasina government. However, in January 2002 the Begum Khaleda government had released this man on bail.[28]

Thus, when Begum Khaleda again came to power in October 2001, it raised the prospects of a rejuvenation of this benign indifference towards militant activities; during this tenure, Bangladesh has faced a series of fundamentalist activities across the nation. Anti-India feeling was high and India remained as an enemy country for some politicians in Bangladesh.

In December 2008, after assuming the power, Bangladesh Prime Minister Sheikh Hasina assure India that Bangladesh would not allow militants to operate from her soil and the agreements signed with India would lead to cooperation in combating terror. She is keeping her words in curbing the insurgents on her soil, she took action and handed over some Indian insurgent leaders including Arbind Rajkhova, the chief of ULFA to India in December 2009. In addition to that she arrested two most senior leaders of the ULFA, one the 'foreign secretary', Sashadhar Choudhury, and 'finance secretary', Chitraban Hazarika, on 1 November 2009. Bangladesh has been launching a number of active operations against Indian terrorists on its soil since Awami League in power this time. So now, Bangladesh is not a safe haven for terrorists any more. However, due to social and political reasons, some training camps which are providing logistics support and safe havens are still functional. Fencing work is continuing but borders with Meghalaya and Assam (in the area of Dhubri along the Brahmaputra River) due to geographical constrain continue to be porous. The Indian Border Security Force (BSF) has given a list of 66 'camps of north-east insurgents' to the Border Guard Bangladesh (BGB), seeking actions against them.[29] Political ups and down of the governments in Bangladesh and their personal orientations in terms of its policies towards India and Pakistan make it simple for Pakistan to utilize Bangladesh as a proxy war base against India.

Demographic Changes in India

Although, no Indian Government study has been conducted regarding illegal migration so far, but as per a rough estimate the yearly illegal immigration from Bangladesh is approximately 300,000 and the total number of Bangladeshi citizen in India is supposed to be around 15 to 17 millions. It is true that there is barely any state in India, where Bangladeshi citizens are not residing. This is the right time for the Indian Government to reach out for some amicable solution as it is having unpleasant implications on the demographic composition of India, especially in border states of India and this might pose grave consequences in the future. This phenomenon of immigration has got impetus with the growing assault over the secular and religious minorities by fundamentalist elements in Bangladesh and requires strong action in the form of policy on the part of Government of Bangladesh.

Conclusion

As a counter to India's influence on socio-politics and culture, there has developed a strong proclivity among neighbours to assert the separateness of their identity. This may find recourse in the adoption of an ideology that contrasts with that of India as when Bangladesh adopted Islam as the state religion and criticized India for what it called an attempt to foist an alien culture that obliterates the distinct culture of the Bengali Muslims. Or, it may lead to demonstrative distancing, a refusal to settle issues on terms which seem reasonable. Indians often bewail this. Commentators from India continue today to bewail the passing of secularism but to do so is an anachronism. They are of a mind with those who call Bangladesh 'an anachronism within an anachronism'. Such comments lead to further feelings of insecurity in Bangladesh. Thus, Bangladesh swung between the two poles of secularism and Islam, Bengali and Bangladeshi; the so-called forces of 1971 and those of 1947, pro-India and anti-India.

NOTES

1. M. Franda (1982), "Bangladesh: The First Decade", South Asian Publication, New Delhi.
2. A. Salam(2008), "Role of Indian People in liberation war of Bangladesh", *Dialogue*, 10(2):137-144.
3. Ibid. p. 3.
4. F. Marcus (1982), "Bangladesh: The First Decade" South Asian Publication, New Delhi.
5. T. Maniruzzaman (1994), "Politics and Security of Bangladesh", University Press, Dhaka.
6. B. Chatterjee (1985), "*I*nside Bangladesh Today", S. Chand and Co. Pvt. Ltd, New Delhi.

7. B. Chatterjee (1973), *Bangladesh Today*, S. Chand and Co. Pvt. Ltd., New Delhi.
8. T. Maniruzzaman (1982), *Group Interests and Political Changes: Studies of Pakistan and Bangladesh*, South Asian Publications, New Delhi.
9. Ibid.
10. L. Ziring (1992), *Bangladesh: From Mujib to Ershad An Interpretative Study*, Karachi: Oxford University Press, Karachi.
11. P.S. Ghosh (1989), *The Cooperation and Conflict in South Asia*, Manohar Publication, New Delhi.
12. S.S. Pattanaik, Smurty S (2005), "Internal Political Dynamics and Bangladesh's Foreign Policy towards India", *Strategic Analysis*, 29(3), 2005, pp. 395-426.
13. S. Bhardwaj (2003), "Bangladesh Foreign Policy Vis-a-Vis India", *Strategic Analysis*, 27(2):263-279.
14. P.S. Ghosh (2005), "Conservative Ascendency in Bangladesh", *South Asian Survey*, 12(2):248-256.
15. S. Bhardwaj (2003), "Bangladesh Foreign Policy Vis-a-Vis India," *Strategic Analysis*, 27(2):263-279.
16. P.S. Ghosh (2005), "Conservative Ascendency in Bangladesh", *South Asian Survey*, 12(2):248-256.
17. Ibid.
18. RNP Singh (2002), "Root of Communalism in Bangladesh", *Dialogue*, 10(2):80-90.
19. Z.A. Bhutto (1990), *The Myth of independence*, Oxford University Press, London.
20. G. Scott and Dr K. Roy (2014), *Unconventional Warfare in South Asia: Shadow Warriors and Counterinsurgency*, Ashgate Publishing ltd., England, 2014.
21. Ibid.
22. B. Rahman (2003), "Bangladesh and Jehadi Terrorism-an Update",*Agni: Studies in International Strategic Issue*, 7(2):123-157.
23. S. Baruah (2005), *Durable Disorder: Understanding toward Politics of Northeast India*, Oxford University Press, New Delhi.
24. Dhar, M.K. (2007), "Bangladesh: A Need to Rediscover the Secular Forces", *World Focus* 4 (Nov-Dec):18.
25. Ibid.
26. D.S. Gupta and S.K. Singh (2004), *Insurgency in Northeast India: The role of Bangladesh*, Authors Press, New Delhi.
27. J. Saikia (2006), *Bangladesh: Treading the Taliban trail*, Vision Books, New Delhi.
28. Bangladesh is increasingly becoming hostile territory for Northeast groups, says Saleem Samad at http://www.tehelka.com/channels/currentaffairs/2002/mar/25/ca032502bangla.htm.
29. Dhaka Tribune, 11 June, 2014.

3

Bangladesh Border Vicinity for Human Trafficking: An Indian Viewpoint

Awkash Kumar

Introduction

The chapter will examine trafficking of human beings as a security issue. It is one of the largest criminal activities around the world as well as a serious crime against humanity. It will try to explore major causes of trafficking and also the profile of the victims. The paper will also examine India as origin, destination and transit country for human trafficking and also look into the response mechanism and anti-trafficking operations carried out by the state police and border security forces.

Over the last few decades, trafficking in human beings has become a major international concern. Humans are not property, but unfortunately they are being used for Commercial Sexual Exploitation (CSE) as well as for forced labour and also for other purposes after being trafficked. At the global level, human trafficking is recognized as a transnational organized crime in which men, women, children and, in fact, the whole family suffers. Majority of the victims are pushed into sexual exploitation, labour work, organ trade and other forms of exploitation. Human trafficking is defined in various ways by different countries and governmental agencies.

For the first time in the 2000, the Palermo Protocol, the United Nations Protocol to Prevent, Suppress and Punish Trafficking in Persons, Especially

Women and Children, included the international universal definition. According to Article 3 of the Palermo Protocol, *'Trafficking in persons shall mean the recruitment, transportation, transfer, harbouring or receipt of persons, by means of the threat or use of force or other forms of coercion, of abduction, of fraud, of deception, of the abuse of power or of a position of vulnerability or of the giving or receiving of payments or benefits to achieve the consent of a person having control over another person, for the purpose of exploitation.'*[1]

In the South Asian region, trafficking has been defined as *'the moving, selling or buying of women and children for prostitution within and outside a country for monetary or other consideration without the consent of the person subjected to trafficking.'*[2]

In India, the National Crime Records Bureau (NCRB) has defined human trafficking as a *'group of crimes involving the exploitation of men, women and children for financial gain, which is a violation of fundamental human rights.'*[3]

Greater demand and supply has created a healthy business for the traffickers. They choose the illegal trade in human beings because in the trafficking trade overheads are low, they don't have to buy cars and guns for their smooth functioning, drugs you can sell only once and they are gone, but women can earn money for a long time.[4] According to the International Labour Organisation (ILO), there are at least 2.4 million trafficked victims around the world and traffickers earn around more than $32 billion through trafficking.[5] South Asia is estimated to be home to the second largest number of internationally trafficked persons, around 150,000 annually.[6] More than 114,000 organ transplants are reportedly performed every year around the world.[7]

India is considered as source, destination and transit country for trafficking in men, women and children, exposed to forced labour and sex trafficking. Across the world around 80 percent of trafficking is done for the purpose of sexual exploitation and for bonded labour, and India is considered as the hub of this crime in Asia. In 2011, it was estimated that 35,000 children were reported missing, of which more than 11,000 of these children were from Bengal.[8] This is one of the major problems in India. Till date, no concrete study has been conducted to know the exact number of trafficked victims in the country. According to NCRB 2014 Report: West Bengal (1,096 cases) has reported the maximum number of cases related to human trafficking accounting for 20.1% followed by Tamil Nadu (509 cases) and Karnataka (472 cases) accounted for 9.3% and 8.6% respectively during 2014.[9] More than half of cases are from these states. It has been estimated that 27 million adults and 13 million children around the world are suffering as victims of human trafficking.[10]

Bangladesh is also a source and transit country for trafficking in men, women as well as children, both girls and boys. Women and children are trafficked for sexual exploitation to other countries. When India is used as a transit country, victims are sold as prostitutes to the Middle Eastern Countries like Bahrain, Saudi Arabia, UAE (Dubai), Kuwait, etc., and as maids to Europe and USA. However, when India is the destination country, boys are mainly trafficked to provide slave labour in the field of agriculture, brick manufacturing, circus shows and begging, and girls and women are mainly used for slave labour as housemaids and prostitutes.[11] Thousands of girls and young women are trapped and abducted to India each year across the international border. Many victims are forced to work in the tea industry in the north-east part of country. Some women also migrate legally and illegally to gulf countries as domestic servants, but often find themselves in trouble. India is a source, transit and destination country, receiving women and children from Bangladesh, Nepal, Bhutan, Sri Lanka and Pakistan.[12] India and Bangladesh come under tier-2, where both countries do not fully comply with the TVPAs (Trafficking Victim's Protection Act) minimum standards. According to reports of the National Human Rights Commission (NHRC) the registered number of cases and conviction rate of the victims are low due to the insufficient law enforcement in the region. The study also mentions that the corruption rate among police, judiciary and bureaucrats is on increase. Most of the time, victims are even re-trafficked with the help of organized criminal gangs.[13]

Major Issues

India and Bangladesh share the fifth longest international border in world, nearly 4,096.7 km long and with 30 districts on Indian side. It covers Assam (263 km), Meghalaya (443 km), Mizoram (318 km), Tripura (856 km) and West Bengal (2,216.7 km).[14] Out of this a total of 3,286.87 km, or around 60 per cent of the border, is fenced. The area along the border is a mix of topographical features making the border extremely porous. It runs through rivers, ponds, agriculture fields, villages and even houses where the entrance is in India and the backdoor is in Bangladesh. Patrolling in border areas is not an easy task as there is lack of proper roads and also a lot of geographical difficulties, consequently criminal groups misuse these porous stretches along the border. They cause many problems ranging from illegal migration, drug and arms smuggling, dealing of fake currency, terrorism, trafficking of animals, trans-border movement of insurgent groups, human trafficking, etc. These problems pose serious challenges to peace and security. The porous nature of the border, lack of economic opportunities, poverty and underdevelopment, attitude of the people towards many petty crimes, laxity in vigilance, nexus among criminals, the police and border guarding forces of both India and Bangladesh all contribute to the escalating trans-border crimes.

Cross Border Trafficking

As per 2011 estimates, the population density of Bangladesh is 964 persons per sq km and it is the most densely populated country in South Asia. Among 80 percent of Bangladesh's population lives in the rural areas and 53 percent are classified as poor by World Bank.[15] There are many enclaves along the border area which are not patrolled or controlled by any law enforcing agencies. A research carried out by the Bangladesh National Women Lawyers Association (BNWLA) shows that these enclaves have been used as recruitment and collection sites by the traffickers.[16]

There are no reliable estimates of trafficked victims. But it has been estimated by the human rights activists that around 200-400 women and children are smuggled every month from Bangladesh many gulf countries. Further, 10,000 to 15,000 are trafficked to India annually. Most of them end up in prostitution. A large number of Bangladeshi women are involved in the brothels of Kolkata, Mumbai and Delhi. In 2010, 3,517 cases were registered under different acts of human trafficking by the Indian law enforcement agencies, and during 2012 nearly 3,554 cases were registered, with the increase of 1.1 percent.[17] Incidence of cases under the Immoral Trafficking Prevention Act (ITP Act) shows an increase of 5.3 percent during the same period. In the year 2012, out of 3,554 cases, West Bengal alone reported 549 cases of human trafficking.[18] According to 2013 data, maximum crimes, i.e., 65 per cent were registered under the ITP Act. As per the National Crime Record Bureau (NCRB) the number of registered human trafficking cases had increased by 38 percent over the five years from 2,848 in 2009 to 3,940 in 2013.[19] According to United Nations Educational, Scientific and Cultural Organisation (UNESCO) report in 2000, around 30,000 women were taken from Bangladesh and sold in the last decade.

Purposes of Trafficking

South Asia has reported the second highest number of trafficked persons in the world in the last decade. According to an estimate, 90 per cent women trafficked from Bangladesh are forced into prostitution. Children of sex workers especially girls are also forced to work as prostitutes.[20] Some of them are engaged in pornography and forced beggary through use of violence. Many of Bangladeshi men are trafficked for the purposes of forced labour or debt bondage. They are trafficked to work overseas with fraudulent condition of forced labour or debt bondage. A group of anthropologist from the United States claim to have reported the case of kidney theft in Bangladesh.[21]

Bangladeshi children are engaged in construction sites, carpet trade and glass bangles industries in Kolkata, Uttar Pradesh and Karachi. Camel racing is also one of the profitable sports in some of middle-eastern countries, particularly in Dubai. This sport requires lightweight jockeys and has also led to an increase in trafficking of young boys from Bangladesh. Human trafficking is done for agriculture, mining, logging, construction, fishery, sweatshop factory, domestic servitude, begging, drug peddling, janitorial, food services, etc.

Factors behind Human Trafficking

There are numerous factors behind human trafficking. Lack of sustainable resources of livelihood forces people to seek employment elsewhere. Limited natural resources, underdevelopment, natural disasters such as floods, droughts and cyclones causes population to migrate and human trafficking is one of the inadvertent consequences thereof. Lack of education and awareness, inadequacy of government policies and ineffectiveness of rural development schemes are some of the other reasons behind trafficking. Poverty, social inequality and deep rooted discrimination are the most commonly identified factors for trafficking. According to a UNICEF report, most of the guardians of trafficked women and children are landless, of them 45 per cent are farmers and 16 per cent work as daily wage labourers.[22] Gender discrimination and poverty are primarily responsible for the massive women trafficking. Discrimination and low status of women within societies excludes them from development opportunities.

Bangladesh has experienced a significant increase of nearly 60 per cent in urban population in the last two decades which is attributed to migration from rural areas. Uneven regional development and massive rural urban migration have also contributed to the growth of urban poverty.[23] The practice of dowry system is another mechanism of trafficking, when a dowry is not paid by the girl's parents the husband or other family members may abuse the girl to pressure the girl's family to pay the dowry payment. In the process the girl may flee to escape the abuse thus becoming vulnerable to trafficking more easily.[24]

Routes of Trafficking

Out of 4,096.7 km of international border, around 40 per cent area is still unfenced and is vulnerable for criminal activities. Among Indian states, Meghalaya, Tripura and West Bengal are the most vulnerable for trafficking and other illegal criminal activities along the India-Bangladesh border. The forest areas of Tripura and Meghalaya provide traffickers ideal routes to move in and out of Indian territory. In recent years, Bangladesh has become the major conduit for illegal arms and ammunition for insurgents in North-east India. Twenty eight of 64 districts of Bangladesh have common borders with India. There are 18 transit points at the India-Bangladesh border through which children and women are trafficked out of country. Road routes are most preferably used for trafficking of human beings followed by water and airways. According to a study, almost half of the trafficking from Bangladesh to India takes place through Benapole in Jessore district of Bangladesh. The major points like Thanurbairi Chandurila, Kaiba Sultanpur, Chodarpur, Chapainaababguj, Hill Akhwara, Chuadangaand Poladanga are other entry points for trafficking in India.[25]

Victims of Trafficking

There is no single profile of trafficked victims. They may be men, women, girls and children, foreign or national citizens, irrespective of their age and mostly from rural and suburban societies. However, records of trafficking indicate that the poor women and children are the key target group of trafficking because of their marginalization, limited economic resources and predominance in the invisible informal sectors.[26] The extreme poverty in areas adjoining the border makes people more vulnerable for trafficking. It has been estimated that more than 10,000 to 15,000 women and children are trafficked from Bangladesh to India, annually. In the last 18 months, since 2014, approximately 1.5 lac people have been trafficked through the Bay of Bengal. Within the first 3 months of 2015 more than 25,000 people have been trafficked through different transit points such as Teknaf, Ukhia, Cox's Bazar Sadar and Maheshkhali. In June 2015, the Bangladesh Cost Guard teams have rescued 116 people from Bay of Bengal and of the total around two third were between 16 to 25 years age group.[27] Mostly young women are vulnerable for being trafficked as they are defined in sexual category. There are many of victims trafficked below 18 years of age. They are frequently lured by false promises of lucrative jobs, education or marriage. If the demand of global labour market is investigated, there are major demands for bonded labour, rented soldiers and sex workers. Furthermore, only women and children are more compatible with these demands and they are easily targeted. Runaways and homeless youth are also frequently targeted by traffickers. Mostly men are being trafficked for the purpose of bonded labour.

Profile of Traffickers

A lot of criminals focus on organized crime as a market of illicit trafficking rather than as exclusive form of criminal organization, as this approach transforms their network model from a transactional to a social network model. An individual can serve as a recruiter, transporter, protector, or in any number of other roles. So according to them, the network model is used for the purpose of trafficking in human beings.[28] Agents recruiting the victims are known as traffickers, they can be anyone known in the community including family members, husbands, wives, parents, friends, neighbours, community representatives, employees, gang members or strangers. It has been estimated that more than 30 percent of the total number of girls and women trafficked have been abducted under the pretext of false marriages or good jobs. A study of traffickers in India showed that of 160 traffickers, one third stated that their family members were involved in their trafficking activities. Of these, around 43 per cent said that their spouses were involved in their trafficking business and 21.6 per cent traffickers involved their children.[29] It is estimated that traffickers have their own professional occupation aside from their criminal trafficking activities. They work as lawyers, doctors, policemen, politicians, drivers, sports people, chefs, and mechanics, etc., and side by side they run their other business of trafficking in human beings.

There are also other stakeholders supporting the main trafficking structures, including financers who finance at various levels and also the goons who provide security at various stages, the hoteliers who provide the safe accommodation during their transit, the transporters who provide transportation of victim from one place to another, doctors or pharmacists who attend the illness of the trafficked victims during the trafficking process, governmental officials who provide immigration clearance and security services.

Roles and Responsibilities of Criminal Justice System

The Criminal Justice System (CJS) comprises the set of agencies and processes established by the government to control crime and execute penalties for law violators. It is comprised of three major institutions which process a case from inception, through trial and towards punishment. In this the state police are the most visible symbol of the administrative authority and have the supreme power to respond first, arrest and investigate any situation. In India, each state and Union Territory has its own separate police force. The police forces are governed by the rules and regulations framed by the state government. Tackling law and order problem is the prime responsibility of the state and the state police plays an important role in maintaining peace, control of crime, protection of life and property of the community. As the police are a state organisation, they reach out into every corner of the country and have long experience of close contact with the population.[30] Manifestation of Internal and external security threats to India's stability are ranging from communal/ sectarian violence to Jihadi terrorism, separatist insurgency, organized crime, human trafficking, drug trafficking, and arms smuggling. It is becoming difficult and challenging to separate internal and external threat for the CJS. Furthermore, both have become grave challenges for the security forces in maintaining the stability and security of the country.

In anti-trafficking operations, the state police play a key role as it is handled by local police authority. But some time they do not perform to their potential as they are not able to control human trafficking which is growing every year. The lack of a professional attitude in policing is due to the lack of proper training. Lack of proper equipment, gadgets, protective gear and communication devices for police personal is also an issue. Until our internal security is not up to the mark, we won't be able to take care of any of the threats, either internal or external. By 2050, India will be the most populated country in the world and the second largest economy with around one billion workforce. However India cannot become a global power as long as complex threats afflicting its internal security remain.[31]

Article 34 of the Bangladeshi Constitution bans forced and bonded labour.

Further, it specifies that it is the duty on the State to prevent and curb prostitution and also guarantee the populace fundamental human rights. There are also a number of policies and legal framework against human trafficking. With the help of Integrated Crime Data Management System (CDMS) software Bangladeshi authorities have set up monitoring cells where information regarding trafficking is monitored and preserved. Also, Rapid Action Battalion (RAB) has been put into operation for combating human trafficking. The Bangladesh Coast Guard is actively engaged in combating human trafficking through waterways. The government has also taken necessary steps by linking the relevant ministries in an effort to combat trafficking in persons by formulating the domestic legal framework.[32]

Conclusion

Human trafficking is an organized crime which not only involves the violation of basic human rights of the victim but it is a growing challenge for the state as a threat to national security. Both government and NGOs are implementing various programs for the welfare of trafficked victims and to combat this crime, but due to various reasons these initiatives are not giving the desired result in combating human trafficking, rehabilitation and reintegration of the victims. It is also evident that the existing police infrastructure and laws are not adequate in combating the emerging trend of organized crime. Among the trafficked victims all over the world, around 80 percent are women and 50 percent are children. It is very well known that the human trafficking is a one of the most booming business and ranks third in the world among organized crime, after arms and drug trafficking. Lack of clarity and proper understanding of anti-trafficking laws by the law enforcement officials and lack of availability of resources also restricts them in prosecuting traffickers and protecting the victims. Thus, human trafficking is a crucial area, which needs attention. Numerous victims are being transported from Bangladesh to India the through porous international border and from India to other countries illegally. It has always been considered as only a form of organized crime and not as a national security issue. However, taking into account its gravity and potential threat to internal and external security, it has become very necessary to examine human trafficking from the national security perspective.

NOTES

1. UNODC (2015), "What is Human Trafficking?", [Online: web] Accessed 24 June 2015, https://www.unodc.org/unodc/en/human-trafficking/what-is-human-trafficking.html
2. SAARC (2002), "SAARC Convention of Preventing and Combating Trafficking in Women and Children for Prostitution", [Online: web] Accessed 18 April 2015, http://www.saarc-sec.org/userfiles/conv-traffiking.pdf
3. N. Kamal, R.Rajasekaran and A. Kumar (2011), "Crime in India 2011 Compendium", National Crime Rerecord Bureau, Ministry of Home Affairs, Government of India, New Delhi.
4. Stoecker, S. (1998), "The Rise in Human Trafficking and the Role of Orgnised Crime", *Demokratizatsiya, 8, No. 1,* 129-144.
5. ILO (2008), "ILO Action against Human Trafficking in Human Beings", International Labour Organisation, France.
6. UNODC (2007). "South Asia Regional Conference: Responding to Trafficking for Sexual Exploitation in South Asia", United Nations Global Initiative to Find Human Trafficking, New Delhi.
7. US Department of State (2014), "Trafficking in Persons Report 2014", [Online: web] Accessed 24 June 2015,http://www.state.gov/j/tip/rls/tiprpt/2014/226646.htm
8. Nirmala, V. (2013), "Gender Relate Violence: With Special Reference to Human Trafficking", *International Journal of Advanced Research*, 2(2), 834-837.
9. http://ncrb.nic.in/StatPublications/CII/CII2014/Compendium%202014.pdf
10. US (2007), "Trafficking in Persons Report", U.S. Department of State, [Online: web] Accessed 20April 2015, http://www.state.gov/j/tip/rls/tiprpt/2007/index.htm#
11. JICA (2015), "Country Gender Profile: India", Japan Development Service Co, LTD (JDS).
12. Troubnikoff, A.M. (2003), *Trafficking in Women and Children: Current Issues and Development,* Nova Publishers, USA.
13. UNODC (2007), "South Asia Regional Conference: Responding to Trafficking for Sexual Exploitation in South Asia", United Nations Global Initiative to Find Human Trafficking, New Delhi.
14. MHA (2007), "Annual Report",Ministry of Home Affairs, New Delhi.
15. Medhi, B. and Saikia, S. (2014), "Impact of Climatic Change and Rise of Sea Level to Trigger Bangladeshi Exodus in Assam: A Review on the Problem of Climate Induce Migration and Environment and Demographic Situation of Assam", *Asia Pacific Journal of Research,* I(XVIV), 33-43.
16. Liu, J., Hebenton, B., and Jou, S. (2012), *Handbook of Asian Criminology,* Springer Science & Business Media, United Kingdom.
17. NCRB (2013), "Crime in India", Ministry of Home Affairs, New Delhi, [Online: web] Accessed 24 June 2015, http://ncrb.nic.in/CD-CII2011/cii-2011/Chapter%206star.pdf
18. MHA (2013-2014), *Annual Report,* Ministry of Home Affairs, New Delhi.
19. NCRB. (2014). *Crime in India,* New Delhi: Ministry of Home Affairs, [Online: web] Accessed 20 March2015,http://ncrb.nic.in/CD-CII2014/cii-2014/Chapter%206star.pdf
20. Rahman, M. (2011), "Human Trafficking a Security Concern for Bangladesh", Bangladesh Institute of Peace and Security Studies, Dhaka.
21. Hughes, N.S. (2011), "The Organ of Last Resort", UNESCO Courier.
22. Rahman, M. (2011), "Human Trafficking a Security Concern for Bangladesh", Bangladesh Institute of Peace and Security Studies, Dhaka.
23. Hogg, C.L. (2006), "Child Recruitment in South Asian Conflicts: A Comparative Analysis

of Sri Lanka, Nepal and Bangladesh", Chatham House and Coalition to Stop the Use of Child Soilder, London.

24. ECPAT (2006), *Status of Action against Commercial Sexual Exploitation of Children. Bangladesh,* Swedish International Development Corporation Agency.
25. Sareen, T.R. (2004), *Socio-Economic and Political Development in South Asia,* Gyan Publishing House, New Delhi.
26. Ruhi, R.A. (2003), "Human Trafficking in Bangladesh: An Overview", *Asian Affairs,* 25(4), 45-56.
27. Biswas, S. (2015), "Human Trafficking in Bangladesh: An Overview", [Online: web] Accessed 2 December 2015, http://fairbd.net/human-trafficking-in-bangladesh-an-overview/
28. Picarelli, J. (2009), "Human Trafficking & Organised Crime in the US & Western Europe"in Friesendorf, C. (ed), Strategies Against Human Trafficking The Role of The Security Sector, 123-145, Geneva, Centre for the Democratic Control of Armed Forces and Austrian National Defence Academy.
29. Nair, P.M. (2002-2003), *A Report on Trafficking in Women and Children in India,* National Human Rights Commission, New Delhi.
30. Epstein, D.G. (1968), "Police Role in Counterinsurgency Efforts", Journal of Criminal Law and Criminology, 59(1), [Online: web] Accessed 22 December 2015, http://scholarlycommons.law.northwestern.edu/jclc
31. Manoharan, N. (2013), "India's Internal Security Situation: Threat and Responses". India Quarterly: A Journal of International Affairs, 69(4), 367-381.
32. MHA (2012), "Bangladesh Country Report", Ministry of Home Affairs, Government of the People's Republic of Bangladesh, Dhaka.

4

India-Bhutan Relationship: An Overview

Shivendra Shahi

Bhutan was the first country that Prime Minister Narendra Modi visited after becoming the Prime Minister of India. This action itself signifies the importance attached to India-Bhutan relations. India is a country which has antagonistic neighbours. India and Bhutan have friendly relations. India signed a friendship treaty with Bhutan in 1949 which was revised in 2007, wherein it was stated that the nations shall cooperate closely with each other on issues related to their respective national interests, and would prohibit the use of territories carrying out of activities harmful to the security interests of each other. The two economies are closely related to each other. However, China, for instance, has been trying to win over Bhutan and reduce India's growing influence. Further, Bhutan has made a conscious effort to avoid taking any decision contrary to India's national interests. This paper is an attempt to give an overview of the relationship between India and Bhutan and to provide probable suggestions to strengthen the relationship.

Bhutan lies in the eastern Himalayas with India to its south and China to its north with a total area of 18,147 sq miles (47000 sq km) and population of 700,000 people. It came into existence in 1656 with mixed monarchical-parliamentary system. It shares its border with China (470 km), and state of Sikkim (32 km), West Bengal (183 km), Assam (267 km) and Arunachal Pradesh (217 km). It is one of the poorest countries in the world and is largely closed to the outside world for protecting its culture to the extent that

Television (TV) was banned until 1999. It became the first country in the world in 2004 to ban smoking and the sale of tobacco.

Bhutan is a hereditary monarchy without a written constitution. The King shares power with a council of Ministers, the National Assembly, the head of Bhutan's 5,000 Buddhist monks with 151 members in the National Assembly, and 106 are directly elected by universal adult suffrage for a three-year term, the remainder include the Royal Advisory Council, the Ministers and religious representatives. There are no political parties. National population council of Bhutias, who live in the eastern part of the country (migrated from India), the Drukda in western Bhutan are of Tibetan origin and many other minority groups which are distributed in seventeen administrative districts. There are 20 languages in the country with Dzongkha as the official language. Bhutan was under Tibetan influence from the 16th Century which was followed by Chinese over lordship up to 1720. In 1774 border friction with British-India led to annexation of some of its territory which was returned to Bhutan by India in 1949. This treaty termed the basis of bilateral relations between India and Bhutan, which provides for, ;perpetual peace and friendship, free trade and commerce and equal justice to each other's citizens.' The much speculated Article 2 in the treaty, in principle, calls for Bhutan to seek India's advice in external matters, while India pledges non-interference in Bhutan's internal affairs.[1]

Historical Overview

In 1958, the then Indian Prime Minister, Jawaharlal Nehru, stated that though Bhutan is a small country, it should remain independent in choosing its own way of life.[2] The policy is continued by the succeeding governments in India. This policy enunciated by Nehru has played an important role in enabling Bhutan getting the international recognition that it deserves. Earlier, in 1947, the relationship between Bhutan and India was suddenly subjected to question, especially after the absorption of some former princely states by Indian Union. At some point, Bhutan even considered joining with Sikkim and Tibet in order to guard against Indian expansionism. In 1948, a Bhutanese delegation was sent to India and got assured that India did not have any desire to encroach on Bhutan's sovereignty. The 1949 Treaty, was not only a continuation of the relationship between both, but in the treaty India acceded to three requests of Bhutan: the yearly 'annual payment' India made to Bhutan be increased, a portion of the land captured in the Duar War be returned, and the King of Bhutan be addressed as the Druk Gyalpo rather than the Maharaja of Bhutan.[3]

The 1949 Treaty indicates Bhutan's complete control of its internal affairs, but external affairs of Bhutan are to be 'guided by the advice of the Indian Government'. But Bhutanese sensitivity of Indian presence was indicated in Rustomji writings in his book 'Crisis in the Dragon Kingdom':

> They fear that foreign influences, starting with the British, have brought about a degeneration of values in Sikkim, the indigenous culture of the Sikkimese has been contaminated by ill-advised contact during the past half-century, and lost its power for good: the present development programme is also being guided, mainly by Indian, who, for all their good intentions, cannot always be expected to appreciate the basic needs of the people and find difficulty in adjusting themselves to conditions in the hill areas. The Bhutanese are determined, therefore, to train up their own people, and feel it would be wiser, in the long view, to accept a few years of delay rather than risk a break-up of their social fabric. This is an understandable attitude which causes no surprise.[4]

Rustomji clearly argued that even though the Bhutanese were forced to take Indian personnel and the critical planning process itself was crafted by Indian Advisors, the Bhutanese from the beginning were looking to reserve complete control of their country.

Indo-Bhutan Treaty of 1949 (revised in February 2007) further provides leverage to India to look after Bhutan's foreign affairs and defence, in terms of:

— Bhutan's Hydropower potentials and generation of electricity;
— Economic Ties through border trade and 95 per cent export and 79 per cent import;
— Human resources (skilled or unskilled);
— Bhutan's tranquillity and peace;
— Combating Insurgencies in the North East India; and
— Security issues

India and Bhutan both have strong cultural and historic ties. There is a smooth flow of people from Bhutan to India for education, employment, medical care, etc. The social interaction amongst the people of the two nations has been cemented over the years, through these exchanges.

Diplomatic relations between India and Bhutan were established in 1968 with the appointment of resident representative of India at Thimpu. Before this, India's relations with Bhutan were looked after by Indian political office in Sikkim. The basic framework of India-Bhutan bilateral relations is the Treaty of Friendship and Cooperation signed in 1949, which was renewed during the visit of His Majesty Jigme Khesar Namgyel Wangchuck to India in February 2007.[5] Both the countries are working together to enhance security bilaterally and regionally, and also need to find ways and means to cope with security challenges, be it money laundering, international economic crimes, cyber crimes, military, narcotics, terrorism, arms smuggling and illegal migratory flow.

Economic Cooperation

Mutually beneficial economic linkages between India and Bhutan have been an important element in the bilateral relations. India continues to be the largest trade and development partner of Bhutan. Planned development efforts in Bhutan began in the early 1960s. The First Five Year Plan (FYP) of Bhutan was launched in 1961. Since then, India has been extending financial assistance to Bhutan's FYPs. The 10th FYP ended in June 2013. India's overall assistance to the 10th FYP was a little over INR 5000 crores, excluding grants for hydropower projects.[6] In the fiscal year 2012-13, India's budgetary support to the Kingdom country stood at USD 600 million (around INR 30 billion). Bhutan's new Prime Minister, Tshering Tobgay, secured an additional aid package from India worth INR 54 billion (USD 819 million, as per the exchange rates at the time of signing the deal) for his nation during his visit to New Delhi in August 2013. It steadily rose over the years to reach USD 985 million (INR 30 billion) in 2015-16 making Bhutan the largest beneficiary of India's foreign aid.[7]

Economic Interests

The two nations are irrevocably bound through massive economic interests. India is Bhutan's largest trade and development partner. India gives aid to Bhutan and is also involved in a variety of projects there. India accounts for 98 per cent of Bhutan's exports and 90 per cent imports.[8] Indian businesses are also active in Bhutan. Major items of exports from Bhutan to India are electricity, ferro-alloys, carbides, bar and rods, cement, copper wire, semi finished products of iron and non-alloy steel, Dolomite, gypsum, agriculture products such as oranges, cardamom and potatoes. Major exports from India to Bhutan are high speed diesel, ferrous products, motor spirit including aviation spirit (petrol), rice, ferrous waste and scraps, wood charcoal, hydraulic turbines, coal, briquette and similar solid fuels of coal, coke and semi coke of coal, bar and rods of iron and non-alloy steels, corrugated iron and non-alloy steel sheet, soybean oil, milk powder, etc.[9]

Hydropower Cooperation

The India-Bhutan hydropower cooperation is a classic example of successful bilateral cooperation; however, the two countries face a range of other challenges that have been straining the ties. Prime Minister Narendra Modi's recent visit did make a strategic mark because he covered most of the short and long-term issues that point towards further development and cooperation between the two states.[10] India operates multiple hydroelectric projects in Bhutan, and is in the process of building a few more projects. Also, during summer, Bhutan produces more electricity than it requires. During such months, Bhutan supplies electricity to India, which faces huge energy deficiency.

Power sector engagement has been the primary avenue for India and Bhutan in taking their relationship forward. Power diplomacy with Bhutan has been India's successful stray. Cooperation in the hydropower sector between the two countries is a true example of mutually beneficial relationship. Hydropower is one of the main pillars of bilateral cooperation. Three Hydro-Electric Projects (HEPs) totalling 1416 MW, (336 MW Chukha HEP, the 60 MW Kurichu HEP, and the 1020 MW Tata HEP), are already exporting electricity to India. In 2008, the two governments agreed to further develop a minimum of 10,000 MW hydropower generation capacities by 2020 and identified ten more projects. Of these, three projects totalling 2940 MW (1200 MW Punatsangchu-I, 1020 MW Punatsangchu-II and 720 MW Mangdechu HEPs) are under construction and are scheduled to be commissioned in the last quarter of 2017-2018.[11] During his visit in June 2014, Indian Prime Minister Narendra Modi laid the foundation stone of Kholongchhu HEP, followed by the Indian President laying the foundation stone for the Jigme Wangchuk Power Training Institute during his state visit to Bhutan in November, 2014.[12] Power is an important sector of Bhutanese economy. It contributes 14 per cent to the GDP. It is the most important export item contributing 35 per cent of Bhutan's total exports. Druk Green Power Corporation, which controls all electricity generation plants of the country, is the highest tax payer of the country.[13]

Initially, economic aid given by India is said to have been influenced by security concerns in enabling Bhutan to have the essential infrastructure, but currently it is followed by a policy of mutual benefit from the projects which are being undertaken in Bhutan by India. India operates multiple hydro-electric projects in Bhutan, and is in the process of building a few more projects. Further, these projects fulfil India's energy needs and, to some extent, also ensure the development of the North-east region of India. In return, India ensures the sustainable development of Bhutan.

Critical Issues within Bhutan

Challenges

Constrained by geo-Strategic and socio-economic factors, environmental degradation and climate change, Gross National Happiness has remained merely a philosophical term; to sustain the democracy along with Monarchy. The pro-democratic movement and issue of Bhutanese refugees, youth aspirations, difficult in coping with balancing tradition with modernity, unemployment in 80% population between 15-25 years, rural-urban migration due to uneven development, problems in land distribution and acquisition, regional economic disparities, uneven development, currency crunch, corruption, increasing public debt, high fiscal deficit mainly due to a dependent economy, small domestic market, problems in public delivery service, high transportation costs, limited exports, etc., are some of the challenges facing the country.

Some external challenges which Bhutan is facing are political violence at the borders with both India and China; Vulnerabilities of sensitive Borders and Borderland Communities; External Aid comes with pre-conditions; Donors from West may try to use political strings; International Agencies may dictate their agenda; Preservation of Culture and unique ethnic identity due to the influx of International Tourists.

Recommendations for India

- Keep engaging Bhutan in economic assistance/Official interactions/ Help in the sectors like health, education, developing infra-structure.
- Open Multi-track Diplomacy, India-Bhutan Friendship Council, Academic Exchanges.
- Maintain 'Non-reciprocal' relations with spirit of Beneficial Bilateralism.
- Develop and inculcate confidence among Bhutanese people about its friendly gestures.

— Provide an access for Transit and Trade with other SAARC nations.

— Respect and support Bhutan to protect its national pride and culture.[14]

Conclusions

It can be said that Bhutan is not interested in using China as a counter-balance for Indo-Bhutan relations, whereas it is more inclined to maintain reasonable relations with China without offending India's interest in the region. Moreover, being sandwiched between two powerful countries, such a policy cannot but be ambivalent and non-antagonistic. A small state has little choice other than to maintain a low profile in dealing with its larger and more powerful neighbours. This is the strategic stand taken by Bhutan vis-a-vis China.[15] India should facilitate Bhutan to grow politically and economically in a liberal democratic atmosphere. If not allowed, then one day Democratic Bhutan may question India and its policies towards Bhutan.

There is much scope and real convergence of interest between India and Bhutan in the economic, financial and commercial areas. As one of the largest and fastest growing economics of the world, India offers unique cooperation possibilities for the mutual benefit of the two countries. Both countries will have to shed their old entrenched mindsets and evolve a new partnership based on their unique convergence and for mutual benefit.

Some initiatives are suggested to improve the relationship between the two countries:

- Both countries should increase mutual defence and security cooperation.
- Both countries should promote and strengthen further cultural, religious, tourism, and educational links with help of setting up high level autonomous forum and through institutionalized cooperation mechanism.
- In consonance with their emerging strategic partnership they should upgrade and institutionalize mutual dialogue through regular annual meetings and exchange of visits at the highest level.
- With the objective of making relationship more meaningful, they should enhance their economic and commercial ties and resolve differences on policy and procedural matters.

The growing partnership with Bhutan exemplifies India's recent policy under Modi, giving priority to its close neighbourhood. An increasingly assertive

China and its growing interest in the region are forcing Indian policy makers to relook their policy towards the region. To counter the pressure emanating from terrorism it is necessary for both countries to expand the scope of their strategic cooperation by establishing stronger economic and strategic partnership. There is tremendous potential of cooperation between India and Bhutan in various fields including trade, health, science and technology, tourism, human resource and infrastructure development. Rising cooperation trends will create a congenial atmosphere which eventually will facilitate large economic benefits for the people of both the nations. The future of Bhutan-India partnership holds ample potential.

NOTES

1. Government of India(2015), "India-Bhutan Relation", Ministry of External Affairs, New Delhi, [Online: web] Accessed 25 December 2015, http://www.mea.gov.in/Portal/ForeignRelation/Bhutan_2015_07_20.pdf
2. Murthy, P. (1999), "Indo-Bhutan Relations: Serving Mutual Interests", [Online: web] Accessed 09August 2015,http://www.idsa-india.org/an-apr9-8.html
3. Ibid. p. 481.
4. Ibid. p. 489.
5. Government of India (2015), "India-Bhutan Relation", Ministry of External Affairs, New Delhi, [Online: web] Accessed 25 August 2015, http://www.mea.gov.in/Portal/ForeignRelation/Bhutan_2015_07_20.pdf
6. See http://www.worldfocus.in/articles/india-and-neighbours/india-bhutan-relations-survey/ for details
7. Macramé Consultants(2015), "India-Bhutan Bilateral Relations", Macrame Consultants Pvt. Ltd. [Online: web] Accessed 25 November 2015, http://macrame.in/wp-content/uploads/2015/06/GST.pdf
8. See http:// http://www.worldfocus.in/articles/india-and-neighbours/india-bhutan-relations-survey/ for details
9. see http://www.indianembassythimphu.bt/pages.php.?id=83
10. Hukil, R. (2015), "Modi's Thimpu Visit: Deepening India-Bhutan Relations", [Online: web] Accessed 3 November 2015,http://www.ipcs.org/article/india/modis-thimpu-visit-deepening-india-bhutan-relations,
11. See http://www.indianembassythimphu.bt/pages.php?id=83
12. Government of India (2015), "India-Bhutan Relation", Embassy Of India, Thimphu [Online: web] Accessed 5 August 2015, http://www.indianembassythimphu.bt/pages.php?id=83
13. http://www.indianembassythimphu.bt/pages.php?id=83
14. http://www.jnu.ac.in/SIS/MakingSISVisible/Presentations/Understanding%20 Bhutan.%Kharat.pdf
15. Khrat, Rajesh (2009), "India-Bhutan relation", in *Himalayan Frontiers of India: Historical, Geo-Political and Strategic perspectives* edited by K. Warikoo, Routledge publication, New York.

5

China's Comprehensive National Power and Security Objectives: Impact on India

Shekhar Adhikari and Atul Mishra

To understand China's Comprehensive National Power (CNP) it is essential to go deep into its history, philosophy and stated policies. The important elements of the growing CNP of China have to be re-examined in the light of recent developments in international politics. As such, the following issues become important in enhancing the status of China in world affairs. These are: history of strong national values, culture and long term vision; the economic strength; China's grand strategy and geo-strategic compulsion; China's plans and strategic initiative; China's demographic dividend; and security implications for India.

China's Cultural History and Values

After a protracted struggle within and outside, China was proclaimed as People's Republic on 1 October 1949 and soon created the People Republic of China. It was Mao Tse Tung who understood the needs of Chinese society. China at that time needed reforms. Mao, as Chairman of Communist Party of China (CPC), initiated the land reforms, the Great Leap Forward as a socio-economic plan and the Cultural Revolution between 1966 and 1976. These reforms strengthened the party's communist ideology. Later on, Deng Xiaoping took a socialist path to match an 'open door' foreign policy. Jiang

Zeming's policy was focused on establishing 'three major' historic tasks—modernisation, national reunification and safeguarding world peace and development. Jiang's successor, Hu Jintao, emphasized the need of 'balanced development.' Further, Premier Wen Jaibao felt that 'China for its development needed first an international environment of long term stability and a stable surrounding environment.' This meant that China needed 'peaceful periphery' for the formulation and implementation of its foreign policy. The slogan was 'peaceful rise of China.'

At the 18th National Congress Meeting of the Communist Party of China on 8th November 2012, Hu Jin Tao linked the increasing corruption in the country to social unrest. He spoke of the need for social, economic and political reforms in the country by laying much stress on maintaining harmonious relations within the society so that social contradictions could be minimized. In March 2013, Xi Jinping was elected as President and Le Kequiang as Prime Minister. Before departing, the Prime Minister Wen Jaibao had warmed the country to face another cultural revolution if China does not undertake political, social and economic reforms. To carry Hu Jintao's ideology of harmonious society and scientific development as a counter to Mao's theories, China would need to sustain the ideology through liberalization on many fronts, including human rights. Thus, on the eve of the 18th Party Congress, China focused on the following security issues:

- Taiwan, Tibet and Tibet related policies became important.
- Since 2010, China had made it clear that South China Sea is important and if provoked then it would resort to use of force.
- On the sovereignty of East China Sea, its military confrontation with Japan was to be avoided because of the US-Japan Security treaty in East China Sea.

Chinese Strategic Culture: Chinese history is embedded with two metaphors, 'the Great Wall' and the 'Empty Fortress.' It is the symbol of an intermingling of both weakness and strength. One can also interpret China in terms of 'strategic deception,' this phrase was much in tandem with Sun Tzu's strategic doctrine that 'war is based on deception.' Even today, Sun Tzu's military writing is important in shaping Chinese military policy. He believed that 'a clever fighter is one who not only wins but excels in winning with ease.' Furthermore, 'victorious warriors win first and then go to war while defeated warriors go to war and then seek to win.' This symbolizes the 'idea of wining without fighting.' In the modern age one finds changes in the connotation of key concepts in the writings of Chinese military experts. They consider strategic contemplation at four levels the military thought, military strategy, military campaign and military tactics. These concepts form the vital core of Chinese national culture.

Mao Tse Tung and others did provide a room for strategic thinking by emphasizing China's relations with the Soviet Union, Five Principles of Peaceful Coexistence and Three World Construct. Later on, Deng Xiaoping focused on economic development. The objective was to engage all the countries for the proper investments and technologies in China to raise its CNP. In other words, China wanted to enhance its CNP by increasing economic and military power in the new world order system.

The Economic Strength

Since the disintegration of the Soviet Union, there was a political vacuum in the international system. Some scholars even suggested that bipolar or multi-polar world has come to an end and the world once again became uni-polar led by the USA. But this kind of thinking did not last for long because the world's focus, after 1991, was more on economic development rather than on military power. We also saw globalization and liberalization had become more important for major powers in assessing their national power capabilities. The impact of globalization was also seen in China. This has not only improved China's economic stature but also restored the balance of power in world politics by giving much scope to multilateralism. The key to success was to sustain economic progress while building strategic capabilities.

In 1978, under Deng Xiaoping's leadership, China embarked on a path of economic reforms by laying emphasis on market oriented economy. In recent years, one has witnessed a vital change in Chinese economy. This shift is from centrally planned system to a more market oriented economy. Now China has a fast growing private sector, though CPC has an important role to play. Thus, China has also become a major economic player in the international system.

As per projection by the Economist (London), China would surpass USA as the most prosperous nation somewhere between 2018 and 2021. China's gross domestic product (GDP) has also improved. This GDP transition from number 2 to number 1position will also enhance its political-military and strategic-security policies. However, the per capita income status of China is still low and the US will retain its military superiority for at least two more decades. However, the restructuring of the Chinese economy has contributed to a phenomenal increase in GDP since 1978. Its GDP has surpassed Italy in 2000, France in 2005, UK in 2006, Germany in 2007 and Japan in 2010. Now China is the second largest economic power after the USA. So far as purchasing power parity basis is concerned, China's GDP in 2012 stood at $11.44 trillion. If this happens, many strategic experts predict that China's economy will be larger than that of the USA by 2049.

Trade with India

Bilateral trade between India and China increased from $23 billion in 2000 to $51 billion in 2008 and $76 billion in recent times with a trade surplus in favour of China at about $27 billion. In 2007, iron ore comprised 52 percent of Indian exports to China. Overall, raw materials made up to 85 percent of India's total exports while the Indian market was flooded with cheap Chinese goods. Thus, it seems that in the economic sphere of Sino-India relations, trade, hailed as making tremendous progress, is a fiction.

However, there is no Sino-Indian congruence on geo-political issues. That is why 'India-China strategic cooperative partnership for peace and prosperity' remains devoid of any content other than a fast growing trade relationship. It seems that Sino-Indian relations will be more as business partners rather than friends. Neither country, today, wants military confrontation. Managed competitions or China's 'Peaceful Rise' will define the relationship between them in the coming years.

It is quite evident from the Chinese security perspective that India is not the only country with which it can maintain relations. In South Asia, Pakistan is important to China. It is important to note that China has succeeded to draw Nepal, Pakistan and Sri Lanka into its strategic orbit.

China and ASEAN

China's relations with ASEAN are not only in political, military and economic fields but also in diplomatic field. In 2012, China made a decision of opening a permanent mission in Jakarta. This has indicated endorsement of an ASEAN driven regional cooperation. In term of economic activities, China has offered assistance to ASEAN for infrastructure projects. It has also argued to set up a fund for maritime cooperation to ensure environmental protection, navigational safety and protection against transnational crimes.

In the year 1820, the contribution in share of world income by India and China was 49 percent, i.e., 33 percent by China and 16 percent for India. 135 years later the share came down to 9 percent. In 2012, the Chinese accounted for more than 40 per cent of global trade and India almost 10 percent and combined together they generate more than half of the world's economic growth. Nevertheless, by 2025, it is predicated that there may be some restoration in the share of India and China to 38 per cent. Furthermore, how China will behave towards India will have to be seen in the growing economic and military competition worldwide. China feels that Modi's Act East Policy will lead to competition in capturing the economic markets in East Asia. India has improved its relations with ASEAN. Thus, one sees China's rapid rise in economic and military spheres have made them to play more dominant roles in the Asia-Pacific region, Europe and other international forums.

So far as trade with ASEAN is concerned, China is ASEAN's biggest trading partner and ASEAN is China's fourth biggest partner. China's trade with region stood around $500 billion. This will grow more in the coming years. Trade with them indicates an upward trend. Thailand is China's largest trading partner and second largest importer. Trade with Vietnam stood at $70 million in 2011.

China's Grand Design

The concept of the New Great Game means competition for acquiring more power, indulging in hegemonistic design for working for profits in the Pacific region, South Asia, Indian Ocean and Central Asian regions. The Oceanic elements are also a geo-political factor in Sino-Indian relations. It has even evoked Alfred Thayer Mahan's concept of sea power as projection of power and control of LOCs, the Sea Lanes of Communication. These are also some elements of Halford John Mackinder's Heartland theory, Nicolas John Spykman's Rimland and Mahan's sea power paradigm which are quite visible in Sino-Indian relations. Both Asian powers aspire for great power status.

There are three competitive areas for India and China. These are security, economic and diplomacy. The opening of Lhasa to Golmund railway in 2006 was seen by Indian strategic experts as 'China strategic master stroke' as the most important strategic development since 1950s. It has altered the military balance in favour of China. Missile systems have been installed and discontent among the Tibetan people has been curbed. Such kind of power projection makes India more vulnerable to Chinese pressures. But, in recent years, India too has improved its military capabilities by testing Agni V which has 5500 km range and can reach Beijing, Shangai and Guanghou. There is a major shift in India's defence policy, i.e., from being passive to assertive. India's military posture has become more offensive. India, today, is capable of facing both Pakistan and China if provoked.

China's rise, is perhaps, due to her naval presence in regions. In military term, the process of China's military modernization lies in the development of CNP. It is poised to further extend its political influence by becoming a significant arms player in the near future. Moreover, Chinese military spending has been increasing sharply, faster than its economy. But, sustained economic prosperity supported by managed domestic situation allowed the resolute CPC to play a more assertive role in international affairs. From the Horn to Africa to South America and South and South East Asia, China's presence is visible. It has also built strong relationships with Indian Ocean region littoral states, supported anti-US posture and supported North Korea, Iran, Sudan, Pakistan, Sri Lanka, Bangladesh and Myanmar on various issues.

National Objectives/Policies as Part of CNP

There seems to be a contradiction in the Chinese national policy. It is difficult to accept what China says and what it does? China wants to regain its lost position in the world by the expansion of CNP. Accordingly, the core elements are:

- To maintain peaceful international environment so that it can gain time to develop its strategic strength;
- To prevent unilateral declaration of independent Taiwan and the rise of militarist Japan;
- To ensure regime stability;
- To continue efforts for national unification and improve relations without giving up territorial claims;
- To ensure economic and trade development which is important for the development of national power;
- To ensure domestic cohesion and regime stability by minimizing inter-region disparities and improve inclusive growth, human development index and standard of living of citizens;
- To ensure overall development in Tibet Autonomous Region and

Xinziang province by having loyal party workers to keep the state of affairs in tight control under it;

- To build military capability and expand its influence over South China Sea and then approach to Indian Ocean region for trade and energy routes and;
- To build a dominant position in the Asia-Pacific region in the short term and then try to attain the status of global power in the long run.

China's Soft Power as Element of CNP

CNP for China is not measured in terms of political, social, economic and military security but it also takes into account 'soft' capabilities. On 15 October 2007, at the National Congress of the Communists Party of China, President Hu Jintao stated that CPC 'must enhance its culture as part of the soft power of our country, a factor of growing significance in the competition in overall national strength.' The CPC is determined to develop its soft power and wants to see the attractiveness of Chinese civilization and political system as well as economic reforms undertaken in 1978. China has funded more than 270 Confucius Institutes in 75 countries teaching mandarin and the party version of history to more than 100 million foreigners. China aims to have more than 1000 such institutes by 2025. As compared to China, India has only 25 cultural centres in 21 countries. At present, China has more diplomats than any other country including the USA. In China's state dominated society, diplomats are chosen as elites and are give extensive language and cultural training.

Chinese cultural diplomacy, economic development, public diplomacy or humanitarian assistance and its soft power tools are seen in almost all parts of the world. It is interesting to note that without compromising on hard power, Chinese foreign policy had made efforts to engage countries far and near. Cultural diplomacy influence in the USA, Europe, Australia, New Zealand, economic engagement involving developing countries like Africa, Pacific Islands countries, South and South East Asia, role of public diplomacy in the world and even humanitarian assistance to various countries indicate China's effort to project a benign image to the international community.

Demographic Dividend

There is a clear cut indication that India has an edge over China so far as demography in concerned. India has a large quantity of young population to take the best out of them and China is burdened by senior people. This advantage should be exploited by India properly. In theory, it will erode China's comparative advantage in labour intensive manufactures by 2025. However, in India, one finds poor domestic and national policies, poor governance, low political will, corruption, slow procurement and investment procedures and regional and major national parties' rivalries which act as sources of weakness rather than strength. Further, overall adult literacy in India is roughly 61 per cent as compared to China's 91 per cent. China sends more than 19 per cent of its young people for higher education to foreign countries while in India it is only 11 to 12 per cent. This shows that though China is ahead of India but it does not mean that Indian cannot improve and, thus, challenge China in this field.

Elements of China's CNP to Obtain National Interest

The India-China Border: It is fifty three years since the two countries fought a border war and the entire frontier from Kashmir to Arunachal Pradesh remains a daunting task to them. It was in 1988 when efforts were made by then Prime Minister Rajiv Gandhi to resolve the border dispute. But no substantial results have been seen to resolve the disputes even having several rounds of talks between representatives of both countries. In the era of globalization, the focus today is more on trade and economic development rather resolving the crucial border issues.

With regard to border settlement, some developments have taken place. Both the countries have concluded several major or bilateral agreements in finding a fair solution to the problem. These agreements are: a Joint Working Group (1988), the Peace and Tranquility Treaty (1993), the CBM Agreement (1996), Appointment of Special Representative (2003), Strategic and Cooperative Partnership for Peace and Prosperity and Political Parameters and Guiding Principles for settlement of the Boundary Question (2005), Promotion of Civil Nuclear Cooperation (2006) and Shared Vision for the 21st century (2008).

Territorial Claims: China appears to be in no hurry to resolve the border issue. From time to time, China has taken a more assertive position on the entire border problem, particularly Tawang in Arunachal Pradesh. China had intimidated the Indian population who were engaged in repairing subsidiary roads and water channels and sometimes back had also issued stapled visas to Indians of Kashmiri origin on the ground that Kashmir is a disputed area.

Visa was also denied to Lt. Gen. B.S. Jaswal in August 2010 because he was in charge of the disputed territory in Jammu and Kashmir.

Besides this, there is another issue which had become a bone of contention between India and China. China has linked Tawang in Arunachal Pradesh with Tibet. China is no mood to recognize a successor to the present Dalai Lama who is operating from India. If the successor is appointed it would place China in an uncomfortable position. In such a case, China has started claiming Tawang as part of its territory. The 134 km Pangong Tso Lake in Eastern Ladakh extends from India to Tibet. Two-third of the area is controlled by China. One has seen the surge of Chinese intrusions on several occasions. To counter these foot, motorized and boat patrol transgression in the hundreds by the Peoples Liberation Army, the MOD has already processed 17 Quick Reaction Teams, Patrol Boats for reconnaissance and area domination.

Chinese strategic intrusion from time to time on our land and the earlier inability of our diplomacy to counter them is a cause of great concern. In its strategic calculation, its ability to prevent a military conflict with India would depend on a strong military capability in Tibet and equally a strong Pakistan's military capability in nuclear and conventional fields.

Is China A Hegemonic Power?

China is still a communist country. It supports brutal regimes that are driven by capitalist considerations. While exploiting commercial opportunities, it has also made strategic in roads. China has signed tens of billions of dollars worth of energy and arms contracts in recent years with such problem riddle states like Myanmar, Bangladesh, Iran, Sudan, Venezuela and so on. Then, there is the China-Nepal-Pakistan nexus which has become a cause of great concern to India. This nexus will cover India from the North West to the East at the eastern sector of the Sino-Indian borders. There is also a strong Chinese presence in the Asia-Pacific region. The Australia 2009 Defence White Paper, USA Quadrennial Defence Review 2010 and National Military Strategy 2011 have indicated that economic relations with China is an important aspect of China's military hegemonic threat in the region which can pose a threat to the natural and legitimate interests of major and small countries.

The repercussions of Chinese foreign policy initiatives have also endangered the security of India. In 1998, George Fernandes, the then Defence Minister, had asserted, 'China is potential threat number one....China is and likely to remain the prime security challenge to India in the medium and long term....the potential threat from China is greater than that from Pakistan and any person who is concerned about India's security must agree with that.' Similarly, the then Indian Prime Minister Atal Bihari Vajpayee explained to the US President Clinton that the nuclear tests was necessary because China is an 'overt nuclear state on our borders, a state which committed armed aggression against it in 1962' with whom 'an atmosphere of distrust persists.' Thus, the Chinese hegemonistic design had made the neighbours more alert and these states have started realignment with such powers which are anti-China.

Conclusion

The above analysis of China's development of CNP leads to an important question. What will be the likely impact of its on Indian security? It is true that China, after hard struggle, structured their social, economic, political and military systems in such a fashion that it is capable of playing a more assertive role in international politics. It was quite evident that after the disintegration of the Soviet Union, China became a more active player, thereby changing the nature and structure of international politics.

If the disintegration of the Soviet Union which had placed China in a more confident and assertive position, India is not far behind. This could be seen from the developments taking place in South Asia. India made a remarkable progress in the development of her economy. The end of the 20th century also saw the nuclear test explosion and efforts made by her to establish strategic partnership with the developed and the developing countries. In such a situation, can India be really be threatened by Chinese progress in various fields. Since the Cultural Revolution, China's foreign and security policies have been bold and it is in a position to play her cards well in international politics.

Though it is true that India-China fought in 1962 and since then both the countries have not agreed to any kind of agreement to solve the border issue. But, what they have done, instead of resolving the border issue, they have focused more on economic and trade relations. In this sense, one can say that China and India, the two fast growing giants, are trapped in a zero-sum strategic rivalry. The present leadership in both countries realize that they can lay the foundation for a stable Sino-India relations. China must reassure India that its ambitious infrastructure programme will not pose a threat to Indian national security. On the other hand, Narendra Modi must also assuage Xi's worries that India will not to be used as a pawn of the US in balancing against China.

Recently, on 14 May 2015, Prime Minister Narendra Modi visited China, Mongolia and Korea. The critics felt that nothing concrete will come from Modi's visit. But, Modi has made a bold effort in recasting Sino-Indian relations. As usual the focus was on economic cooperation with China. Although the border dispute cannot be solved overnight but a beginning has been made. At present, both the leaders preferred status quo on border management and working in other fields. Narendra Modi and Xi Jinping are making efforts to take India-China bilateral relations to new heights. One can hope that both the countries succeed in achieving some measured progress as Deng stated once, 'there is enough space for both the countries to prosper.'

In the last few years, we have seen remarkable changes in the world and India's security. The world needs India to be set up as a global power. On the one hand, India's relations with the USA have improved and on the other hand, India has played her cards well in not antagonizing powers like the erstwhile Soviet Union and China. This is quite evident from India's participation in SCO and BRICS. In both the organizations, India had to play an important role because all these three countries, today, face the problem of religious fundamentalism, separatism and terrorism. In July 2015, India and Pakistan were made members of SCO to fight against terrorism which has affected all members' internal and external security. In BRICS also, both India and China have concrete roles in reshaping the economic destiny. Thus, one can say that in spite of China's development of CNP and projecting her strategic objective in an assertive way, this will in no way result in further conflict with India. But, probably, both India and China, acting together, and making a positive presence in world politics will be a reality in the coming years.

NOTES

1. A. Sahgal and P.Palit (2005), "The Singh Doctrine", Armed Forces Journal, May, [Online: web] Accessed 16 November 2015, http.//www/armed force journal .com / 2006/05/ 1677960/.
2. National Economic and Social Development (2015), National Bureau of Statistics of China, [Online: web] Accessed 13 October November 2015, http://www.stats.gov.cn/english/news and coming events/ 20090226-402540784.htm.
3. D.S. Saibal (2012), "China Meet Acquire Anti US Tone", *Times of India*, 8 June, Delhi.
4. A. Bhattacharya (2011), "Sixty Years of India-China Relations", *Strategic Analysis*, Vol. 34, No. 5, September, New Delhi.

5. South China Morning Post, 19 November, 2011 in BBC Monitoring Global News line-Asia-Pacific Policy, 20 November, 2011.
6. A.T. Mahan (1918), "The Influence of Seapower upon History, 1660-1783", Boston.
7. M.Pugh (1996), "Is Mahan Still Alive? State Naval Power in the International System", *Journal of Conflict Studies*, 26/2:101-233.
8. Chung Chi'ieng-ping (2004), *Domestic Politics, International Bargaining and China's Territorial Disputes*, Routledge, London.
9. J.S. Nye (2010), "American and Chinese Power after the Financial Crisis", The Washington Quarterly, October, [Online: web] Accessed 4 December 2015, http://ir.rochelleterman.com/sites/default/files/Nye%202010.pdf
10. http://www.livemint.com/Opinion/Nb7KkZ3yOVSNW3vHf9K1oM/World-history-bu-per-capita-GDP.html

6

India-Maldives Relationship: An overview

T.C. Karthikheyan

Introduction

India and Maldives have had a good working relationship for decades and it is on the basis of acknowledging the mutual importance of one towards the other. In fact, Maldives is the only country in South Asia which has never succumbed to the attitude of portraying India as a big brother that threatens and intervenes in its stability and internal affairs. India has played a vital role in strengthening the security and safeguarding the sovereignty of Maldives as was witnessed in 1987. India is also having one of its long standing vibrant defence engagement programmes with Maldives that has stood the testing times. The economic relationship between these two nations has also been good. The general cordial relationship witnessed some aberrations only in recent times manly due to the compulsions of Maldives' domestic politics and that too has subsided now.

The Maldives is not only a busy holiday destination it has its own relevance and importance in international relations. Though its location is at a vantage point in strategic parlance, Maldives had never been a part of any military alliance in international affairs even during the Cold War period. This has to be seen in the context of two compelling reasons. The first one being, given its inherent vulnerabilities in the form of its geographic structure, lack of natural resources and economic disadvantages—where everything had to be imported except for fish, coconuts and some variety of melons, they had always maintained good relations with their neighbours, including regional and world powers. This eventually helped them to avail economic assistance from both the blocks during and after the Cold War. The second one is its policy of non-alignment. Maldives adheres to the policy of non-alignment, deriving the most possible benefit and assistance for its well-being from the international community. After granting independence to Maldives in 1965, the British maintained their Royal Air Force base in the Gan Atoll of the archipelago till they vacated the facility in 1976, in line with its new policy of abandoning defence commitments east of the Suez Canal. Maldives eventually turned off a million dollar offer for the Gan island from the erstwhile USSR to be used for their 'fishing vessels.'[1] Even after the end of the cold war, Maldives did not contemplate letting any regional or world power to utilize their islands for military activities.

Military and Security Relationships

Maldives plays an important role in India's scheme in the Indian Ocean Region. Given its strategic importance and the emerging competition between the regional powers, the vast Indian Ocean and its contiguous waters present a wide range of security issues to India ranging from military threats, piracy, economic interests in its exclusive economic zones. The Indian Ocean is also located at the crossroads of terrorism originating from 'two banks' to its west and east that are hotbeds of Islamic fundamentalism, thus making it a *de-facto* 'lake of jihadi terrorism.'[2] Given the established links of some regional groups like the Somalian pirates with global terror groups in the region, like Al-Qaeda, security concerns for the Indian Ocean littorals are running high.

Commensurate with the recent developments like piracy and seaborne terrorism, India has now taken the role of a leader in its sphere of influence using its naval capabilities. The Indian Navy is helping the Maldives to tackle piracy and it has become increasingly important to secure the island territories, especially the ones that are uninhabited which could be used by the terrorists.[3] India has initiated the process of putting viable cooperative mechanisms with other like minded nations to harness the collective strength of states to secure the maritime domain in its vicinity. Consequently, it has beefed up its defence cooperation with Maldives commendably in recent years. After the 2008 Mumbai 26/11 attack, the defence community took stock of the need to seal the permeability of India's costal security apparatus. The Indian Navy too is in midst of putting in place a combined security grid by installing a number of radars throughout its vast coastal region for effective real time information gathering and surveillance. Consequently, India has installed radars in some of the islands in Maldives to monitor the movement of ships and other activities in the India Ocean Region. These radars are having their operating stations in India.

Cooperation with Maldives brings three important benefits for India. They are, extension of Indian military and economic influence in the South Asian region, curtailing possible Chinese influence on Maldives, thereby pre-empting the further strengthening of the Chinese strategy of forming 'string of pearls' and achieving and maintaining a strategic balance with China in the Indian Ocean Region.[4] India has always been more receptive to the demands of the Maldivian government for its security needs. The best example is the flying of the Indian Air Force squadrons and the Indian Navy interceptor vessel on receiving a distress call from Maldives, to thwart the attempted coup on the Maldivian government in 1988 by some mercenaries led by a prominent Maldivian businessman. India has contributed towards the security assets of Maldives hugely. It has transferred a Indian naval ship '*Tillanchang*',[5] the Indian Navy also took the responsibility of assisting Maldives in maintaining the ship in its lifetime. Likewise it has donated numerous of surveillance helicopters, boats and ships. The Indian Army also conducts a joint exercise '*Ekueuvrin*' (meaning friends) with the Maldivian National Defence Forces (MDNF) from since 2009 on counter-terrorism.[6] The effective implementation of the combined Indian Navy-MNDF (Maldivian National Defence Force) exercises, hydrographic surveys, integrated surveillance and coordinated patrolling between the two nations would address the security concerns of both the countries phenomenally. The Indian Coast Guard also conducts an exercise on maritime rescue operations and patrolling of seas around Maldives called '*Dosti*' (meaning friendship). Though India helps Maldives in upgrading its security, ties between the two are not uni-dimensional but also encompass the political, economic, cultural and educational fields, which have a lot of scope for further development.

Political Relationship

The political relationship between India and Maldives has been consistent for decades compared to India's relationship with other countries in the region. Though there was an autocratic regime in Maldives for three decades headed by Gayoom, India has never made any attempt to change that abruptly. Rather, it had always remained receptive to its security and economic needs. In fact, it is India that voluntarily stepped in to help Maldives when it faced a coup attempt in 1988.[7] Political relationship between the two got strengthened tremendously after that incident. At the same time, it is with India's help that the pro democracy activities took deep roots and made a strong impact in the island nation. India supported the democracy movement right from the beginning since the year 2004 through institutional cooperation and guidance. The Election Commission of India was involved in helping and training the Maldivian government/authorities in the successful completion for the electoral process. They are also involved in each and every elections held in Maldives, whether to the parliament or to the local bodies or to the office of the President. The 2008 Presidential election saw substantial involvement of Indian authorities in the successful conduct of the election. India has regularly conducted training programmes for the Maldivian administrators and executives, and also played a major part in bringing democracy in Maldives through institutional cooperation. It was this kind of assistance in times of both peace and crisis situation that built mutual confidence and has kept India–Maldives relations intact. This is not possible without a strong political understanding among the two countries and their leadership.

But things got to a different trajectory when the former President Nasheed took refuge at the Indian High Commission to evade an arrest warrant. India got involved into the domestic political crisis unintentionally and after discussions among the stakeholders the issue was sorted amicably. The background of this crisis shall be tracked back to the events that happened on 7 February 2012 when the transfer of power took place in Maldives under controversial circumstances, when he stated that he resigned his Presidency 'under duress'. Right from February 2012, the relationship between the two countries was not commendable and the ruling regime in Maldives had its interests on the Chinese side, whereas the opposition parties had other opinions. This visibly showed the tense and volatile domestic political conditions of the Atoll Island State. Throughout that political crisis in Maldives, India had sought to maintain a balanced approach by giving equal importance to both the serving and the former Presidents of Maldives. Whenever they requested a meeting with the higher officials of the Indian government they were treated equally, though the former president Mr Nasheed had enhanced existing cooperation by bringing in various initiatives that took India-Maldives relations to a new plane during his stint as President.

As both the concerned parties in Maldives valued Delhi's support, India's intervention made the task of restoring democracy easier and earlier.

Nevertheless, India clearly stated its perspective without any ambiguity and any preference for one person or the other, during the 2014 Presidential elections in Maldives, by reposing the faith on the Maldivian people. From India's point of view, Nasheed taking refuge in its Male' office had provided an unintended and unprecedented occasion to restore contacts with the then Maldivian government and political leadership after the cancellation of the GMR contract on airport development.

Economic Relationship

Vulnerability in terms of economic factors has played a vital role in Maldives' relationship with any country and it has greatly influenced its foreign policy. Almost all the essential goods for the day to day needs of the people of Maldives have to be imported as it has no rivers and lacks proper agriculture. Most of its needs are imported from Sri Lanka and India only. Thus, India plays an important part in the Maldivian economy too. It has also provided long term and short term loans and grants for millions of dollars. Maldives is exposed to an array of external economic fluctuations that are usually beyond its control, aggravated by environmental and topographical factors that can cause sudden and highly disruptive shock effects in a small land area. The manufacturing sector has only a limited influence on the economy[8] because of lack of mineral resources and a strong domestic market to sustain production. For centuries, Maldives was isolated from much of the international community with its remoteness and peculiar geographic features. It was untouched by the fierce political and economic domination which has been witnessed throughout the region. The economy greatly relied on subsistence fishing and agriculture, exchanging the few products they produced with Indians and Sri Lankans for rice, cooking oil and other basic necessities.

Maldives has a huge deficit between its imports and exports. The difference has only widened along with its developmental process, thus making it an extremely open economy. This openness and the country's dependence on a small number of sectors makes Maldives susceptible to economic shocks over which it has no control. For more than four decades, since it opened its economy, Maldives has been required to adjust to a succession of shocks with their origins in the external environment that have affected key sectors of the nation's economy and hence its growth performance. The disruptive effects are particularly pronounced when external shocks coincide, as happened in the early 1990s, when the decline in revenue from tuna exports coincided with several negative developments in tourism.[9]

The impressive annual growth in the economy since the latter part of the 1980s, particularly after the opening up of its economy in 1989, has been due largely to the increased receipts from tourism and fishing as well as government investment in infrastructure. The seemingly high level of per capita income and HDI fail to capture the true vulnerability of the Maldivians, the insecurity of the population and the extraordinary challenges for ensuring sustainable human development. The economic progress recorded in Maldives has been considered the highest (16.2 per cent in 2004 before the tsunami hit) among members of the South Asian Association for Regional Cooperation (SAARC).[10] But after the tsunami of 2004, it witnessed some setbacks from which it has recovered gradually before it was hit again by the global economic meltdown in 2008. Maldives is extremely dependent on the outside world, primarily for aid and concessional trade, and this has resulted in high external debt. The risk of the public and external debt ratio moving on to an unsustainable trajectory would significantly endanger the economic security of the state. This is in addition of the burden of narrow source of resource generation and wider expenditure of social services as the islands are scattered and amenities have to be provided in almost all the islands. The 2004 tsunami and the 2008 global economic crisis only accentuated its economic problems.

India's Assistance to Maldives

India has been a committed partner ensuring non-traditional security of Maldives in various aspects, in a variety of fields such as education, health, infrastructure, technology and equipment, environment, etc. The Indian government has provided Rs 5 billion worth of aid to the Maldives during the three-year period 2009-2011. In addition, line-of-credit facilities, bond purchase, standby credit facility and items, equipment and financial assistance worth $268 million was provided to hold the SAARC summit in Addu, according to the statistics of the Indian High Commission in Malé.[11] The largest contribution from India in those three years was to the construction of Faculty of Tourism and Hospitality building. $2.5 million was granted as free assistance of the Indian government to assist in the development of human resources. India also agreed to assist with the military hospital established by the Maldives National Defence Force (MNDF). Private Indian companies also invested in major projects in the Maldives in the fields of construction, communication technology, wind energy, tourism, etc. During his visit to Maldives for the 17th SAARC summit in November 2011 the Indian Prime Minister announced a standby credit facility of $100 million for Maldives and promised help in setting up the Maldives Police Academy. The State Bank of India also subscribed fully to the $100 million in bonds issued by the Maldives Monetary Authority. Ambitious plans to enhance connectivity between the two countries to enhance trade and people-to-people contact were also signed. But the cancelation of the $500 million GMR airport project by the Maldivian government created an uneasy relationship between the two nations not only in terms of economic cooperation but also affected the political relationship between the two for some time.

Conclusion

Strategic cooperation between India and Maldives is indispensable in the Indian Ocean Region, based on each state's dependence on the other and optimum utilization of their knowledge, resources and capacities. The Indo-Maldives maritime cooperation provides the much needed focus for India in improving its capacity to defend its vital interests in the Indian Ocean, as well as to reinforce its regional strategic pre-eminence. The very limited options to diversify its products and markets apart from the two main sectors of tourism and fishing have stagnated the Maldivian economy. In recent years, fisheries have not been doing well and there has been a decline in fish catch due to internal and external reasons. Though tourism continues to provide most of the country's revenue, but that too depends on favourable climatic conditions and a secured environment. In ensuring the economic security of Maldives too, the international community plays a major role, by providing timely financial assistance and policy recommendations for prudent management of resources. The Maldivian government's agreement with the IMF to reduce its fiscal deficit and to bring in tax reforms is a case in point, where the government's autonomy in decision-making according to its own interests is compromised. The Indian role in the mediation process between the opposition parties in the aftermath of the alleged 'coup', further reiterates that Maldives is in need of external influence to sort out their domestic issues and that shows that they are vulnerable to external pressures.

The dependent structure of the state of affairs in Maldives makes it more vulnerable to external forces. The problems faced by Maldives are enormous and it shall be met only with the international cooperation and India has been playing a huge role in this aspect. Though Maldives has ventured outside the region to gain support for its economic development particularly with China, it has also been wary of not antagonising India. Nevertheless, the huge amount of financial assistance given by India and the cultural linkages between the two nations has limited Maldives' option to form an engaging relationship with other big powers of the world.

NOTES

1. U. Phadnis and E. D. Luithui (1985), "*Maldives, Winds of Change in an Atoll State*", South Asian Publishers, New Delhi, p. 75.
2. G.S. Khurana, "Maritime Security in the Indian Ocean: Convergence Plus Cooperation Equals Resonance", *Strategic Analysis*, vol. 28, no. 3, 2004, p.414.
3. Karthikheyan, "Strengthening India's Strategic Depth in the Shallow Waters of Maldives", *Sarjana*, Vol. 26, No. 2, 2011, pp.15-32
4. Ibid. p. 22.
5. S. Dikshit, "India transfers naval ship to Maldives", *The Hindu*, 17 April, 2006, [Online: web] Accessed on 25 Sep. 2015 URL: http://www.hindu.com/2006/04/17/stories/2006041706371200.htm
6. Ministry of Defense, 'India and Maldives to tackle sea-borne terrorism', *Press Information Bureau*, India, 2009, [Online: web] Accessed on 12 Aug. 2015 URL: http://pib.nic.in/newsite/erelease.aspx?relid=47230
7. P. Sahadevan (1999), "Maldives", in Banerjee, Maj.Gen.Dipankar (ed.), *Security in South Asia*, Manas Publications, New Delhi, pp.248-284.
8. H.W. Armstrong, (et al.) "The Economic Performance of Microstates", Report for the UK ODA, 1996.
9. Ministry of Finance and Treasury (2010), "Republic of Maldives", [Online: web] Accessed 23 May 2007, URL: http://www.finance.gov.mv/v1/datanstat?id=25
10. ADB, Strategy and Programme Assessment, "Maldives: Poverty Assessment", Asian Development Bank, Manila, 2007.
11. Minivan News (2012), [Online: web] Accessed 18 September. 2015, URL: http://minivannews.com/news-in-brief

7

Cementing Indo-Myanmar Strategic Ties and Act East Policy

Mohinder Pal Singh

As major powers of the world are vying to engage Myanmar, the recent visit of the Indian Prime Minister for the ASEAN summit in 2014 and visit of Myanmar's Foreign Minister in 2015 for India-Myanmar Joint Consultative Committee in New Delhi is a step in the right direction to stymie China's designs. After almost two decades of launching, India's 'Look East' policy (LEP) has engaged Myanmar slowly and cautiously, mainly because of over assertiveness of China which openly supported the oppressive military regime with benevolent aid. Though a considerable progress came with expanding border trade and infrastructure development projects, India did not think it prudent to delve into the realm of providing military aid. The important requirements of their military hardware were replenished only by China and so it became the single largest trading partner and a mentor who protected Myanmar's right in international forums. China openly vetoed a UN resolution against Myanmar for abuse of human rights of pro-democratic supporters. The Myanmar Army (*tatmadaw*), which is continuously engaging in a long drawn internal strife with various ethnic groups, needs to equip its armed forces with sophisticated equipment. The morbid state of Myanmar's economy forced it to go in for the 'aid route' rather than the 'trade route' for military assistance. It is a known fact that in Myanmar the Military not only exercises control over the military but also the government and the decision making matrix of the economy.

In a closely contested 1990 elections, the National League for Democracy (NLD) led by Noble laureate Aung San Suu Kyi won a clear majority defeating the military backed party and other parties. In a swift coup (third in the history of Myanmar) the military junta refused to hand over the power and exiled over 1000 elected members and their supporters. The world shunned the military regime of Myanmar due to incessant human rights abuses. At the appropriate moment, China not only became its saviour and a key ally but also the main arms supplier. It had supplied arms amounting to $1.4 billion in 1989 followed by another deal of $ 400 million in 1994 which proved to be a shot in the arm for the waning military prowess of *Tatmadaw (*myanmar military*)*. However after the 2011 elections and establishment of a democratic Government under President Thein Sein which brought about revolutionary reforms, USA and countries of EU moved in swiftly in re-establishing the snapped ties. Recently, United Kingdom has invited 30 Myanmar officers to a prestigious defence conference. Australia is also pledging basic military engagement to support security sector reforms. The US wants to restart defence training for Myanmar that was cut 25 years ago after a ruthless crackdown on protesters in 1988. It must be remembered that before sanctions were applied, the USA had financed $4.7 million in military sales between 1980 and 1988 and trained 167 officers at American military schools under the International Military Education and Training (IMET), a program jointly managed by the State Department and Defense Department that helps more than 120 countries. Even today the IMET alumni occupy some important positions in the military hierarchy including a current vice president.

India's position vis-a-vis other developed nations is unique, as it not only shares common historical ties but also 1643 kilometer of border with Myanmar. And tranquillity of the border is a prime concern of both the countries. Due to its rugged terrain the border management can only be effective if both nations assiduously cooperate. The problem of the border gets compounded because some insurgent groups which have known to seek safe havens across when chased by the Indian Armed forces. Good military ties with our eastern neighbour means better border management and better control over the insurgent groups operating in the North East of India. It also strengthens bilateral ties with the present Chair of ASEAN community of nations.

In the last decade, India too has taken many steps to help Myanmar in its development process. Government of India is actively involved in over a dozen projects in Myanmar, both in infrastructural and non-infrastructural areas. These include up-gradation and resurfacing of the 160 km long Tamu-Kalewa-Kalemyo road; construction and up-gradation of the Rhi-Tiddim Road in Myanmar; the Mega Rs 1500 Crore Kaladan Multimodal Transport Project, which is going to link the north-eastern states via the Bay of Bengal and Myanmar route. An ADSL project for high speed data link in 32 Myanmar cities has been completed by TCIL, ONGC, GAIL and ESSAR are participants in the energy sector in Myanmar. M/s RITES is involved in development of the rail transportation system and in supply of railway coaches, locos and parts. In September 2008, NHPC signed an agreement for development of the Tamanthi and Shwezaye Hydro-Electric Power project in Chindwin River. A heavy turbo-truck assembly plant set up in Myanmar by TATA Motors with GOI financial assistance was inaugurated on 31 December 2010. Other projects include revamping of the Ananda Temple in Bagan, upgradation of the Yangon Children's Hospital and Sittwe General Hospital. India has also assisted in the reconstruction of one high school and 6 primary schools in Tarlay township, the area worst affected by the severe earthquake that struck north-eastern Myanmar in March 2011.

In December 2013 the Indian Army Chief visited Myanmar. He handed over two war gaming software packages called 'Combat decision resolution' and 'Infantry company commander's tactical trainer' which have been customized for training for the Myanmar's Army. He also gave five hand-gliders for the Defence Services Academy at Pwin Oo Lwin. Another gesture was to incorporate Myanmar's armed forces special training packages in the Indian Army's counter-insurgency and jungle warfare school at Vairengte in Mizoram.

Indian media also reported that Myanmar army displayed keenness for courses in mechanised forces like tanks and infantry combat vehicles, information technology, intelligence and English language, among other areas. The most significant part of this visit was the establishment of an Army training team at Myanmar. Till now, Myanmar has not permitted any country to establish any such training establishment, not even China, the closest known ally of the last two decades. This should not only be seen from the military perspective but strategically as it is likely to give India an edge to further steer its economic and strategic ties to new horizons.

The election year, 2015, in Myanmar saw a spate of visits of leaders between the two countries which gives further credence to the increasing fervour of bilateral relations. Most significant was the visit of Myanmar's foreign minister U Wunna Lwin to India to participate in the first meeting of the India-Myanmar Joint Consultative Committee in New Delhi, co-chaired by External Affairs Minister Sushma Swaraj and Myanmar's Foreign Minister U Wunna Maung Lwin. In this forum the Indian External Affairs Minister offered New Delhi's commitment to help Nay Pyi Taw build 'a professional and capable Myanmar Navy to safeguard and ensure its maritime security.' India also offered to assist in modernization of Myanmar's Army, thus taking the military cooperation to next level. The statement also gave commitment of India in the field of IT and dealing with emerging security challenges and military training. Dipanjan Roy, reporting for the Economic Times, mentioned that the joint consultative Commission of the two countries discussed ways and means of having better coordination between the security forces to deal with insurgent groups in the North East region of India. The visiting foreign Minister also met the Prime Minister Modi, who offered all support and cooperation to the eastern neighbour. The Indian PM is likely to visit Myanmar ahead of the elections in November 2015.

These bilateral talks become more significant in view of the recent coordination seen during the Indian Army's surgical strikes along the border in June 2015 on the insurgent camps operating from Myanmar. The world was agape at the Indian army's blietzkrieg in neutralizing the militants in their camps across the border as also the support which was provided by the Myanmar authorities for this operation. Writing about this operation of 16 June 2015, Bertil Lintner, one of the best known experts on Myanmar, says, 'The Chinese may not want to set India's northeast ablaze, but it is in Beijing's interest to cause frictions and disruptions in Burma's relations with India.' Over the past four years, Burma has distanced itself from its old ally China, and established closer contacts not only with the West but also India. A closer, more cordial relationship between Burma and India is not in China's interest. Instability along the border—rebel raids into India and retaliatory, Indian cross-border attacks—would serve that purpose."

This was a significant development in view of the recent slide in Sino-Myanmar ties due to skirmishes of Kokang rebels spilling over into China and also the large scale involvement of Chinese nationals in timber smuggling, in which Myanmar Army caught 153 Chinese nationals with hoards of illegal timber in January 2015. Subsequently, all of them were meted out with very harsh punitive action, which did not augur well with China. All 153 were given life imprisonment in June, 2015.

From Look East to Act East Policy

India's 'Look East' Policy (LEP) was introduced in the early 1990s by the then Prime Minister PV Narasimha Rao. Subsequently, it was endorsed by Prime Ministers Atal Bihari Vajpayee and Manmohan Singh. During the ASEAN meet in June 2015, Prime Minister Narendra Modi told the world leaders that his government accorded high priority to turn India's erstwhile 'Look East' policy into an 'Act East' Policy.

It should be noted, with credence, that since coming to power in 2014, the government of Prime Minister Narendra Modi has lent India's Look East Policy even greater momentum, leading to unveiling an upgraded 'Act East Policy' during the India ASEAN Summit in Myanmar in November 2014. This gives a clear message that India is becoming increasingly willing to play a more active and prominent strategic role in East and Southeast Asia. It goes beyond doubt that Myanmar is 'door to ASEAN' for trade and strategic depth. Modi's three day visit to Myanmar brought ASEAN and Myanmar back in the Indian focus. The shift from LEP to AEP does not merely show a departure from LEP but rather a implementation phase and 'commitment' to implementation of the projects.

The important aspect of the visit was the focus given to the three C's: culture, commerce and connectivity. Tourism being one of the important aspect of cultural sharing and religious tourism of the Buddhist circuit like linking Bodh Gaya to Yangon would act as a boost to increase people to people contact between India and Myanmar.

On the commerce aspect, the India-ASEAN Free Trade Agreement has already been operationalized and includes both services and investments. On the issue of connectivity, there is an urgent need to move forward with the plans that have been in the pipeline. The completion of the Tamu-Kalewa-Kalemyo sector of the India-Myanmar-Thailand Trilateral Highway is poised to create a new dynamic in India's multi-faceted ties with the region. Whilst both Myanmar and India are focusing on the development of the border regions, these projects will act as vital catalysts to deliver on the proposed outcomes

In order to provide an accurate strategic foresight of Indo-Myanmar relations and its implication for India, it is necessary to understand the historical and present context, national ambitions, and the current means available to achieve these goals. The paper concludes that the period of the next 5-10 years, from an Indian standpoint, will be one of balancing between securing its economic investment through bilateral relations with the government which comes into power after 2015 elections. India, in its ernest quest to improve the relations with Myanmar, is likely to give stiff challenge not only to China but also the other western countries. Also, China will have to face growing resentment of local Chinese presence in Myanmar, border instability, weak Myanmar governance, and stronger international commitments.

Alternatively, considering the military Junta's controversial history, it wants to prove to the regional and international community that it is a legitimate government elected by the people. Through the Seven Step roadmap to Democracy and the election in 2015, the Junta wants to show its credibility as the government of Myanmar. The Junta has been successful at making regional actors compete for its natural resources and its strategic importance works in its favour. When China, India, and ASEAN compete for access to Myanmar, they are supporting the Junta financially, which gets translated into political support. Also, the Junta does not want direct foreign involvement in its national affairs. India's policy being less assertive is more conducive to Myanmar's objectives.

NOTES

1. A. David (2001), "China-Burma Relations, Challenges to Democratization in Burma" International Institute for Democracy and Electoral Assistance (International IDEA) Stockholm, Sweden.
2. D.R. Chaudhury (2015), "India to help modernise Myanmar Army and Navy to broad-base defence partnership", *ET Bureau*, 17 July 2015, New Delhi.
3. T. Kean (2015), India Looks to Improve Defence Ties with Myanmar", *Myanmar Times*, 17 July, New Delhi.
4. I. Bagchi (2015), "India-Myanmar Agree to Fight Terrorism Jointly", *Times of India*, 16 July, New Delhi.
5. L. Thant (2013), "Burma and China to Build on Strategic Military Relations", *The Irravady*, July 25.
6. R. Pandit (2013), "India Steps up Aid to Myanmar to offset China's Might", *TNN* Nov 1.
7. S. Sundararaman (2014), "Modi in Myanmar: From 'Look East' to 'Act East'", *IPCS*, 17 November, New Delhi.
8. M.A. Myoe (2007), "A Historical Overview of Political Transition in Myanmar Since 1988", Asia Research Institute, National University of Singapore.
9. M.S Martin (2010), "Burma's 2010 Elections: Implications of the New Constitution and Election Laws", Congressional Research Service.
10. B. Paul (2004), "Burma: International Affairs and Defence Section", House of Commons library, London.
11. K.Y. Hlaing (2011), "Political Impasse in Myanmar", Working Paper No 111, City University of Hong Kong.

12. M.A. Myoe (2007), "Sino-Myanmar Economic Relations Since 1988", No.86, Asia Research Institute, National University of Singapore, April.
13. L. Jagan (2009), "Border War Rattles China Myanmar Ties", *Asia Times*, 01 September.
14. Y. Sun (2012), "China and the Changing Myanmar", *Journal of Current Southeast Asian Affairs*, 31 (4):51-77.
15. B. Tea (2010), "China and Myanmar: Strategic Interest and Road Ahead", IPCS Research paper, New Delhi.
16. B. McCartan (2011), "Partial peace in Myanmar", *Asia Times Online*, 12 October, 2011.
17. S. Yun (2012), "China's Misjudgement in Myanmar", *Journal of South Asian Studies*, 2012.
18. U.B. Singh (2012), "An Assessment of Manmohan Singh's visit to Myanmar", *IDSA Issue Briefs*, June 1, New Delhi.
19. M.A. Myoe (2011), "In the Name of Pauk-Phaw: Myanmar's China Policy since 1948", Institute of Southeast Asian Studies, Singapore.
20. H.K. Yin (2012), "Understanding Recent Political Changes in Myanmar", *Contemporary Southeast Asia: A Journal of International & Strategic Affairs*, 34(2).
21. Y. Sun (2012), "China and the Changing Myanmar", Journal of Current Southeast Asian Affairs, 31 (4):51-77.
22. https://mea.gov.in/Portal/ForeignRelation/myanmar-july-2012.pdf
23. http://timesofindia.indiatimes.com/india/India-Myanmar-agree-to-fight-terrorism-jointly/articleshow/48099886.cms
24. http://www.bbc.com/news/world-asia-33632291

8

Non-Conventional Security Issues between India and Nepal: An Exploratory Study

B.C. Upreti

Nature has placed India and Nepal in a position which can hardly be seen anywhere else in the world. The two countries share a common geographical, socio-cultural and economic landscape. There are common historical and political bondages. The open border between the two countries is a unique arrangement that facilitates the people of the two countries to move across the border. In fact, there are few countries in the world which maintain an open international boundary. The open border itself has facilitated the growth of deep rooted social and economic inter-linkages and the people of the two countries have been enjoying it for centuries. However, the people of the two countries not only share the deep rooted geographical, historical, socio-cultural and economic inter-linkages, but there are several challenges and problems, which the people of the two countries face equally. In fact, there are many problems which have cross-border implications. These problems and challenges can be resolved on the basis of mutual cooperation and a mutual understanding between the two countries.

This paper intends to explore some issues and challenges under the category of non-traditional security threats, which can be best dealt with collaborative approach and actions.

Non-Traditional Security: A Note

The whole approach to security has undergone a massive change over the last few decades.[1] The traditional notions of security based on the security of the state and its territory through military means is not considered to be sufficient. It is now believed that it is not only the state which needs to be secured, particularly from external aggression, but the people or the subjects of the state also need to be protected.[2] It does not mean to suggest that the traditional issues of security have become irrelevant. The state, identity and autonomy these are very much relevant and the security of the state has to be ensured. But the core of the security today is the security of the people. Since the activities of the people have several dimensions, social, economic, political, and environmental, they need to be secured in respect of all the dimensions of their lives and activities. Thus, the comprehensive approach to security has become a vital issue in the whole discourse of security in the contemporary phase. The issues relating to social, economic, political and environmental security, etc., fall under the category of non-traditional security issues. In this context, one may argue that the non-traditional issues are much more important as they have direct implications for the well-being or even survival of the people.[3]

Non-Traditional Security Issues between India and Nepal

The non-traditional security issues have acquired importance in international relations, both in terms of their cross-country implications and the cooperation on a bilateral or multilateral basis to contain such threats. In fact, there are certain issues which cannot remain confined to the national boundaries of a country. They are bound to have cross border implications such as the climate change, spreading of vector borne disease, floods, sedimentation, etc. Therefore, cooperation among the concerned countries becomes a necessity in such cases in order to ensure protection against such problems. The most important aspect of the India-Nepal relations is that the two countries not only have formal politico-diplomatic relations but there are several other dimensions of relations, which are informal, much more wider, deeper and age old in nature.[4] In fact, as mentioned above, the historical linkages and the open border has given way to these informal dimensions of relations and many of them have become a way of life for the people of two countries. In the context of these multi-dimensional relations and the people to people linkages, there are several areas where security issues are involved and which have cross border implications. There are two important aspects with respect to India-Nepal relations:

- India-Nepal relations cannot be understood merely on the basis of formal political aspects. The informal dimensions are equally important and at times these become much more significant in comparison to formal politico-diplomatic issues.
- There are several factors giving rise to both traditional and non-traditional security issues, which are equally significant to both the counties. The two countries have been sensitive to many of these non-traditional security issues and these have, at times, been cause of conflict between the two.

The factors that have made non-traditional security issues prominent between the two countries may be categorized as following:

- India and Nepal form an integral part of a contagious and compact geographic region. The Himalayas the Gangetic reverie soil zone are shared by the two countries. Therefore, the eco-system is same in both the countries.
- There is a contiguity of forest resources, bio-diversity, river water resources, etc., across the international borders between India and Nepal.
- Gangetic Plain/North Indian River Plain and the Tarai region of Nepal form one of the most densely populated regions of South Asia. On both the sides it contains the richest agro-industrial belt of the two countries. Therefore, there is larger flow of people in this region.
- The international border between the two countries is open and easily accessible. The border between the two countries helps them in numerous ways; a number of security risks are also associated with the open border, which are both traditional and non-traditional in nature.[5] The open border has not only given way to social and economic patterns across the border for a long time but, in recent decades, it has also been responsible for various abuses-containing security risks for both the countries.

It may be emphasized here that there have been a peculiar geographical, environmental and socio-economic patterns that are shared by both India and Nepal. It is obvious, therefore, that any of the security challenges arising out of it will be faced by both the countries.

It may be noted here that after the Chinese occupation of Tibet in 1950, China reached right up to the south of the Himalayas, forming the border with India, Nepal, Bhutan and Sikkim at that time. Except India rest of the countries of the Himalayan region are small in size and vulnerable in terms of socio-economic development. It naturally posed serious security challenges for India also due to the fact that China had historical claims over a large part of the territory south of the Himalayas and it had already occupied Tibet. It also became imperative for India to ensure security of other Himalayan states against any possible northern invasion. India's policy towards the Himalayan states was guided by this security perception for a long time.[6] While this security perception of the Himalayan region may still be relevant for India, many other security issues, non-traditional in nature, have become significant in the modern times.

Non-Traditional Security Dimensions

Some of the important dimensions of non-traditional security issues which are shared by the two countries may be mentioned as below:

Energy Security

Energy security is an important aspect. In fact, energy security has become a global concern in modern times, as energy is the core to modern economic development. Energy security is a major challenge for the South Asian countries due to population pressure, growing economies and shortage of energy resources, particularly oil and petroleum products.[7] These countries are largely dependent on imports of oil from West Asian countries, involving economic burdens due to oil price rise and oil politics. There is a need to develop alternative sources of energy that calls for bilateral and regional cooperation among the countries of the region.

Nepal is among those countries of South Asia which have limited energy resources. However, it is rich in river water resources. Nepal's estimated hydro power potential is 83000 MW, next only to Mexico. All its rivers have a north-south direction and flow into India after crossing the Nepalese territory. These rivers provide vast scope for India-Nepal cooperation for hydro-power generation that can meet the needs of Nepal and India to a considerable extent. The two countries have already entered into a number of projects for hydro power development. However, much has still to be done to exploit the hydro-power potential of Nepal. The country is highly deficit in electricity. It has not been possible to implement the Mahakali Treaty which was signed as early as in 1997. Many other projects are still pending. Actually, Nepal has become oversensitive about its river water potential and the whole issue of river water cooperation is politicized. It is true that it is a significant wealth of Nepal. But the country has not been able to realize that the untapped waters are of no use and the waters lost today are a loss for ever.

The Indian Prime Minister, during his visit to Nepal in September 2014, emphasized the need for energy security in the South Asian region. He also stressed upon activating hydro power projects and their timely completion. India has concluded the Power Trade Agreement and Power Development Agreement with Nepal. There are some other areas like development of solar and wind energy. India has done some progress in the development of these alternative sources of energy. Nepal can learn from India's experiences in this direction and seek her cooperation in developing her own alternative pool of energy resources.

Environmental Security

The environmental security is yet another issue which is being confronted not only by the South Asian countries but elsewhere in the world as well.[8] There are several environmental issues being confronted by India and Nepal together. Since both the countries form part of the same environmental zone, the adverse environmental implications are faced by both the countries. The Himalayan region forms a fragile and highly sensitive ecological zone. The seismic disturbances, glacier melting, garbage pools, etc., are serious threats to the environment of the hills. The recent incidents of Uttarakhand hills in India in 2012 and the devastating earthquake in Nepal on 25 April 2015 are a clear indication of the environmental challenges in the Himalayas. There is lot of tourism in the Himalayas due to which development is also taking place. The interference of human beings in the affairs of nature has caused ecological disorder. It may be noted here that the environmental destruction in Nepal has its implications in India as well, both social and economic, due to the open border between the two countries.

The landslides, drying up of water resources, deforestation, etc., are other environmental hazards, which cause problems for both the countries and these have cross-country implications. The two countries can learn from each other's experiences and also formulate a joint action plan to manage the environment. The fact remains that the environmental threats do not have any state boundaries and it is not possible to contain them within the state boundaries.

Therefore, such problems must be tackled through a bilateral or multilateral approach.

There has been a worldwide concern about the implications of climate change. The developing countries are considered to be more prone to the adverse implications of climate change due to the larger emission of carbon dioxide (CO_2) and other greenhouse gases. These countries are also faced with the problems of fast depletion of natural resources. The fast depletion of forests and biodiversity is a common problem in both the countries. The Gangetic plains of India and Nepal form densely populated agro-industrial belt. Urbanization has taken place very fast in this region. The air pollution, industrial wastes, CO_2 emission, etc., are causes of environmental challenges in this region. All these challenges have cross-border effects.

Problem of Floods

The problem of floods has been a major issue between India and Nepal. All the rivers of Nepal have a north-south direction and after crossing the steep hills of Nepal they enter into the plains of India. These fast flowing rivers when entering the plains areas with full force can cause havoc in the Nepali Tarai and Indian Gangetic plains. The floods of the river Kosi have been a perennial problem for India and Nepal.

In 1954, the Kosi Agreement was concluded between the two countries, which apart from various schemes of water utilization included flood control mechanism. However, it has not been possible to control the floods of Kosi. Every year it causes devastating floods and a huge area gets submerged with flood waters in Bihar, India, and parts of the Tarai region of Nepal. It causes loss of human beings, animals, houses and other property and agriculture land. India has to bear a great loss every year. Therefore, it has tried to control floods by embankments along the river side. Nepal's complaints are that due to India's unilateral decision to construct embankments she has to face more floods.

It is strange that despite huge losses every year the two countries have not been able to reach to a sustainable formula of flood management. The two countries have agreed many times to work together for flood management, but nothing substantial has come about. One problem is that the river water management is a state subject in India, while the sharing of international river waters is an issue of foreign policy conducted by the central government. This creates problems. Nepal has been complaining that India creates problem for her, while for India it is a huge loss every year due to the floods of Kosi, Gandaki and other rivers. The people of the region have to be secured against these floods whether in India or Nepal. It is possible only through the combined efforts of the two countries.

Social Security

There are several aspects of social security where the two countries need to cooperate in order to ensure security of the people of the two countries. Actually, due to the open border there is free flow of people across the national boundary. It has also given rise to a number of social security issues.

The problem of human trafficking is very serious. A large number of women and children are brought to India or to other countries via India to work as labourers, house hold helpers, sex workers, etc. The women and children are more prone to trafficking and are the worst sufferers. These people are subject to abuse, harassment, poor and unhygienic living conditions. They are denied basic human rights and their rehabilitation is a challenging task. It is a matter of insecurity for a large number of people.

Similarly, there are problems of communicable diseases or vector born diseases on both sides of the border area particularly diarrhoea, malaria, jaundice, etc. Because of a close interaction between the people of the two countries and the non-existence of any kind of natural barriers in the border region, these diseases are easily transmitted across the border, creating problems for the people of both the countries. In the border areas there are problems of organized crimes, social abuse and other anti-social activities. These criminals and other anti-social elements easily move to the other country after doing a mischief in one country. Such activities pose serious security challenges for the people of two countries.

A large number of people move across the India-Nepal border for various social and economic purposes. The 1950 Treaty of Peace and Friendship concluded by the two countries has facilitated such unabated migration. In the border regions there are large numbers of daily commuters looking for employment, education, market, health services and so on. However, despite the treaty there have been problems relating to migration, particularly in Nepal due to the provisions relating to citizenship, labour rules, industrial policies, etc. The involvement of migrants in anti-social activities in certain cases has also been a cause of concern for the two governments.

Economic Security Issues

Nepal is a landlocked country and India alone provides the sea route to her through its territory. Apart from this, India is the largest trading partner of Nepal. In the border region, a large section of the population looks towards India as an alternative source of earnings and employment generation. There is a well knitted border economy between the two countries. However, there are serious problems of smuggling and illicit trade through the India-Nepal border, thereby posing challenges of economic security for the two countries. There are reports to suggest that the unofficial trade along India-Nepal border is at such a high volume that it is like a parallel economy. How to ensure security against illicit trade, fake currency, smuggling, etc., are serious issues.

Terrorist Trespassing and Security Risks

The rise of terrorism in South Asia and India being one of the major targets of the terrorist agencies has become a major security issue, not only for India but for the smaller states of the region as well. Due to the open border, it has been easily possible for the terrorists to move across the India-Nepal border and seek their hideouts in Nepal. At the local level also, the India Nepal border is used by insurgents, criminals and other miscreants. It has serious security risks for both the countries. India and Nepal can work together to control movement of terrorists and other such elements across the border and finding out their hideouts.

Looking Beyond State Centric Approach

It is clear from the above brief survey that:

- There are a number of non-traditional security issues between India and Nepal.
- The two countries are equally affected by these security challenges.
- Some of these non-traditional security issues have serious implications for the bilateral relations of the two countries as the one country blames the other giving rise to these challenges.
- Many of the non-traditional security issues are directly or indirectly related to the open border between the two countries. Hence, it needs proper and adequate management.

From the perspective of sustainable development, peace and stability, these security issues need to be resolved. While the two countries can take up their own measures to tackle these problems, there is a need to go beyond the state centric approach. It is necessary to follow a cooperative approach. In fact some of the problems like floods, climate change, environmental degeneration, and terrorist trespassing cannot be contained without adequate cooperation and understanding between the two countries. Therefore, India and Nepal need to collaborate with each other to deal with all these issues. Further, not only an inter-state cooperation is required but there is also a need for the involvement of the people of the two countries to deal with the non-traditional security issues. There are problems like human trafficking, rescuing and rehabilitation, prevention of vector born disease, deforestation, etc., where involvement of the civil society and the masses can be effective.

NOTES

1. A.R. Khan (ed.) (2001), *Globalization and Non-Traditional Security in South Asia*, RCSS, Colombo, 2001; Also see R.M. Basrur (ed.), *Security in the New Millennium*, India Research Press, New Delhi.
2. L.R. Baral (1999), "Non-Military Threats and Governance" in Muckund Dubey and Nancy Jetly (eds), *South Asia and its Eastern Neighbourhood*, New Delhi, pp. 243-267; B. Buzan (1997), "Rethinking Security after the Cold War", *Nordic Journal of International Studies*, vol. 32, no.1 March.
3. Mahbub ul Haq (2006-07), *Human Security in South Asia, Human Development in South Asia 2005*, Human Development Centre, Oxford University press, Karachi.
4. B.C. Upreti (2001), *Uneasy Friends, Readings on Indo-Nepal Relations*, Kalinga Publications, New Delhi.
5. B.C. Upreti (2009), "The India-Nepal Open Border: Nature, Issues and Problems", in K. Warikoo (ed.), *Himalaya Frontiers of India, Historical, Geo-Political and Strategic Perspectives*, Rutledge, New York.
6. B.C. Upreti (1988), *Dynamics of Foreign Aid: A Case Study of Indian Aid to Nepal*, Printwell Publishers, Jaipur, 1988, pp. 1-17. Also see, K.R. Singh (1986), "Geo-Political Consideration" in Gautam Sharma et al. (eds), *India's Northern Security*", New Delhi.
7. V. Gupta & Chan Suan Kwa (eds.) (2010), *Energy Security: Asia-Pacific Perspectives*, Manas, New Delhi.
8. B.C. Upreti (2006), "Environmental Security in South Asia: Dimensions, Issues and Problems" in Dev Raj Dahal and Nischal Nath Pandey (eds), *Comprehensive Security in South Asia*, Manohar, New Delhi.

9

India-Nepal Open Border System Debate amidst Natural Calamity and the Constitution Making Process

Shreesh Kumar Pathak

In diplomatic circles, on varied grounds, some countries may be labelled as weak or strong nation but the ultimate power lies with Mother Nature. Science is still unable to predict Nature's course and impacts. The devastating quake jolted Nepal very deeply in the year 2015. The calamity has definitely shaken the humanity but not its will. Nepal is trying hard to recover from the calamity and to reconstruct the essential structures.

Nepal's first democratic Constitution was promulgated on September 20, 2015. Constitution making is not an easy exercise, especially if the nation has varied populations and different colours of pages in its history book. Before the process of constitution making reaches its culmination, Nepal had to face a profound degree of natural calamity. The international community, which maintains the belief in humanity and in global fraternity, helped open-heartedly. In the process, a country can understand the significance of cobweb of relationships with other countries. For the meaningful conduction of relationships the role of an effective and strong political system cannot be denied.

As the dust settled; with undying spirit, the people of Nepal have come in a position to initiate the process of restructuring almost everything which was ruptured, a long-expected consensus on constitution making among the stakeholders of political society has also surfaced recently.[1] Calamity has definitely played a significant role in this consensus. Amidst the calamity and constitution making process, this would not be improper to discuss an old but relevant debate about the open border system of India and Nepal. A nation must want to explore varied possibilities of cooperation through its borders for further development in all other fields as the chances of establishing polity are improving. Nepal is geographically surrounded by its traditional friend India. India and Nepal enjoy an open border system following the India-Nepal Friendship Treaty, 1950. Open border system has its own pros and cons. It is high time to settle the debate by concerned stakeholders that in which way India and Nepal are going to manage the border with its associated prospects and problems.

India-Nepal Open Border System

There are at least three reasons which make the border with Nepal so special. At first, Nepal is a land-locked country. The 3222 km of its frontier and it has no access to any open sea or ocean.[2] This landlocked status has a great impact on the economy of Nepal, as it relies on its neighbours for importing goods from third countries. The second is that Nepal has only two neighbouring countries, which are the countries with the biggest population of the world, China and India. Nepal's northern Himalayan region borders with the Tibetan autonomous region of China, in the south, east and west it is surrounded by India's states of Uttar Pradesh, Bihar, West Bengal and Sikkim. Thirdly, the open border between Nepal and India permits people of both countries to cross the border without a visa and to take goods, even for everyday usage across the border without paying any sort of customs duty. Besides the economic relations across the border, Nepal and India's people are closely tied with cultural and social threads, especially in their border areas. Therefore, the open border gives the opportunity for people to live their social life unrestricted despite the frontier.

In an advance stage of political development, a well bounded ethnic entity may evolve where people and groups inside the boundary are likely to exhibit 'opportunism' in their alliances, interaction patterns and cultural borrowings, as they seek personal and group advantage unhampered by border restrictions of rigid loyalty.[3]

But this inter-connectedness and interactions can make changes in the ethnographic profile of the border areas, which may generate political risk and threats for social and cultural entity of the area and the country. People from both countries are free to enter each other's territory from any point on the border, while the movement of goods is allowed along 22 designated transit points.[4] People in border areas of both sides often develop a natural interdependence in case of an open border system and geographical compulsions justify the relationship. Open borders are also very much open for criminals, smugglers, terrorists and wrong doers in the absence of strong border security and management. In this way, the people with ill intentions can use the facility of open border in order to fulfill their ill purposes.

Hence, open border has its own pros and cons. The open border system shows greater mutual trust, strong bond of relationship, natural interdependence and deeper cultural and social affinity. But the facility of the open border system can be exploited by wrong persons as well. This exploitation of the open border system can jeopardize the bilateral relationship. Often, neighbouring nations get involved in allegations and accuse each other for any bad happenings in the border region. Rather than improvise the internal security system for each nation, it is easy to accuse and make further allegations. The open border system is a positive development, but due to the fragile system of border mechanism and management, all the bad things are credited to the open border system. Some voices, especially concerned politicians, security establishments, and academia from each side of the border criticize the system of open borders and advocate for either closing or tightly regulating the border.

The open border system can prevail between two countries only based on mutual understanding, good neighbourly relations, religious sentiment, the same topography, social similarities, and family relationship. These factors are evident in case of India and Nepal; and that's why the open border system has been prevailing for more than sixty four years. Some political elites of both nations share a very close contact. In India's long struggle for independence, many Nepalese leaders made contributions against the colonial ruler. Many Indian leaders too helped a lot in the process of establishing democracy in Nepal. Institutionalization of democracy in Nepal is vital not only for Nepal but it also in the greater interest of India. This open border system was a convenience even for officials and bureaucrats. They can roam easily across the borders and this makes them efficient to formalise any policy level advancement which is important for the bilateral relationship. The people in border areas of both sides are even connected socially with nuptial ties and they share in-laws relationship across the borders. The open border system offers the very convenient facility to them and because of it, they are easily able to do their social and family duties without any bureaucratic hurdles.[5] So, similar to the strong economic relations, there are close social linkages across the border. People on both sides of the border are deeply related to each other through kinship, culture and religion, which may be due to the history of the creation of the frontier and migration to the border area. The two countries are tied together in many ways, the differences are hardly visible in the border areas and entering the other country is so easy, that the national border even seems to disappear.

The Nepal-India border, let it be repeated, stands up as the ideal frontier of South Asia. It is open, porous, and respectful of identical demography and sensibilities on the two sides, allows unimpeded commerce and yet keeps national identities and respects sovereignties.[6]

The concept of an open border between India and Nepal was institutionalized in the Treaty of Peace and Friendship that the two countries signed in 1950. Provisions in the treaty,[7] wherein citizens of both countries are provided equal rights in matters of residence, acquisition of property, employment and movement in each other's soil, provide for an open border system between India and Nepal. The open border system between India and Nepal has not been functioning for centuries as common people have the perception. Actually, the concept of an open border formally began in the 19th century after the delimitation of the India-Nepal boundary in 1816 and the restoration of Naya Muluk in Nepal in 1860.[8] During the period of colonialism in the Indian sub-continent, the British continued the open border system policy arguably for two reasons: Firstly, like Maharaja Ranjeet Singh, the English had seen the undying spirit and bravery of the Gurkha and they too recruited them in Indian Army and another reason might be economic. Though small, but Nepal was a new market for the finished goods of Indian factories. Hence, the British had sufficient reasons to let the open border continue. It was essential to afford unhindered cross-border movement of not only for goods but also for the people; therefore, the idea of an open border system prevailed.

Independent India continued this practice to nourish and further the established and continuing linkages. The emergence of China and its continued interest in the region justifies India's stand on the open border system. For the security complex of India, the Himalayas are always considered as a natural boundary/barrier, which prevent attacks on India from the north.

Nepal in its north shared some portion of the great Himalayas and hence both nations are very much integrated with their security interests. The open border system hence is the best suited policy decision by both countries which effectively addresses the security concerns of the two countries. Cross-border interactions through open borders has made possible over the years the fusion of ideas, religions, social customs and helps to make settlements of people in each other's territory. Without the unrestricted flow of people across the borders, it would not be possible. In both countries, religious places and several institutions have played a very significant role in strengthening the social and cultural relations between India and Nepal. Places like Pashupatinath, Lumbini, Janakpur, and Muktinath in Nepal and Kashi, Gaya, Rajgir, and Haridwar in India are visited by people from both countries.[9]

With the open border system, the two countries enjoy the same level of economic and trade freedom. Bilateral trade and micro level trade inputs are flourishing due to the unrestricted flow of people. "One major aspect is the income that accrues to Nepal in the form of salaries, remittances, and pensions from the Gurkhas recruited into the Indian army. As part of the tripartite agreement between Nepal, India, and the United Kingdom, Nepal allowed the recruitment of Gurkhas in the Indian army, because it faced the burden of rehabilitating 200,000 soldiers discharged from the British Indian army at the end of World War II.[10]

As a landlocked country, Nepal has to depend on India to access to the sea through a passage. Maximum part of its import has to pass through India. India, as a trading partner, shares a major chunk of its global trade and is its biggest trading partner. India is the largest trading partner of Nepal in terms of both export as well as imports. India absorbs 67.5% of total trade consisting 66.9% of total exports and 67.6% of total imports.[11] With the expansion of globalization, Nepal too has accepted the impact of liberalism and consumerism. This growing consumerism and increasing aspirations of the new Nepal have offered opportunities in countries like India to get benefited by the growing market in Nepal. And India is taking all the necessary steps to strengthen the Indo-Nepal trade ties even more and along stable lines. Due to availability of cheap labour, Indian merchants and entrepreneurs have invested heavily in Nepal, which also offers them tax breaks for setting up joint ventures.

On a different note, an open border system is not a good idea if the region has problems like terrorism, illegal migration, fake currency, drug trafficking and human trafficking, etc. An open border system demands continuous coordination, cooperation, and transparent intelligence sharing between the two states. The instability of Nepal in its political affairs often brings great uncertainty and it affects the mutual trust and bilateral mechanisms like the open border system badly. In this scenario, the disadvantages generally outnumber the advantages of open border mechanism. Then, security analysts often reiterate the ill effects of the open border system and they advocate a regulated border or the complete closing of the open border system. Some prominent disadvantages of this system are as follows:

- Territorial disputes and encroachments
- Transgression of the border by insurgents and terrorists
- Spilling over of domestic unrest in Nepal across the border into India
- Cross-border illegal activities like smuggling, gunrunning, trafficking in drugs and humans, etc.

Cross-Border Movement of Terrorists, Insurgents, and Criminals

An open border allows easy egress to insurgents and terrorists. In the late 1980s, at the time of the beginning of cross-border terrorism at a larger scale, Sikh and Kashmiri terrorists sneaked into India via Nepal as the border between India and Pakistan was fenced, making infiltration through it difficult. In later years, many insurgent groups in the northeast, such as the United Liberation Front of Asom (ULFA), the National Democratic Front of Bodoland (NDFB), and the Kamtapur Liberation Organization (KLO), also misused the open border.[12] In 2003, these insurgent groups are reported to have shifted their base to Nepal after being chased out of Bhutan. It has also been reported that they are increasingly sneaking into the Nepalese territory and forging links with the Maoists. Their plan is to establish a safe sanctuary in Nepalese territory and engage in the supply of arms and ammunitions to various insurgent groups operating in northeast India and in the red corridor in the country. In recent years, it has been reported that many terrorists involved in numerous bomb blasts in the country had sneaked in through the porous and poorly guarded Indo-Nepal border. Yasin Bhatkal, co-founder of Indian Mujahideen, had been nabbed by Indian authorities in August 2013. He was allegedly behind 11 major bomb attacks in Indian cities that killed many people, including in New Delhi, Mumbai, Bangalore, Ahmadabad, Pune, Surat, etc. He was arrested from the porous border between India and Nepal. This was another big catch for Indian security agencies after Abdul

Karim *alias* Tunda, a key Lashkar-e-Tayyaba operative and expert bomb-maker, who was also arrested from the India-Nepal border on 16 August 2013.

Apart from insurgents, many hard-core criminals pursued by Indian security forces escape into Nepal through the open border. There they set up criminal syndicates and smuggling gangs and carry out the smuggling of drugs, fake currency, arms, gold, and explosives.[13] It was reported that Dawood Ibrahim visited Kathmandu several times and utilized his connections with Pakistan's Inter-Services Intelligence (ISI), business houses, Nepalese politicians, and the criminal underworld for large-scale hawala transactions. Similarly, criminal groups operating in Bihar and Uttar Pradesh use Nepal as a sanctuary from where they mastermind crimes like kidnappings, extortions, car-theft, etc. Minor criminals, too, cross over to the other side to keep away from the Indian police. The increasing madrassas along the Indo-Nepal border is also a source of major concern for the Indian security agencies. It is reported that nearly 1,900 madrassas have come up along the border, 1,100 in India and 800 in Nepal.[14]

Along with madrassas, many Islamic non-governmental organizations (NGOs) have cropped up in the Muslim majority areas in Terai region. Although most of these madrassas and NGOs cater to the social and educational needs of the local people and the waves of Bangladeshi migrants who are settling along the border areas, but under the influence of the ISI, in the guise of madrassas and NGOs, some are engaged in anti-India activities. The use of Nepalese territory by the ISI as a base to carry out anti-India activities since the 1990s is also another matter of serious concern for India's security establishment.[15] The ISI has been so far able to establish a wide logistical network in Nepal to help its agents enter India to carry out insurgent activities.

Significant investigations on the hijacking of Indian Airlines plane IC814 convincingly proved the ISI's involvement in that episode.[16] Intelligence reports also suggest that the ISI is funding many madrassas along the border, which are often used as a stage for anti-India propaganda and as recruiting centres for terrorists. In the past few years, there have been reports alleging the ISI's involvement in pumping fake currency notes into India to destabilize its economy. Arrests of persons involved have provided clues into how many Nepal-based criminal syndicates are used by the ISI to smuggle in fake currency through the open Indo-Nepal border. In 2005–2007, Pakistan and China had shown interest in opening consulates in the Terai. This was, however, not permitted by the Nepalese government on India's request. The fact that

Nepalese soil, which is misused by external agencies, is corroborated by the patterns of global terrorism and assisted by many non-state actors.[17]

The terrorist and Maoist rebels have gained benefits from the open border. They have misused it for the transaction of illegal arms and ammunitions. However, the common people of Nepal and India fear insecurity for their life and property. Not only the Indian and Nepali nationals cross the porous border without any restriction, but these days some Pakistani, Bangladeshi, Sri Lankan and even Afghan and Iranian nationals infiltrate into Nepalese territory, misusing the open border to some extent. Their similar face, attire, posture and behaviour resemble the Nepalese and Indian nationals. Some of the Pakistani, Iranian, and Myanmar infiltrators are in quest of refuge in mostly western nations through the United Nations High Commissioner for Refugees (UNHCR) office in Kathmandu.[18] In one sense, the porous border has helped to initiate rebellious activity in both nations to some extent. Therefore, Indo-Nepal open border management system is going to be difficult for the common people of both countries.

Unrestricted migration over the years has produced territorial pockets dominated by people originating from the other country. According to official estimates, there are 2.2 million Nepali citizens residing in India. Unofficial estimates put the figure at approximately 6 million.[19] Nepalese generally come to India in search of better employment opportunities. There are three types of movements from Nepal. The first is that of people who come on a daily basis to buy goods for domestic needs. Such movement is usually confined to the border region. The second type is that of seasonal migrants, who generally travel to India to find work during agricultural off-seasons. The third type of migrants moves on a long-term basis and generally settles down in India. In the second and third cases, migrants spread out both to neighbouring areas as well as further away from the border. In recent years, due to the intensification of the Maoist movement and the consequent threats to their livelihood and security, the number of Nepalese migrating to India has increased. The net effect of such migration, in extreme cases, is the clamour for a 'homeland', as was witnessed in the hill district of Darjeeling adjoining the Indo-Nepal border. In the 1980s, these Nepali speakers demanded a separate homeland under the aegis of the Gurkha National Liberation Front. It is believed that the agitation received support from across the border.[20]

A similar phenomenon is also unfolding in Nepal's Terai region, which is preponderantly inhabited by Madhesis. Madhesis are of Indian origin and constitute a substantial portion of the population in the Terai region. They are highly dissatisfied with their present state of affairs and are agitating for a fair representation in Nepal's political, administrative, and military establishment. If this problem is not addressed urgently, the incipient Madhesi movement might flare up into a major secessionist movement in Nepal. An open border and a sympathetic population across the border, along with repressive government measures, could lead to its spilling over into India, causing severe unrest in the border region.

Illegal activities, such as the smuggling of essential items and fake Indian currency, gunrunning, and trafficking in drugs and people, are quite rampant along the Indo-Nepal border. Smuggling of essential items from Nepal to India takes place because of the differential tariff rates that prevail in the two countries. This problem is compounded by Nepal's decision to import these goods far in excess of its requirements. A portion of these goods get diverted to Indian consumption centres even before entering Nepal. In addition, a number of other items are smuggled in, including Ganja and hashish, different types of herbs, vegetable ghee, and cardamom, as well as goods from third countries. Conversely, urea, sugar, industrial explosives, gutkha, etc., are being smuggled from India into Nepal.[21]

The Indo-Nepal border is an easy route for the smuggling of arms and ammunition as well. Arms ranging from sophisticated AK47s and 56s to country-made weapons are smuggled across the border through the districts of Pilibhit, Lakhimpur Kheri, and Bahraich. Insurgencies in the two countries and the emergence of criminal gangs, especially in the states of Bihar and Uttar Pradesh, create a demand for these weapons. Various Indian insurgent groups, Maoists, various criminal syndicates, and individual couriers are actively involved in such arms smuggling.[22]

Another illegal activity that has emerged as a major concern for law enforcement agencies is the trafficking of women and children from Nepal. Hundreds of women and children are smuggled in from Nepal for commercial exploitation.[23] According to some estimates, approximately 200,000 Nepali women are in Indian brothels and nearly 7,000 Nepali girls are sold in India every year. This trafficking takes place, especially via the border districts of Bihar and Uttar Pradesh. A voluntary group has mapped around 1,268 unmanned routes along the Indo-Nepal border, which facilitate human trafficking.[24]

Demands for Closing the Open Border

The adverse consequences of an open border have led from time to time to demands for its closure. A demand for closing the border first came from people in the northeast, who did not view favourably the continued migration of Nepalese into their region. Nepali migrants in the northeast basically followed the Gurkha soldiers who were recruited by the British Indian army to guard the north-eastern frontiers. These settlers worked as labourers in the coal mines, oil refineries, and tea plantations, and also as dairy farmers and kitchen helpers. There was harmony between them and the locals till the late 1970s, after which the 'sons of the soil' movement swept Assam and the adjoining states. Locals began to express resentment at the presence of Nepali 'foreigners' amongst them and demanded their expulsion. The agitation against the Nepalese first started in Assam and then spread to other states.

In 1980, violence against Nepalese was witnessed in Manipur for the first time. Meghalaya soon followed suit. In 1986–87, in Shillong, Jowai, and other parts of Meghalaya, Nepali settlers were targeted and hounded out of the state. Such violence also spread to other states such as Mizoram and Nagaland. All this resulted in a large-scale exodus of Nepalese from these states.[25]

In subsequent years, the misuse of the open border by criminals, terrorists, and smugglers provided the spark for the demand to close the border. The ISI's increasing use of Nepalese territory to launch anti-India activities have provided further ammunition to such a demand. Advocates of this course of action argue that security considerations, one main reason for keeping the border open, no longer exist given the improvement in Sino-Indian ties. Moreover, given that international crime and cross-border terrorism have now become fundamental security concerns, an open border is seen as a hindrance in tackling these threats.

In the case of Nepal, it has been a more vocal proponent of a closed border.[26] The Nepalese people have generally been apprehensive about being inundated by Indian migrants through the open border. This fear has been compounded by the fact that it shares borders with two of the most densely populated Indian provinces, Uttar Pradesh and Bihar. These states also suffer from intense population pressure on agricultural land and provide meagre employment opportunities—factors that invariably force people to migrate in search of land and economic opportunities. Everybody in the border area does not have social relations with India or do not get the benefits of the open border. A special example is the Tharus, an ethnic group living spread across the Terai. Many Tharus are rice farmers and as people have the possibility to purchase cheap rice in India; it is hard for them to get good prices on rice. Generally, Tharus don't have social relations across the border. They do not appreciate the open border system. Politically, two sorts of views are generally prevalent.[27] One favours an open border system and the other is against it. Obviously, there are two possibilities of judging the open border, a positive and a negative one. Both are deeply connected to different images of Nepal-India relations and constructions of the two states. There are different perspectives on the border and on India, some people feel close to India, for some it seems to be a threat.

Given the close social, economic, and cultural linkages that exist between the two countries, closing the border is not a sensible or feasible proposition. Such a step would be a retrograde and adversely affect people at the individual level as well as the economies of the two countries. A more prudent step would be to better manage and regulate the movement of goods and people across the border. Aware of the enormous costs involved in closing the border and realizing that what is actually needed is better management of the border, the government of India has been adopting a three-pronged approach in this regard. Firstly, it has put in place, along with its Nepalese counterpart, bilateral mechanisms to better manage the border in a coordinated manner. Secondly, it has begun to deploy security forces to supplement state forces that hitherto have been principally engaged in guarding the border. And, thirdly, it has begun to initiate the building up of better infrastructure in the border regions to improve connectivity and enhance the accessibility of these areas to security forces.

An open border has proved beneficial for both India and Nepal. It has resulted in the forging of close social-cultural ties and economic interdependence has made their relationship special. The open border can be the symbol of friendship and cooperation between the two countries and for closer economic and social relations with the local population, as well as it can symbolize a threat to personal business and for the independence and security of the nation. The existence and contents of these different views also gave the impression of an internal separation in Nepal and the importance of being original Nepalese. Presently, India and Nepal both have new security concerns and challenges to meet. For India, the ISI of Pakistan using Nepal as a launching pad for terrorist activities in India is becoming an issue of grave concern. The open Indo-Nepal border facilitates free movement of such people once they reach Nepal. Here it is not the open border, but weak governments, who do not cooperate in an adequate way, which leads to border problems. Now in the changing scenario, one can expect better coordination at the diplomatic level and better cooperation at the policy and population level between India and Nepal in order to get benefitted mutually over the border issue.

NOTES

1. Pokharel, Krishna (2015), *Nepal Parties reach consensus on Constitution*, Wall Street Journal, [Online: web] Accessed 12 June 2015,URL: http://blogs.wsj.com/indiarealtime/2015/06/10/nepal-parties-reach-consensus-on-constitution/
2. B. Hans (2012), "Nepal's Border to India", [Online: web] Accessed 2 July 2015, URL: http://www.uni-bielefeld.de/tdrc/ag_sozanth/downloads/hans.pdf.
3. R.A. Levine, and D. T. Campbell (1972), "Ethnocentrisms: Theories of Conflict, Ethnic Attitudes and Group Behaviour", John Wiley & Sons Inc., New York.
4. Pushpita Das (2008), "Securing the Northern Coast of Gujarat: Challenges and Responses", *IDSA Reports*, 2008, p.879. [Online: web] Accessed 2 July 2015, URL: http://www.idsa.in/reports/GujaratCoastSeminarReport011208.htm.
5. H.L. Shreshtha (2006), "Proliferation of Small Arms and Light Weapons in Nepal: A Discussion" in Shiva K Dhungana (ed.) *The Maoist Insurgency and Nepal-India Relations*, Kathmandu: Friends for Peace, Kathmandu.
6. K.M. Dixit (2012), "Lights are the border", [Online: web] Accessed 15 Sept. 2013, URL: http://nepalitimes.com/news.php?id=11897.
7. GOI (2012), "Annual Report 2012", MEA, New Delhi, India. pp. 273-75.
8. Pushpita Das (2008), "Towards a Regulated Indo-Nepal Border", *Strategic Analysis*, Vol. 32, No. 5, September,New delhi
9. V.B.S. Kansakar (2006), "Nepal-India Open Border: Prospects, Problems and Challenges", 2006,[Online: web] Accessed 15 Sept. 2013, URL: http://www.fes.de/aktuell/focus_interkulturelles/focus_1/documents/19.pdf.
10. S.D. Muni (1992), *India and Nepal: A Changing Relationship*, Konark Publishers, New Delhi, 1992, pp. 180-82.
11. WB (2012), "World Bank Trade Policy Review Report 2012", p.13.
12. H.L. Shreshtha (2006), "Proliferation of Small Arms and Light Weapons in Nepal: A Discussion" in Shiva K Dhungana (ed.) *The Maoist Insurgency and Nepal-India Relations*, Friends for Peace, Kathmandu, p. 63.
13. GOI (2000), *Annual Report-MHA 1999-2000*, New Delhi, India.
14. A. Riaz (2008), *Faithful Education: Madrassahs in South Asia*, Rutgers University Press, Washington, p. 187.
15. G. Das (2011), "Securing India's Borders: Challenges and Policy Options", Centre for Land Warfare Studies, New Delhi, p. 18.
16. GOI (2003), Press Release-MHA 2003, New Delhi, India.
17. Pushpita Das (2008), "Towards a Regulated Indo-Nepal Border", [Online: web] Accessed Sept. 22, 2007, URL: http://www.academia.edu/3203966/Towards_a_Regulated_Indo-Nepal_Border.
18. H.L. Shreshtha (2006), "Proliferation of Small Arms and Light Weapons in Nepal: A Discussion" in Shiva K Dhungana (ed.), *The Maoist Insurgency and Nepal-India Relations*, Friends for Peace, Kathmandu, 2006.

19. Pushpita Das (2008), "Towards a Regulated Indo-Nepal Border", *Strategic Analysis*, Vol. 32, No. 5, September,New delhi
20. Ibid.
21. GOI (2013), "Annual Report-MEA 2013",New Delhi, India.
22. Ibid.
23. G. Pradhan (2007), "Innocent Victims: Trafficking of Women and Girls across Indo-Nepal Border", [Online: web] Accessed Sept. 22, 2007, URL: http://www.cwin.org.np/resources/issues/ trafficking.htm.
24. UNICEF (2014), "UNICEF reports 7,000 Nepali women and girls trafficked to India every year", [Online: web] Accessed 22 July 2012; http://www.ungift.org/knowledgehub/en/stories/September2014/unicef-reports-7-000-nepali-women-and-girls-trafficked-to-india-every-year.html
25. L. Nath (2006), "Migration, Insecurity and Identity: The Nepali Dairymen in India's. Northeast", *Asian Ethnicity* 7(2): 44.
26. Pushpita Das (2008), "Securing the Northern Coast of Gujarat: Challenges and Responses", IDSA Reports, 2008, p. 888. [Online: web] Accessed 21 June 2009; URL: http://www.idsa.in/reports/GujaratCoastSeminarReport011208.htm.
27. B. Hans (2010), "Nepal's Border to India", [Online: web] Accessed 22 July 2012; URL: http://www.uni-bielefeld.de/tdrc/ag_sozanth/downloads/hans.pdf.

10

Pakistan's Socio-Political Disorder Threatening India's Security Scenario

Sanchita Bhattacharya

For decades, Pakistan's domestic problems and scuffles have influenced or rather threatened India's security scenario. Though, the domestic crises of Pakistan are mainly the result of combination of factors: the failure of state institutions, over enthusiastic Army and supra-state entities, yet cross cultural relationships among the two nation states are being used maliciously to destabilize the other country, sometimes politically and sometimes economically. Pakistan's domestic politics remains intimately linked to political relations with Pakistan's neighbours. Any analysis of threats to its security must emphasize on this overlapping phenomenon between external and internal problems.[1]

The state of Pakistan suffers from a host of domestic concerns which not only threatens the fabric of the state, but also try to hamper India's security, both external and internal. In addition, a turbulent neighbour with unstable political history has been a challenge for India. Apparently, the problem seems to be concentrated within the domestic politics of Pakistan. But, a deeper analysis shows the extent or reach towards Indian territory. The disorders are mainly the work of non-state actors, over-ambitious army, American funding and presence, counter-currents of Balochistan and Kashmir, War on Terror, Money laundering, nuclear arsenal, etc.

Non-State Actors

One of the important components of Pakistan's domestic strife challenging India's security domain is the non-state terror actors. There are three sets of non-state actors dynamic in Pakistan. The first set of non-state actors include the various factions of the Taliban, Quetta Shura, Haqqani network and the Tehreek-e-Taliban (TTP). The second set of non-State actors include those India (and Kashmir specific) militant organisations, especially the Lashkar-e-Toiba (LeT), Jaish-e-Mohammad (JeM) and the Hizbul Mujahideen (HM). The third set of non-state actors are sectarian, belonging to multiple Sunni groups including Sipah-e-Sahaba, Lashkar-e-Jhangvi, etc.[2] The presence of non-state actors (Islamic extremists) associated with Pakistan or working on Pakistan's land with impunity is considered a threat to the peace of the world and to India's security as well.[3] In a somewhat covert manner, the state has supported such elements to fulfil the unwarranted ambitions. The decadent approach has given unlimited power and mobility to terror groups to publicly pronounce their demands exemplifying the 'actual' foreign policy of Pakistan. Moreover, apart from the so called India-centric groups, other terror organizations are also somewhat vocally anti-India. In the month of January 2013, top TTP leader Wali Ur Rehman, in a rare video appearance, pledged to send fighters to Kashmir and wage a struggle for the implementation of *Sharia* rule in India. 'The practical struggle for a *Sharia* system that we are carrying out in Pakistan, the same way we will continue it in Kashmir, and the same way we will implement the *Sharia* system in India too. And this is the only solution for people's problems,' said Rehman.[4]

One can very well state that post 9/11, Pakistan's engagement in the War on Terror in combating Al-Qaeda and Taliban was motivated by its domestic security consideration in terms of containing terror groups. The then Pakistani President Musharraf was prompt in extending full support to America in the ensuing war. The most probable reason for his forthright response was his recognition that America and Pakistan could join in quelling the radical religious and terrorist elements growing within the region.[5] Moreover, Musharraf was also interested to neutralize the sectarian terror elements in Pakistan. Groups like Tehreek-e-Nafaz-e-Shariat-e-Mohammadi (TNSM); Sipah-e-Muhammad Pakistan (SMP); Tehreek Nifaz Fiqah-e-Jafria (TNFJ); Sipah-e-Sahaba Pakistan (SSP), etc., have been very antithetical to the domestic stability of Pakistan and they take refuge in sectarian biases to inflict terror. Confronting the sectarian challenges to the writ of the state, Musharraf was content to exploit the opportunities offered by the War on terror to crackdown on these groups and suppress them once and for all.[6]

The Kashmir policy of Pakistan (i.e., destabilizing India) is the result of domestic strife and tension in terms of exploitation of Jihadi sentiments and showing off of the 'Islam Pasand' policy of Pakistan. The policy of amalgamating the entire Kashmir within Pakistan does not have a direct impact on the internal problems. But, it does entertain a hate culture and militant outfits do exploit the mindset and become preachers of the state policy. Terrorist groups use a range of instrumentalities to raise finances and worse state institutions are deeply complicit in a wide range of terror financing operations.

Huge amount of donation has been is collected by them in the name of Kashmir and Jihad. Militant groups like JeM and LeT, infamous for their 'state-sponsored' terror activities in Kashmir, are active players in terror-funding within Pakistan. One notorious trust, Al Akhtar, an offshoot of JeM, for instance, has been designated by the US Treasury Department as a Foreign Terrorist Organization (FTO) since 2003 and by the UN since 2005. Saud Memon, a financier of Al Akhtar Trust, was found to be involved in the kidnapping and murder of Wall Street Journal's reporter Daniel Pearl. Al Rashid Trust (ART) also deserves mention in this context; it was listed by the US Department of Treasury on September 23, 2001 and by UN on October 6, 2001. ART was known to have been supporting Jihadi activities in Kashmir along with Chechnya, Kosovo, Afghanistan under the leadership of Mufti Mohammad Rashid. ART was linked to LeT, JeM, Al-Qaeda and Lashkar-e-Jhangvi, among others.[7]

The situation is becoming unfortunate with each passing day as in order to appease and legitimize its non-state actors, the government is shelling out its own resources which, in turn, will be used against it apart from obviously percolating down to the anti-Indian terror elements. The appeasement, therefore, is counter-productive, but Pakistan has a long legacy of consecutive governments that have willingly or unwillingly appeased terrorists in order to survive in the short term.[8] The political inconsistency of Pakistan and the lack of legitimate governments often provided ample scope for terror groups and their parent radical organizations in asserting domination and taking political mileage.

Domination of Army

Pakistan has been in a frail political situation, and government policies are making it weaker. Its disastrous economy, worsened by a series of corrupt leaders, is at the root of many of its problems.[9] Pakistan lacks economic development and political stability, which keeps on making the country dependent on international players and financial institutions.[10] The imbalance in the civil-military aspect of the country is well reflected in the economic sphere. The Army in Pakistan is itself an economic enterprise, along with the corrupt 'Families'[11] of Pakistan, who control more than 70 per cent of the economy. The lack of economic stability and rampant corruption of the political leaders, provide leverage to the Pakistani Army in conducting affairs of state, both in the forefront and backstage as well. The domination of the Army, especially threatens the security condition of India as the former has been against a viable and practical rapprochement between the two countries. Therefore, one assumes that the Kashmir issue will not go away easily as the interests of the Army will not allow things to move in a positive direction beyond a point. However, at the moment, Pakistan seems to be using talks with India is way of gaining legitimacy at home and abroad.[12] The Army of Pakistan has not been supportive of the cordial relationship between the two countries. ISI, the intelligence wing of the army, is the notorious protégé of the state, to keep a close eye on India's security scenario and domestic state of affairs. The domination of military in practically every aspect of state politics of Pakistan has repercussions for India and its security.

The military in Pakistan is also antagonistic about India's role in Afghanistan. India's commitment to a strong and stable Afghanistan and its investment in the country's reconstruction are a cause for concern in Pakistan, particularly among the security agencies. From Pakistan's viewpoint, India's goals are to deny Pakistan 'strategic depth' in Afghanistan, to deny Pakistan the ability to block India from the trade and other connections to Central Asia and beyond, and to prevent militants in Afghanistan from attacking Indian targets in Afghanistan.[13] The Army resents Afghan calls for military aid from India due to fears of Military encirclement, even though Pakistan Army appears to have realized the folly of seeking 'strategic depth' in Afghanistan in military terms. To counter the perceived attempts at encirclement, the Pakistan Army and the ISI have begun to reach out to members to the erstwhile Northern Alliance. Pakistan believes that it needs powerful allies within Afghanistan to combat Indian influence and that the Afghan Taliban and their allies in the Haqqani Network and Gulbuddin Hekmatyar's Hizb-e-Islami are the only ones available.[14]

American Donations

Due to dilapidated economic growth, the country has to deal with the hovering presence of American donations and the greater risk of its 'own' interest in Central and South Asia. Pakistan has long since been part of US military alliances in the region, unlike India's Non-Alignment policy. Therefore, from 1950-60s onwards, US presence in Pakistan was for countering Soviet influence in the region. India being a natural ally of the Soviets was seen suspiciously by the US Administration. Moreover, the China-US rapprochement also brought Pakistan into the forefront of US diplomacy. Pakistan was the needed friend of US to contain Soviets and mend ties with China. The flow of money, which came with political affiliation, has therefore become a measure of success, when it comes to US-Pakistan relations. The funds and aid provided by the US to Pakistan has been utterly misused in training of militants belonging to various assemblages, partly causing a serious security challenge for India. The Mujahideen story took a serious turn towards Kashmir, post the Soviet evacuation of Afghanistan.

The focal story of donations started with the Soviet invasion of Afghanistan in 1979. After the invasion, US reconsidered its position and began supporting (along with generous funding from Saudi Arabia) Pakistani and Afghan Mujahideen in their fight against the Soviet Union. In 1981, the US provided Pakistan with a USD 3.2 billion Five Year Military and Economic Aid package.[15] It was followed up in 1986 with another USD 4.02 billion given out over the next six years. Level of US aid to Pakistan has waxed and waned since the 1980s, according to American Geo-Political initiatives. Since 9/11, the country has received USD 19.34 billion in economic and military aid from US for its cooperation in the so-called 'War on Terror.'[16]

Recent conspicuous news thus shows that US made decision to release more than USD 1.6 billion in military and economic aid to Pakistan that was suspended when relations between the two countries disintegrated over the covert raid that killed Osama bin Laden and deadly US air strikes against Pakistani soldiers.[17] Officials and congressional aides said ties have improved enough to allow the money to flow again. It also becomes easier for the donor to entice Pakistan for its own benefit in terms of financial gains. The crippled domestic economy, thus, leads to a fractured foreign policy. Unfortunately, it has become pertinent that the 'welfare aid' is often siphoned to the official face of militant organizations for fulfilling their activities and agenda, which definitely is used for anti-India activities, in connivance with the Army and the ISI. Moreover, the public sentiment in Pakistan is extremely dangerous for US and they are strongly opposing the US role in the War on Terror and also its presence in Pakistani polity in lieu of the War. The people of Pakistan are not taking such liaison cordially and the killing of fellow Muslims in the Af-Pak areas is further worsening the domestic theatre of Pakistan.

US presence, politically and financially, caused overall strain and mass resentment and an easy pretext for terror groups with global Islamic agendas to validate their claims. Islamic extremist forces, which were well entrenched in Pakistani society, posed a great challenge to the Pakistani state. Anti-Americanism has emerged as a dominant trend in Pakistani society. It has been explained under the following three models: Firstly, the Friendship-Betrayal Model based on the historical experiences of engagement and estrangement in Pak-U.S relations. Secondly, Anti-Imperialism which reflects the capitalist, resource oriented US policies in the developing countries. Thirdly, Anti-Islamism based on the pro-Israeli and pro-Indian US policies.[18]

The unstable nature of the Pakistani State due to US donations and presence has an overbearing effect on India, as the groups working to destabilize Pakistan with the pre-text of US money, only abuse the finances to aggravate Jihad towards the Indian State. The common hatred of people are further amplified by anti-India and anti-US speeches of the army and religious leaders inciting people to fight against these two countries. US may think the amount of money flowing into Islamabad will buy friends for the US cause, but generally the funds reach to people fighting against such cause.

Balochistan-Kashmir Counter-currents

The Balochistan issue is a one of the major irritant in the domestic sphere of Pakistan. It is the largest among four provinces, with an area of 347,190 sq km. The province has rich natural resources, especially energy resources, including an estimated 19 trillion cubic feet of natural gas and 6 trillion barrels of oil reserves.[19] Balochistan also holds extensive deposits of gold and copper at Reko Diq in the district of Chagai. The strategic importance of nearing the Arabian Sea with a coastline of 760 km has created further problems. The Gwadar port (Pakistan-Iran border) and the NATO supply lines have redefined its importance in terms of Pakistan's policies with the US and China.

Crucially, the ethnic imbroglio of Balochistan has been infamous for 'kill-and-dump' operations. The tension emanated from the course of events during the independence of Pakistan. The forces of nationalism in Balochistan are a threat to national integration and federation of Pakistan.[20] Groups like the

Baloch Liberation Army, Baloch Republican Army, Baloch Liberation Front, etc., are continuously challenging the establishment. Moreover, since 2009, Balochistan has come under increased scrutiny, with the Americans alleging that Quetta and its environs are a safe haven for the Taliban leadership, including Mullah Omar. The Americans are also keeping a close tab on the Quetta Shura.[21] Other militant groups like Lashkar-e-Jhangvi (LeJ), Taliban, Jundullah also known as the Iranian People's Resistance Movement, are also active in Balochistan. Interestingly, on 9 February 2012, the Oversight and Investigations Subcommittee of the United States House of Representatives Committee on Foreign Affairs convened a hearing on Balochistan, chaired by Congressman Dana Rohrabacher. The fact that the Balochistan issue has made it to the legislature of the world's most powerful country is no small development.[22]

In terms of Indo-Pakistan relations, the latter has always 'blamed' India for covertly supporting the Baloch insurgents fighting the Federal Government. Accordingly, the Kashmir question from Indian side is often countered by the Baloch ethnic problem. And, at the same time, India has her own stakes in the region due to the proposed gas pipelines of Iran-Pakistan-India (IPI) and Turkmenistan-Afghanistan-Pakistan-India (TAPI). Pakistan trying to equate the two situations and causing further political purges in Balochistan in the name of Kashmir, cause political discomfort for India, especially in dealing with terrorists in the Kashmir valley.

Change in Pakistan's Internal Dynamics following the Afghan War and War on Terror

Pakistan always considered Afghanistan to be strategically important and in order to access Central Asia, Afghanistan is high in the priority list. However, as a matter of fact, as long as Pakistan sees a stable Afghanistan as suspiciously synonymous with an encircling Indian-Afghan alliance, then Pakistan will oppose stability in Afghanistan.[23] So, the situation is not at all comfortable for Pakistan and it cannot keep on justifying the existence of such elements only in the name of Islam.

The Afghan policy of Pakistan has deep-rooted repercussions on the already existing tumultuous domestic situations within the country seeping into Kashmir. As was experienced during the 'Mujahideen Experience', the free flow of Kalashnikovs along with drugs, organized criminal activities and disgruntled Talibans-Pashtuns amalgamated into the domestic milieu of

Pakistan. The Mujahideens trained and brainwashed in Afghanistan, soon found themselves turning towards the 'Kashmir issue.' The brutally trained warriors fighting for God's cause became an eminent threat for India's security establishment with their infiltration and training programs of militants to fight in Kashmir. The steady flow of terror recruits eulogizing the Mujahideen saga in Afghanistan and their success story wanted to repeat the same in the Kashmir valley.

Post 9/11, the situation has worsened due to double-edged Pakistan policy on Afghanistan. Up to a point, the leadership of Musharraf was very upright in helping the US against Al-Qaeda and Taliban but, in reality, a huge population of Pashtun refugees with a 'certain bent of mind' are the reality of Pakistan. They are generally found in KP, FATA, Quetta, Capital of Balochistan, Lahore, Rawalpindi, etc. A substantial number of them are also active participants in the Karachi quagmire. Moreover, Pakistan's involvement in Afghanistan has also brought the havoc of US Drone attacks. The American establishment is determined to kill terrorists, but in the process common people are brutally injured and killed. Since 2004, Drone attacks by the US on Pakistani civilians have created destruction in the Pashtun areas. According to *South Asia Terrorism Portal,* since 2005, about 2590 people have been killed in Drone strikes in Pakistan.[24] The attacks and rampant killings have increased anti-American sentiments of the common Pakistani people. According to a poll of Pakistani public opinion carried out by the Pew Global Attitudes Project in 2009, it was found that only 16 percent of Pakistanis have a favourable view of the United States.[25]

The international war against terrorism has caused more agony, deaths and destruction to the people of Pakistan than any other country of this world.[26] Pakistan has paid a heavy price in its war on terror. Its then High Commissioner to Australia, Abdul Malik Abdullah, said in June 2012, 'We are talking about 43,000 Pakistani people who have lost their lives, and that's not including the number of those who have been maimed, crippled, incapacitated.'[27] Pakistan's decision to be part of the US War has crippled the country from within. Pakistan's offer to be part of the US coalition fighting al-Qaeda and its later participation has given a better political leverage to Pakistan over India. Close alliance with the US has reinforced US's preference of Pakistan. The Afghan situation has also provided suitable ground for radicals to fight the government. The extremists are indeed on a violent spree to terrorise the people and the establishment.

Money Laundering and unstable Economy

The trail of financial terrorism in the Indian sub-continent has got the countries of Bangladesh, India and Pakistan in this intricate web. In 2012, some LeT militants were arrested with foreign currency of Bangladesh (taka), amounting to 10 crore. Three of them were Pakistanis. Similarly, Pakistani citizens Mohammad Danish and Sabbir, along with Bangladeshi Fatema Akhtar were arrested with 10,00,000 fake Indian currency notes on 18 January 2014. And on 21 January, a Bangladeshi citizen named Zahid Hasan was arrested along with 50,000 forged Indian notes. A Pakistani national Mohammad Imran was arrested at Hazrat Shahjalal International Airport on 15 January 2015 with 80,00,000 fake Indian rupees. He came to Bangladesh allegedly with a fake passport and visa. It is interesting to note that while Pakistan is busy financing terror activities in other countries of the sub-continent and is also very much engaged in smuggling of fake currencies, the State Bank of Pakistan (SBP), itself is devising policies to curb the menace of fake currency in its own country. As part of its campaign 'Rupay ko Pehchano,' the SBP has developed and launched a total of five videos on the security features of currency notes. It has developed one video of Rs 5,000, Rs 1,000 and Rs 500 notes each, while another video sheds light on the security features of all currency notes in circulation.[28]

In addition, the SBP has launched a mobile application to inspect the currency note. The latest application easily identifies the fake currency note. 'After a rising chorus of public complaints by people who unwittingly got duped into accepting these fake notes, the task of SBP was clear,' according to a report issued by the SBP. Mobile app for devices (i-Pad, i-Phones) and Android educates the users about tell-tale signs behind a real and a fake Pakistani rupee note of any denomination.[29]

Earlier, on 6 October 2015, the SBP stated that the presence of counterfeit currency notes is an undeniable fact and the primary responsibility to check their influx lies with law enforcement agencies. The SBP said it has adopted a three-pronged strategy: ensuring state-of-the-art security features in banknotes that are difficult to counterfeit; developing necessary capacity and infrastructure with banks to issue genuine and authenticated bank notes to the public; and creating awareness among the general public. The problem of terror funding and circulation of counterfeit currency is not only crippling the economy of the sub-continent, especially India, but financial fraud has become an important constituent of terrorism. Pakistan, on the one hand, is trying to spread the menace to other parts but there is no denying the fact that on its domestic turf, the situation is gradually getting out of hand. Terror-finance is a major evil to deal with, and it won't be wrong to say that Pakistan itself is now facing the brunt.

Poppy Cultivation and Drug Cartels

Pakistan, along with Iran and Afghanistan, constitute the Golden Crescent, one of the world's biggest drug-producing regions. According to the United Nations Office on Drugs and Crime (UNODC) 2013 Report, global trafficking routes and seizure data in Pakistan indicate that the major trafficking routes run from Afghanistan through the western Pakistani provinces of KP and Balochistan into Iran in the west, and south to Pakistan's coastal cities, including the ports of Karachi and Qasim in Sindh Province. Moreover, according to UNODC, Pakistan itself has over 1,000 hectares of poppy cultivation, concentrated in the restive FATA on the border with Afghanistan. Most Pakistani poppy cultivation apparently takes place in FATA, including its Khyber Agency, Dir, Bannu and in non-traditional areas including Orakzai, Kurram, and the North and South Waziristan Agencies, along with KP and Balochistan. Cannabis is also produced in large quantities in the border provinces, although most of the cannabis trafficked in the region originates from Afghanistan and is then processed for distribution in the inaccessible areas of Pakistan's FATA region.[30] In November 2013, the then Interior Minister of Pakistan, Rehman Malik, focused on the domestic menace of drug abuse caused by Pakistan's participation in the Golden Route. 'It is estimated that in 2010 the total number of drug users in Pakistan reached about 8.1 million; they are abusing opium and heroin, including intravenously, and hashish, among other things,' Malik stated.[31]

For India, Pakistan's narcotics trade has a two-pronged quandary. In the first instance, the border areas of the country not only with Pakistan, but also with Nepal and Bangladesh, have become a significant den of illegal narcotic trade. Secondly, the amount of money generated from selling various narco-products are often used by terrorists and militants for funding their own organizations. In the 1980s, for the first time, drug trafficking posed a serious threat to India's national security. It was an era when India faced trouble from the Khalistani terrorists who were involved actively in the drug trade. The evident results of such trade across the borders are the rampant drug abuse in the bordering states as well as growth of terror and insurgent activities. Illicit drug trade has been a promising source for financing terror activities in India and abroad. Pakistan's ISI, which has been regarded as one of the important agencies in funding global terrorism, has been making rich dividends through the drug trade since the 1980s. Poppy cultivation, in tribal areas of Pakistan has provided a secure base for the ISI and the Pakistan Army to produce, refine and smuggle top quality heroin to the western markets through India.[32]

Moreover, the March 2008 annual report of the International Narcotics Control Board pointed out that the use of courier services for drug trafficking is on the rise in India, and the country is increasingly being used as a major transit as well as destination country for smuggling of banned substances. The report added that Indian law enforcement agencies are seizing an ever increasing quantity of heroin from the India-Pakistan border, indicating a rise in trafficking from neighbouring nations. The quantity of heroin entering India from Pakistan and Afghanistan increased more in 2007 than in previous years. 'Law enforcement agencies in the north-western part of India are seizing ever increasing quantities of heroin originating in Afghanistan and Pakistan and en-route to Europe via Pakistan and India,' the report said.[33]

Threat from Nuclear Arsenal

One of the biggest challenges facing Pakistan is the safety and safekeeping of its nuclear arsenals from falling into wrong hands. The country's main enrichment facility is a centrifuge plant located at Kahuta; Pakistan may have other enrichment sites. Islamabad gained enrichment related technology from many sources. This extensive assistance is reported to have included uranium enrichment technology from Europe, blueprints for a small nuclear weapon from China, and missile technology from China.[34] According to SIPRI Yearbook 2015, Pakistan has about 100-120 nuclear warheads in comparison to India's 90-110.[35] With Chinese assistance, it has also developed land-based ballistic missiles up to the range of 2,500 km, as well as built up the cruise missiles—*Babur* and *Ra'ad*. It is very proud of having developed tactical nuclear weapons (*Nasr*) to be used in the battlefield to further deter India from any form of conventional retaliation. Pakistan has excessively relied on nuclear weapons for the last three decades and is likely to continue to do so since it has failed to build other strengths or overcome its fundamental challenges. Its excessive reliance on nuclear weapons to project its power emerges from its weaknesses within.[36]

The international concerns, including that of India's has been the safety and security of Pakistan's strategic assets are the nuclear weapons and materials.

First and foremost concern from India's security viewpoint is the fear of non-State actors getting access to the nuclear weapons directly, or to the nuclear bureaucracy who in turn would help them build a weapon. Secondly, a major issue over the nuclear safety and security in Pakistan is related to the non-State actors attacking a nuclear installation within the country—either to create unacceptable damage, as a part of their anti-State activities or to procure nuclear materials, or both. Third major issue, is what is generally referred as an insider job, meaning a divide within the security establishment and a section 'going rogue' with taking control of a few weapons or materials.[37]

Pakistan's national security establishment, on the other hand, rejects contentions that its nuclear posture provides cover for militant proxy groups that act against India. The strongest of these groups is LeT, dedicated to preventing normal relations between Pakistan and India. The belief is widely held in India and elsewhere that Pakistani officials continue to view LeT as a necessary asset to be employed against India when the circumstances dictate. As such, the perception abounds that Pakistan finds utility in nuclear weapons as a shield to prevent retaliation when extremist groups carry out attacks on India, characterized colourfully by one analyst as 'jihad under the nuclear umbrella.'[38]

Moreover, the 'insider threat' perhaps from low-level personnel working on nuclear sites, is an ongoing challenge to Pakistan's nuclear security. An assault and takeover of even a single nuclear device or facility, and fear heightened by recent suicide bomb attacks on Air Force bases, reportedly serving as nuclear weapons storage sites, also remains a persistent threat to the nation and India's security as well. Pakistan has dispersed its weapons to several low-profile sites, thereby increasing the challenge of securing these weapons. Similarly, the imperative to protect its weapons would likely lead the Pakistani military to transport these in small, secret convoys, potentially at greater risk of capture from an insider.[39]

Conclusions

The host of common factors like Afghanistan, Kashmir issue, War on Terror, militant groups, internal strife, etc., are very dominant in defining domestic strife of Pakistan. These factors not only disrupt the political order of Pakistan, but also intimidate India's security. The recent attacks on the Indian Air Force base in Pathankot, best explains the internal conflict of Pakistan, where the civilian government, on the one hand, is trying to improve diplomatic ties with India, and the terror organizations which are trying to dislodge the process, as has earlier happened by the 26/11 Mumbai attacks. India's security is much challenged by the activities occurring inside Pakistan and the repercussions on India's side. The two countries are not only related historically but also the contemporary political tug of war is de-stabilizing the two sides as also South Asian region in totality.

NOTES

1. Akbar, Muqarrab (2011) "Pakistan's Foreign Policy: Internal Challenges in the New Millenniem", *Berkeley Journal of Social Sciences,* 1(2): 1-11
2. Chandran, Suba (2012), "The Crisis State Pakistan's Security Dilemma", [Online: web] Accessed 2 Oct 2015 URL: http://www.ipcs.org/pdf_file/issue/IB192-Suba-BGS.pdf
3. Rashid, Qaisar (2013), "Pakistan's foreign policy challenges", [Online: web] Accessed 14 September 2015 URL: http://paktribune.com/articles/Pakistans-foreign-policy-challenges-243163.html
4. [Online: web] Accessed 8 September 2015 URL: http://www.rediff.com/news/report/taliban-vows-to-unleash-jihad-in-kashmir-implement-sharia/20130108.htm
5. Gilani, Tariq (2006), "US-Pakistan Relations: The Way Forward", [Online: web] Accessed 8 September 2015 URL: http://www.army.mil/professionalWriting/volumes/volume5/march_2007/3_07_3.html
6. Tellis, Ashley J. (2008) "Pakistan and the War on Terror: Conflicted Goals, Compromised Performance", Carnegie Endowment for International Peace, Washington DC.
7. Bhattacharya, Sanchita (2013), "Pakistan's Terror-Finance Inc", [Online: web] Accessed 8 Oct 2015 URL: http://newageislam.com/islam,terrorism-and-jihad/pakistan%E2%80%99s-terror-finance-inc/d/10899
8. Bhattacharya, Sanchita (2013), "Can Pakistan stop its people funding terrorism?", [Online: web] Accessed 8 Oct 2015 URL: http://www.eastasiaforum.org/2013/11/16/can-pakistan-stop-its-people-funding-terrorism/
9. Stern, Jessica (2000), "Pakistan's Jihad Culture", [Online: web] Accessed 8 September 2015 URL: http://www.foreignaffairs.com/articles/56633/jessica-stern/pakistans-jihad-culture
10. Rashid, Qaisar (2013), "Pakistan's foreign policy challenges", [Online: web] Accessed 11Nov 2015 URL: http://paktribune.com/articles/Pakistans-foreign-policy-challenges-243163.html
11. In 1968, Dr. Mahbub ul Haq, the then Chief Economist at the Planning Commission of Pakistan, identified 22 families/groups in Pakistan that were dominating the financial and economic life of the country controlling 66% of the industrial assets and 87% of the banking. Interestingly, the number has somewhat increased to 44, over the ongoing decade.
12. [Online: web] Accessed 11Nov 2015 URL: http://www.idsa.in/system/files/strategicanalysis_skumar_0903.pdf
13. Gul, Imtiaz (2015), "Pakistan's persistent security challenges", [Online: web] Accessed 28 September 2015 URL: http://www.eastasiaforum.org/2015/12/23/pakistans-persistent-security-challenges/
14. Kanwal, Gurmeet (2013), "Pakistan's Internal Security Challenges: Will The Military Cope?", [Online: web] Accessed 28 September 2015 URL: http://www.ipcs.org/pdf_file/issue/IB230-Gurmeet-Pakistan.pdf.

15. Aguilar, Fransisco et. al. (2015), *An Introduction to Pakistan's Military*, Cambridge: Harvard Kennedy School.
16. Nevins, Sean (2014), "America Gives Aid to Pakistan, Pakistan Gives Terrorism To The World", [Online: web] Accessed 16 Nov 2015 URL: http://www.mintpressnews.com/america-gives-aid-pakistan-pakistan-gives-terrorism-world/199921/
17. [Online: web] Accessed 16 Nov 2015 URL: http://www.theguardian.com/world/2013/oct/19/usforeignpolicy-pakistan
18. [Online: web] Accessed 8 Oct 2015 URL: http://graduateinstitute.ch/files/live/sites/iheid/files/shared/executive_education/Global%20South%20Workshop/paper_Younus.pdf
19. Alamgir, Aurangzeb (2013), "Pakistan's Balochistan Problem: An Insurgency's Rebirth", [Online: web] Accessed 2 Nov 2015 URL: http://thebalochistanpoint.com/pakistans-balochistan-problem-an-insurgencys-rebirth/
20. Akbar, Muqarrab (2011), "Pakistan's Foreign Policy: Internal Challenges in the New Millenniem", *Berkeley Journal of Social Sciences,* 1(2): 1-11
21. Siddiqi, Farhan Hanif (2012), "Security Dynamics in Pakistani Balochistan: Religious Activism and Ethnic Conûict in the War on Terror", *Asian Affairs: An American Review,* 39 (3): 157-175.
22. Siddiqi, Farhan Hanif (2012), "Security Dynamics in Pakistani Balochistan: Religious Activism and Ethnic Conûict in the War on Terror", Asian Affairs: An American Review, 39 (3): 157-175.
23. Shinwari, Sadaf (2013), "Pakistan Political Crisis, impact on Afghanistan", [Online: web] Accessed 21December 2015 URL: http://www.khaama.com/pakistan-political-crisis-impact-on-afghanistan-1243
24. [Online: web] Accessed 4 December 2015 URL: http://www.satp.org/satporgtp/countries/pakistan/database/Droneattack.htm
25. "Pakistani Public Opinion: Growing Concerns about Extremism, Continuing Discontent With U.S.," The Pew Global Attitudes Project, August 13, 2009.
26. [Online: web] Accessed 11December 2015 URL: http:www.pakistantalk.com/forums/strategic-issues-iisues/6964-war-against-terrorism-its-impact-pakistani-masses.html
27. Strachan, Julieanne (2012), "War exacts its heavy price", [Online: web] Accessed 8 September 2015 URL: http://www.canberratimes.com.au/act-news/war-exacts-its-heavy-price-20120609-202ot.html.
28. Bhattacharya, Sanchita (2016), "Web of financial terror in sub-continent: Pakistan's doing can be its undoing, [Online: web] Accessed 8 September 2015 URL: http://southasiamonitor.org/details.php?type=sl&nid=15074.
29. [Online: web] Accessed 12December 2015 URL: http://www.thenestribe.com/2015/12/22sbp-introduces-mobile-app-to-detect-fake-currency-notes/
30. Drug Use in Pakistan 2013 Technical Summary Report, (Vienna: UN Office on Drugs and Crime, 2013): [Online: web] Accessed 12 December 2015 URL: http://www.unodc.org/documents/pakistan/2013.03.01ab_Summary_Report_Drug_Use_inPakistan_SvdV_v1.pdf.
31. "Around 70 Pc of Taliban's Income Comes from Drugs: Malik," *Dawn*, 13 November 2012: [Online: web] Accessed 8 September 2015 URL: http://www.dawn.com/news/763762/around-7-pc-of-talibans-income-comes-from-drugs-malik. In 2010, Pakistan's population was estimated to be 180 million.
32. "The Golden Crescent and Implications for India's National Security", 2014: [Online: web] Accessed 28 September 2015 URL: https://startegiccultureindia.wordpress.com/2014/12/10/the-golden-crescent-and-implications-for-indias-national-security/

33. [Online: web] Accessed 28 September 2015 URL: http://www.vijayvaani.com/ArticleDisplay.aspx?aid=162.
34. Kerr, Paul K. and Nikitin, Mary Beth (2013), "Pakistan's Nuclear Weapons: Proliferation and Security Issues", [Online: web] Accessed 11 September 2015 URL: https://www.fas.org/sgp/crs/nuke/RL34248.pdf
35. SIPRI Yearbook (2015), [Online: web] Accessed 23 December 2015 URL: http://www.sipri.org/yearbook/2015/downloadable-files/sipri-yearbook-2015-summary-pdf
36. Chawla, Shalini (2015), "Why does Pakistan threaten India so often with nuclear attack?", [Online: web] Accessed 19 September 2015 URL: http://www.dailymail.co.uk/indiahome/indianews/article-3240567/Why-does-Pakistan-threaten-India-nuclear-attack.html.
37. Chandran, Suba (2012), "The Crisis State Pakistan's Security Dilemma", [Online: web] Accessed 19 September 2015 URL: http://www.ipcs.org/pdf_file/issue/IB192-Suba-BGS.pdf
38. Dalton, Toby and Krepon, Michael (2015), *A Normal Nuclear Pakistan,* Washington DC: Stimson Center.
39. Aguilar, Fransisco et al. (2011), *An Introduction to Pakistan's Military*, Cambridge: Harvard Kennedy School.

11

Understanding the Federally Administrated Tribal Areas (FATA) Problem

Ravindra Prasad and Raghvendra Pratap Singh

Agencies and Frontier Regions that constitute the region of Pakistan known as Federally Administered Tribal Areas (FATA) have a tradition of a vast and rich history. The administrated areas are a semi-autonomous tribal region in the northwest of Pakistan. The region lies between Afghanistan to the west and north, and the provinces of Khyber Pakhtunkhwa to the east and Balochistan to the south. The FATA comprises seven agencies and six frontier regions. The seven agencies are: Bajaur, Momand, Khyber, Orakzai, Kurram and North and South Waziristan. There are six frontier regions adjacent to the settled districts of Peshawar, Kohat, Dera Ismail Khan, Bannu and Lakki Marwat which are part of FATA. The area had a population of some 3.1 million people at the time of the 1998 census, and current unofficial estimates range up to 7 million comprising mostly of ethnic Pashtuns tribes who straddle the Durand Line.[1] The territory is dominated by Pashtun tribes, who also live in the neighbouring Khyber Pakhtunkhwa and Afghanistan and are Muslim by faith. The territory is governed through the Frontier Crimes Regulations.[2]

Historical Perspective of FATA

In ancient and medieval periods, FATA was a corridor of early invasions and route for trade between Central Asia and the Indian sub-continent. Alexander (323 BC), Turks (445-550 AD), Arabs (568-900AD), Changez Khan and his successors (1220-1365 AD), Taimur and his successors (1380-1504 AD) and Babur (1526 AD) came through these routes. After the collapse of the Mogul empire, Nadir Shah in 1739 AD, obtained the possession of trans-Indus territory followed by Ahmad Shah Abdali who established the first Afghan monarchy (1747-1818) covering these areas too. Thereafter, the rise of the Sikh rulers (1818-49 AD) with their annexation of Peshawar in 1832 installed them as new rulers of northwest India but they possessed very little influence on the trans-Indus tract and left the tribesmen to manage their own affair.[3]

The area along the British India frontier and Afghanistan border inhabited by Pashtuns of various tribes was the epicentre of the 'Great Game' between the British and the Russian Empires in late 19th and early 20th centuries. The British apprehension of Russian expansion into Central Asia and fear of an Afghan-Russian coalition forced the British to launch two wars on Afghanistan in 1839-42 and 1878-79. The Pashtun tribal belt was also involved in the confrontation. Pashtuns fought along with rulers of Kabul against British and Indian forces. If the first war did not bring any glory to Britain the second war brought most of the Pashtuns tribal belt under the control of the British troops.

Despite the military success, the British government soon realized that constant attacks by Pashtun tribes against forces of the East India Company were very dear and failed to provide security for British interests. In 1893, Britain, while having control of Afghanistan's foreign policy, forced King Abdur Rahman of Afghanistan to accept the Durand Line Agreement. This plan artificially divided the Pashtun inhabited tribal region into two parts. It would, then, fall under the jurisdiction of two unfriendly countries. In the agreement, the 1,610 miles border between Afghanistan and India were drawn from Wakhan in the north to the Iranian border with some adjustment of territories.

Since the enforcement of the Durand Line Agreement, FATA had its own political system and relationship with the national capital under the rule of the British Raj and it continued till these tribal areas became a part of Pakistan in 1947. The Pashtun tribes who checked foreign invasions were given power to run their internal affairs. They were governed by the Frontier Crimes Regulation established by the British through appointed political agents and maliks.

In 1947, the Indian Independence Act annulled the agreements between the British Raj and Tribal Areas. The independent state of Pakistan, then, had to come to new agreement binding Pashtun tribal areas to Islamabad. The Pakistani Government did not curb the rights and privileges of maliks and gave autonomy to the region. In return, the Pashtun pledged loyalty to Pakistan. The conditions of the political relations between FATA and the federal government along with the administrative set up of the tribal areas were formalized by orders and notifications by the Governor General of Pakistan and agreements which were reviewed and, later on, modified to incorporate them in the Pakistan's Constitution of 1973.

The Soviet intervention in 1979 and the presence of their forces in Afghanistan until 1989 had negatively affected the FATA because millions of Afghan refugees fled across the border into the most undeveloped region of Pakistan. The region became a hub for the Mujahideen to fight against the Soviet forces as weapons, money, fighters and Jihadi ideology spread. This was a turning point in their history because these tribes gradually transformed into religious fundamentalism as maliks and traditional clergy lost authority and Mujahideen commanders had the political power to control the resources. Deobandi and Salafi teachings were also accepted because many young frustrated students were fed up with long drawn wars with the Soviet Union. Many madrassas, including militant Jihadi ones, were endowed with religious fundamentalism and secular education had no role in society.

With Operation Enduring Freedom in October of 2001 many Taliban fighters, Al-Qaeda and affiliate groups such as Islamic Movement of Uzbekistan escaped and found safe haven in the FATA. Today, FATA is one of the most important areas in the global war on terror. The history of the region is full of examples where mere military intervention did not bring any long-term strategic success. To understand the complex history, geography, politics and economics of the region, it is important to understand combat terrorism in this region and elsewhere.

Geography

Geographically, the region can be divided into three sub regions, i.e., the Northern, Central and Southern Region. The Northern Region lies between the Swat and Kabul Rivers which is mostly covered by mountains and has a temperate climate which, though, limits agriculture but allows a variety of cash crops including fruits, seeds, etc., to grow. The Central Region comprises

Khyber, Kurram and Orakzai Agencies and the frontier region of Peshawar, Kohat and Bannu has snow-clad Safed Koh Mountains in the North and fertile Khanki, Mastura and Bara River valleys in the South. The Southern Region comprises both the Waziristan Agencies and frontier region of DI Khan, Tank, Bannu and Lakki Marwat and have igneous rock formed Waziristan Hills where a number of important minerals are available in commercial quantities.[4]

In military terms, the area is meant for low-intensity conflict in the form of skirmishes and ambushes and favours, predominantly, small-scale infantry operations. Lack of laterals and difficulty in inter-valley operational movements limits the nature of fighting which is un directional. It is also characterized by lack of mutual flexibility with heavy logistical requirements. Peshawar, being an important communications centre is critical for maintaining the government's writ. The Axes Chitral Mardan Nowshera and Peshawar-Kohat-Bannu-Razmak-Wan az–Zhob constitute the backbone of the communications system. Apart from this, Peshawar-Khyber assumes much importance for movement of logistics for coalition forces deployed in Afghanistan.

The People of the Frontier

The status of the FATA region and its people constitutes a core issue that depends over the bi-national aspects of the Durand Line. The core elements include the political status of the FATA region and its people, their historic disregard for the boundary, and their ties to the border world.

Drawing the Durand Line began a process that resulted in an unusual system of administration in which the peoples on the British side of the line retained stateless autonomy within an imperial system that declared sovereignty over their lands. The British system maintained this indirect control by appointing clan leaders as chiefs of their local communities under the supervision of British tribal agents. Special laws under the Frontier Crimes Regulations (1901) gave the colonial administration sweeping powers to deal with individuals and whole groups outside of the normal judicial process. They could and burned houses, banned people from the region, stopped trade, and imposed large collective fines or other punishments without right of appeal.[5]

When Pakistan became independent, it chose to maintain the anomalous status of the FATA region rather than to incorporate its people into the new state with the same rights and responsibilities as other Pakistani citizens. Thus, even today, Pakistan cites the Frontier Crimes Regulations as its legal justification for imposing collective punishments that apply not only to residents within FATA but also to members of their tribes living outside it. In addition, Pakistan maintains the same system of tribal agencies and indirect rule established by the British. This makes it very difficult for Pakistan to deal with the border question without first tackling its internal administration of the frontier. No international settlement can be expected as long as Pakistan continues to treat the people in the FATA region as colonial subjects rather than as full citizens.[6]

For the people living along the Durand Line, it had never been accepted as an international border. They think as if it does not exist, then crossing from one side to another would have been easier. There are villages located in Pakistan that have their farmland in Afghanistan and vice versa. Governments recognize this fact by not demanding papers from local people even at formal border crossings.

The historical record states that even though there is a bilateral agreement between the Afghan and Pakistani people at the local level it must include a soft border provision that permits regular travel, work and trade by local residents. Afghanistan's vehement opposition to a 2006 Pakistani proposal to fence the border proves this point. The problem arises with such a soft border requiring strong states on either side to contain security problems or criminal activities. Neither side can be in a position to secure the region in accordance with their interests.

The local non-acceptance of the Durand Line is only one aspect of the region's resistance to state penetration in their activities. Although this is not mentioned in the FATA, such resistance also comes from the Pashtun tribes on the Afghan side of the frontier as well. Pashtuns in the region take great pride in asserting their autonomy by declaring their Pashtunwali tradition and tribal jirgas supersede state law codes and courts. Pashtunwali is both a code of honour and a code of conduct that influences individual and group behaviour in a way that helps them for their own governance rather than the formal government. In political terms, it seems they are members of stateless societies that had little political affiliation to political governments which today rule over them. Their identity is not known in terms of the state but in terms of tribes and localities. Even 'tribe' may be not a correct term but the more appropriate term used is *qawm*, or solidarity groups that change from situation to situation. In such a system, individual interests are important and these may differ from people to people. Successes mean to them what and how they can gain from a complex world and then move to achieve the ultimate result. Though they are capable to act collectively only on a temporarily basis but they find it difficult to bring these ad hoc alliances together to form one entity. To them, what may not happen today may well be repeated tomorrow. For this reason, their explanations of events often appear to be rooted in the particulars of persons, places, actions or moments of history. State actors find it difficult to appreciate the dynamics of such a system. They see regularities where they do not exist, attribute to tribes a greater degree of unity than they actually possess and find themselves ill-equipped to deal with personality-driven politics that may be as changeable as the weather.[7]

System of Governance

Administrative System: FATA is administratively ruled by the Governor of Khyber Pakhtunkhwa. He is a representative of the Pakistan President and each Agency has a Political Agent. The role of Political Agent can be better described as half-ambassador and half-governor wherein he administers the Agency with a necessary mixture of tact, patience, wit and sympathy. He is the kingpin of the Agency and his duties encompass the role of magistrate, police chief, director of health and education, and chief engineer, all-in-one. He is assisted by one or two Assistant Political Agents (APA), Tehsildar, naib Tehsildar and Moharra (officials). The other important (tribal) administrative institutions which play important roles are the Jirga System, Nikkat System, Malliki System, Khassadari System, etc. In the tribal areas of the eastern regions, the role of Political Agent is played by District Coordinated Officer or DCO.[8]

Judicial System

Enjoying special Constitutional status which excludes the FATA from HC/SC Jurisdiction, the tribal judicial system hinges on the troika of Jirga System, Political Agent and Federal Crimes Regulation, 1901. In all the disputes (criminal/civilian and even in the case of Frontier Crimes Regulation), the Riwaj (the Customary Law) and Sharia (Islamic Law) form the basis for arbitration. The Frontier Corps, Frontier Constabulary, Khassadars and Levies act as law-enforcement agencies of the civilian administration. Here, the government generally does not interfere in the offences occurring between tribes. The government intervenes when State interest is involved. In such cases, the interference is direct, either by use of force or indirect, i.e., through Maliks/Khassadars or by invoking the tribal/territorial responsibility clause of Frontier Crimes Regulation.

Socio-Economic Profile

FATA is the least developed area of Pakistan with agriculture and livestock as the main livelihood which has approximately 7% of land under cultivation.[9] The region has approximately 1500 primary schools, 180 middle schools, 120 high schools and the eight colleges. It has an overall literacy rate of 17.4% and female literacy rate is as low as 3%. Likewise, in the health sector, the average population per dispensary is 2,893 persons while the average population per doctor stands at 14,949 persons. The transport infrastructure is also in rudimentary form with roads per sq km as low as 0.16% which leaves almost one-third of the area inaccessible.

Fundamentalist Groups in FATA

The Haqqani Network group was headed by Jaluluddin Haqqani and was responsible for the setting up madrassas and military training camps in the border areas between Pakistan and Afghanistan. Their activities in the region, which began in 1978, continue till date and have the support of Al-Qaeda, and other militant organizations. Due to his advancing age and health problems, Jalaluddin Haqqani has passed the mantle of leadership to his son Sirajuddin Haqqani. It is also assumed that Jalaludin Haqqani has passed away. His son operates out of North Waziristan in Pakistan. He carries a five million dollar US bounty on his head. The group has links with foreign fighters, Pakistani Taliban (TTP) and Afghan Taliban. It operates on professional lines and has its own think tank and a political wing. The notable members of this group are Moulvi Gul Ramzan, resident of Miranshah, Moulvi Naeem, resident of Bannu, and Moulvi Muhammad Saleem, resident of Waziristan and also include many experienced guerrilla fighters who hail from Central Asia and the Middle East. The militant wing is overseen by two other sons of Jalaluddin Haqqani—Nasirudin Haqqani and Badaruddin Haqqani, who also supervise the operations in Kashmir. This group is vehemently anti-Shia and anti-Northern Alliance of Afghanistan. The fighters in this group number approximately 15,000.[10]

Tehrik-i-Taliban Pakistan: This group was formed by Baitullah Mehsud, a leading militant in Waziristan, Pakistan. He formed the TTP, which is a coalition of five militant groups set up in December 2007. Reports say that they have commanded at least 5,000 fighters and were behind many attacks in Pakistan including the assassination of Benazir Bhutto, which he has denied.

According to the Pakistani security officials, Baithullah Mehsud, his wife and body guards were killed on 5 August 2009 in a US drone attack in the Zangar area of South Waziristan. He was succeeded by his fellow tribesman Hakimullah Mehsud.

The Taliban of North Waziristan: This group was a part of the TTP earlier. At that time it was headed by Baitullah Mehsud. They were separated in 2008, but returned to the TTP fold in 2009. The amir (head of the group) is Hafiz Gul Bahadur of the Khel Wazir tribe. His deputy is Maulvi Nazeer who operates in South Waziristan, died on January2, 2013. The group has the protection of Mufti Nur, a notable person of the area.

The Mehdi Millitia and Haidari Taliban: These groups comprise of militants of the Shia sect. The Commanders of this group are Hussein Ali Shah and Abid Hussein. They operate in the Kurrum agency against the TTP as well as group called Tehrik-i-Taliban Islami. Both groups have a combined strength of 8,000 to 10,000 soldiers. They are supported by Iran and the Northern Alliance of Afghanistan.

Lashkar-e-Islam: Another important militant group in the Khyber agency, it is headed by a local man of the Afridi tribe named Haji Mangal Bagh. It started off as a vigilante group, prosecuting local criminals and the population.[11] Later, however, it adopted the Taliban practices where people were punished for not attending prayer services, not closing shops at prayer time and committing unsocial acts.

Tehreek-e-Nafaz-e-Shariat-e-Muhammadi (TNSM) - (Malakand Division): This group is active in the Malakand Division and the Swat valley. It is headed by Moulvi Fazlullah who was targeted by the Pakistan army during its operations in the Swat valley.[12]

The Kashmiri Group: Besides the groups, there are others actors who promote Talibanization in the tribal belt of Pakistan as well as other parts of the Khyber Pakhtunkhwa province. These are: Lashkar-e-Tayaba (perpetrators of the Mumbai attack), Lashkar–e-Jhangvi, Sipah-e-Sahaba, Harkat-ul-Mujahideen, Jaish-e-Muhammad and Harkat-al-Mujahideen-al-Islami. They have not only taken active part in the Kashmir liberation activities but are also responsible sectarianism in Pakistan. These groups have moved into the tribal belt when

Pakistan imposed restrictions on their movements. The fighters are originally from the Punjab and Kashmir, and also have links with the Haqqani group and the TTP.

Groups of Taliban Forces in FATA

There was a time when the Taliban were known more as an Afghan entity. Prior to 9/11, when these groups had their active presence on Afghan territory then the real agenda was clearly outlined to their naïve supporters in Pakistan and Afghanistan. To them 'Taliban' was a way of life built around an extremist interpretation of the Quran. The Taliban believed that anyone who differed with them was an apostate and, therefore, deserved to die. That was why when the majority of the Mujahideen fighters returned to Pakistan after the Soviet withdrawal, they preached a version of Islam in which the followers of the Shia sect were declared as non-believers. The Shias were made targets and their places of worship were destroyed. In response to the atrocities committed, two Shia militant groups emerged in the region, where previously there were none. These groups have the support of the Pakistani Intelligence who uses them against the TTP. [13]

The Orakzai Tribal Agency: This is the region where the Shia and the Sunni militants are at war with each other. These factions have supporters in all three neighbouring countries; Iran, Pakistan and Afghanistan.

Kurram Agency: In this agency, Qari Hussien is known for his ruthlessness and is a fearless commander. He also controls a substantial number of suicide bombers. He supports the TTP's cause and is closely related to the Taliban in the Darra Adam Khel area which is headed by Commander Tariq.

The Khyber Agency: The Khyber Agency is like the Kurram agency engaged in fundamentalist activities. The militant groups number more than three. Here also, the adherents of the TTP group headed by Hakimullah Mehsud who died in November, 2013 have made their presence felt.

Mohmand Agency: The Mohmand Agency is well known for their militant activities. When the agitation began in this region, the army began its operation in June 2007 against the residents of Lal Masjid (red mosque) located in Islamabad. Religious extremists including women who were students at the madrassa, located inside the mosque complex, had become vigilantes against prostitution and gambling.

Bajaur Agency: This is the part of South Waziristan, where the Pakistan army carried out an operation against the Taliban towards the end of 2008 in which approximately 1,500 Taliban fighters were killed. Also 950 fighters were arrested, which included a large number of foreign fighters.

In the recent past, we have seen many casualties in FATA. This is shown by the chart given below:

Fatalities in FATA: 2006-15

Years	*Civilians*	*SFs*	*Militants*	*Total*
2006	109	144	337	590
2007	424	243	1014	1681
2008	1116	242	1709	3067
2009	636	350	4252	5238
2010	540	262	4519	5321
2011	488	233	2313	3034
2012	549	306	2046	2901
2013	319	198	1199	1716
2014	159	194	2510	2863
2015	1001	104	356	1424
Total	5341	2276	20255	27835

Source: South Asia Terrorism Portal Assessment – 2015, [Online: web] Accessed 2 November 2015, http://www.satp.org/satporgtp/countries/pakistan/Waziristan/index.html

The International Perspective

Since 11 September 2001, FATA had been viewed as a region of global insecurity. The militant activities can be controlled only when Pakistan takes responsibility for its territory and extends the structures of the state into the region, particularly through expanding opportunities for economic development and education in the FATA region. The task is quite difficult because of the poor security situation and to work for development projects seems difficult. The Durand Line also increases the problem because it prevents such development from occurring in FATA and in the Afghan provinces. Moreover, Afghanistan's denial of de jure recognition to the border has stood in the way of a comprehensive development program that could have a greater impact on the parallel developments in each country.

Having driven the Taliban and Al-Qaeda from Afghanistan, the United States and its allies have become more active to end FATA's ability to serve as the centre of Islamic fundamentalists who promote international terrorism and seek to destabilize Afghanistan. The US, NATO, and Afghan combat troops along the Durand Line have to face grave problems because those fighting in Afghanistan when defeated get shelter in Pakistan with the hope they will not be pursued or attacked across an international boundary.

As the member of the international community, negotiations between Pakistan and Afghanistan can resolve the problems between them only if they tackle them as a set of interrelated issues. Mere discussions would not bring stability in the region even if they succeed. Afghanistan is not in a position to accept the political price for accepting the border unless such an agreement were part of a border package designed to make the country more secure. What is important is that the focus should be on trade, security, and non-interference in each other's domestic affairs? In particular, as a landlocked country, Afghanistan has long-standing concerns about its access to trade through the port of Karachi and obstacles to its transit trade with India.

But Pakistan can also gain from the border negotiation. Pakistan's economy and tax base is disturbed by billions of dollars because of the goods smuggled into the country through Afghanistan. Then there is problem of drug trade. The solution lies in trade with Afghanistan which would in a big way help to overcome this problem. Pakistan is also facing security problems and there is apprehension in the mind of Pakistani government that India might attempt to use Afghanistan as a base to 'encircle' it. Today, Afghanistan is much concerned about Pakistan's support of the Taliban. Earlier it was Pakistan who was concerned about Afghanistan's tacit support of Pashtun and Baluch separatists that a hostile Afghan government could harbour. Thus, it would be in the interests of both the countries to cooperate on issues that threaten their security. With so much distrust between the two countries, it is necessary for the international community to come out and take the lead in bringing them together and in strengthening regional security. What has been noticed is that only a soft border solution would work in a region where local people have historically had right of free passage. Furthermore, soft boundaries require strong states to maintain them. The cooperating states must take tough measure to manage external borders and it could possible by effective regional security cooperation. But such kind of security is currently absent in Pakistan and Afghanistan.

It would have been much easier to maintain security if the Durand Line was not a disputed boundary between these states but rather the centre of a regional cooperation scheme which cooperated in preventing activities hostile to each other. This is more important for Afghanistan because it lacks the economic infrastructure to develop its internal security without massive foreign subsidies. Moreover, relying on foreign powers will not solve its problem. Only an agreement on cooperation with Pakistan could bring reduction in the regional threat. Pakistan should also stop its covert support to the Taliban and from being used as a base for attacks on Afghanistan. Some experts even suggest that Pakistan might manipulate the situation in the FATA region to achieve strategic relationship with the United States that will provide it with military and financial assistance. It is clear that the United States had stopped, to a great extent, its aid to Pakistan soon after the Soviet Union withdrew from Afghanistan and after the attacks of 11 September 2001.

Conclusion

It is generally seen that status quo in FATA will continue to remain for some more time. Therefore, it is in the interest of both the countries to reduce the current tensions and to seek settlement on broad issues. A successful solution will also require the consideration of the need and participation from the people who actually live in the border regions. But in reality neither Afghanistan nor Pakistan has shown their ability to work for a quick solution on the border question. But the process must begin and should start with confidence-building measures. This would help them in reducing tensions. Hence, a series of Track II dialogue could be the best solution, but such dialogues would be largely ineffective unless each side was convinced that the other was serious about seeking a resolution. Hence, small measures are seen as most practical and as providing a better starting point. This include discussion for trade and transport, creating a commission to consult the border communities, and forging closer security ties on problems of common interest. The 'peace jigra' held by the Afghans and Pakistanis in Kabul in August 2007 offers a beginning to such a forum.

FATA's problems can be resolved when following measures are taken seriously:

- Accepting, at least tacitly, that as the Durand Line has served as an internationally recognized border for more than a century. Several debates on various forums on the history of the agreement and its status during various stages have impeded rather than facilitated a settlement. Some changes could be desirable but the wholesale transfer of sovereignty might not be accepted.
- So far, the existing cross-border ethnic ties and difficult topography of the region, are concerned there is a need to recognize the rights of

the local population to cross the border freely as they do today. In order to make it functional, it is the responsibility of Afghanistan and Pakistan governments to demonstrate their ability to control their respective territories. This will require Pakistan to regularize the political status of the FATA region and Afghanistan to respect the choices of the people there.

- All those countries involved in this should come out with concrete solutions and one such method is border-related confidence building measures between Afghanistan and Pakistan, including trade, transit rights, and security measures. These measures will, no doubt, reduce the level of conflict between the two countries and provide benefits to both.
- The Western world must be in a position to bring the parties together and provide the political incentives which are important to maintain progress. Pakistan also needs some assurances from Afghanistan that it will not hinder Pakistan's security problems (particularly in Afghanistan's relationship with India). Afghanistan also needs free access to ports, particularly Karachi, economic security, and non-interference by Pakistan's in its domestic politics.
- In a region when political perceptions are clear then concrete progress will be key to any successful outcome. It is also necessary that some kind of guarantee of international long-term security guarantees and a substantial aid package that benefits both Pakistan and Afghanistan might enable them to minimize their differences and work for a common goal.

NOTES

1. Siddique and I. Khattak (2004), "War on Terror Highlights Development Needs in FATA", *The Friday Times*, January 23, Lahore.
2. S.S. Ali, R. Javaid (2001), "Indigenous Peoples and Ethnic Minorities of Pakistan: Constitutional and Legal Perspectives, Routledge, London.
3. K.M. Hasan (2006), "A Political and Diplomatic History of Afghanistan, 1865-1901", Leiden Boston, Brill.
4. J.F. Murhy (2002), "Sword of Islam: Muslim Extremism from the Arab Conquest to the Attack on America", Promethean Books, New York.
5. Report of a Conference on the Durand Line: History, Consequences and Future (2007), American Institute of Afghanistan Studies and the Holling Center in Istanbul, Turkey.
6. Ibid.
7. Ibid.

8. S.V. Salahuddin (2012), "Militancy in Pakistan and Afghanistan", Pentagon Press, New Delhi.
9. D.S. Markey (2008), "Securing Pakistan's Tribal Belt", Council on Foreign Relations, Center for Preventive Action, Council Special Report No. 36.
10. A. Rabasa and S. Boraz and P. Chalk (2007), "Ungoverned Territories: Understanding and Reducing Terrorism Risks", RAND, California, United States.
11. R.D. Crews and Amin Tarzi (2008), "The Taliban and the Crisis of Afghanistan", Harvard University Press.
12. Ibid.
13. C.C. Fair and J.A. Howenstein (2006), "Troubles on the Pakistan-Afghanistan Border", United States Institute of Peace.

12

Sri Lanka: A Geostrategic Imperative for India

Narender Kumar

Introduction

The Indian Ocean region (IOR) is emerging as a Centre Stage for the 21st Century power play.[1] The Indian Ocean gives India a large manoeuvring space. It extends India's reach to the extremities of strategic boundaries and gives it depth to secure the territorial boundaries as well. It is indeed a springboard for India's quest to be a comprehensive national power. It makes India relevant to the regional and global community and a net security provider to the region. Therefore, the island nations and archipelagos in the Northern Indian Ocean Region become more significant. Erosion of influence in the periphery of the maritime boundary of India certainly will be counterproductive and will also impact the other nations in regional proximity. Sri Lanka, an island nation, has a coastline of 1340 kilometres which makes it as one of the most significant geographical entity in the Northern Indian Ocean in close proximity to the international sea lines of communications. If Sri Lanka allows its coastline to be used by China for military or non-military purposes, it will erode maritime influence of India and thus will create a strategic imbalance in the region. China has incorporated Sri Lanka as a trade and transit partner to pursue the maritime silk route diplomacy. Sri Lanka has given green signal to China in March, 2016 for construction of $1.5 billion China-funded Colombo Port City project.[2] Though Sri Lanka in no way can replace India in the IOR but Sri Lanka has the potential to provide a toe hold to China between Malacca Straights to the African Coast. Geostrategic location of Sri Lanka at the top of the Northern Indian Ocean needs to be examined since it will impact vital national, cultural and economic interests of India.

Sri Lanka has witnessed internal instability in the past on account of Jana Vimukthi Peramuna (People's Liberation Front) a communist uprising in the early 1970s, which took the lives of almost 15000 youth, and later the three decade old Tamil insurgency spearheaded by Liberation Tigers of Tamil Elam (LTTE). Sri Lanka emerged out of the twin uprising primarily by using excessive force to crush the armed rebellion fighting against the state. Sri Lanka has been undergoing international pressure to deal with war crimes allegedly committed in the final stage of the conflict in 2009.[3] Sri Lanka is yet to come to terms with regard to the war crimes since a UN report has found that as many as 40,000 people may have been killed in the last months of the civil war, though the Sri Lankan government has disputed these figures.[4] Sri Lanka has delayed and deferred the process of bringing the guilty to book and at the same time the government has to put in place the reconstruction and reconciliation process. Actions of Mahinda Rajapaksa government were considered not transparent and this remains a challenge to the Maithripala Sirisena government.

In the regional context, Sri Lanka assumes great significance since China is pursuing an aggressive policy for maritime expansion in the IOR. The strategy of the maritime silk route is here to stay and so are the Chinese naval war ships/submarines. In the backdrop of the above, it is unwise to allow Sri Lanka to drift away from India. Entry of China in the Northern IOR has altered the power balance in the region. It has increased direct competition between India and China and has set a race to establish bases and places across the rim nations and archipelagos in the IOR. At this stage, when China is on the hunt for bases and lily pads in IOR, US would like to leverage its position to give strategic balance in favour of India to prevent dominance of China directly or indirectly in the Indian Ocean. Sri Lanka has now become a focal point of regional and extra regional power competition due to its geo-strategic location. The significance of Sri Lanka at the head of the Northern Indian Ocean cannot be ignored and needs to be taken note in the security calculus for the IOR. A politically and economically stable Sri Lanka is important for both India and the region.

Sri Lanka a Fulcrum in Northern Indian Ocean

Sri Lanka occupies strategically the most vital geographical location in the Northern Indian Ocean Region. It directly impacts the maritime and coastal security of India. If favourably disposed toward India, it adds to the strategic significance and if it is unfavourable, in that case it erodes the maritime periphery of India. If China and Pakistan are able to draw out Sri Lanka from the Indian sphere of influence, it will assist Pakistan and China to open the third front (maritime) against India. This will allow both the adversaries to encircle India in collusion with each other. India must look at Sri Lanka as an enabler for maritime security of India. In fact, to a great extent, maritime security and aspiration of India to be a regional power hinges on the posture adopted by Sri Lanka. There is a growing need to deepen military and economic relationship with Sri Lanka to promote regional cooperation and prevention of militarization of the region.

Growth in China and East Asia is slowing down and it has opened opportunities to India and South Asia. The region's rim states do share a number of common interests including security of sea lanes, environmental protection, regulated extraction of raw material from the sea, and rules-based cooperation and competition in the economic fields. Given the diverse and complex demography, economic interests and security paradox, the rim nations are unlikely to become a conglomerate or union of nations to pursue common objectives. As a consequence, the IOR continues to remain fragile and, at the same time, it is also emerging as the most important economic region of the world. In the backdrop of the above, the only option India has is to seize the opportunity to be the leader of regional countries. India should strive to become a caretaker or net security provider in IOR, but if it fails to develop an understanding with the rim nations and, more importantly, archipelagos in Northern IOR, the space will be encroached upon by China or other extra regional powers. Thus, Sri Lanka becomes an important partner of India to protect the economic and maritime interests of India.

Social and Political Inequality in Sri Lanka

Power sharing and unequal distribution of economic opportunities on the basis of demography is a cause of instability and internal conflict in Sri Lanka. It has 74% Sinhalese population, 12% Tamil, 7% Muslims and the balance is other communities. Religious distribution is 69% Buddhist (Sinhalese), 16% Hindus (mostly Tamils), 8% Christians (Tamil and Sinhalese) and 7%

Islam.[5] Internal conflict in Sri Lanka was not due to religion but was attributed to demography, socio-political environment and economic factors. Conflict in Sri Lanka had a direct impact on India with war refugees flooding the Indian state of Tamil Nadu that caused a major law and order situation including spread of the LTTE network in the southern states of India. There are reports that a large number of Tamil refugees have not gone back and settled for good in Tamil Nadu. Sri Lankan Tamil issue is still a roadblock in bilateral relations between India and the Island nation. The Sri Lankan government should acknowledge that although the war is over, but conflict of interest of the minority Tamil community continues to remain in vogue, therefore, peace is not irreversible as yet.

Reconstruction and Rehabilitation of Tamils an Unfinished Agenda

During the 30 years' war, the minority Tamil community was persecuted and subjected to human rights violation both by the government troops and the LTTE. Political and economic rehabilitation of Tamil community continues to remain a point of dissonance and the Sri Lankan government is yet to integrate the Tamil community as part of the mainstream. War criminals have not been brought to justice and rebuilding of lives is yet to pick up steam. Sri Lankan Tamils should not face discrimination as a community wronged by the government, society, and the majority Sinhala population. If the Sri Lankan government allows Tamils in the North and East to remain politically and economically isolated, there are dangers of these areas plunging back into chaos. This time the blame will rest with the Sri Lankan government because the global community is on the side of the Tamil community. While open war may have ended, the physical insecurity remains. Human rights violations in Sri Lanka including extrajudicial killings and disappearances of young Tamil males[6] has not helped the state to integrate the Tamils in the mainstream. The biggest worry is that the Sri Lankan government has not made any serious endeavours to remove the insecurities from the minds of the ethnic, religious and demographic minorities. Therefore, even those who are moderate and sincerely wish peace and stability to return to the North and East are slowly losing faith in the current dispensation as well. The international community including the United States and the United Kingdom have called upon Sri Lanka to ensure accountability for war crimes and removal of social inequality.[7] Internal instability in Sri Lanka has serious implications for India because it creates political overtones in Southern India and also gives an opportunity to adversaries of India to further strengthen their toe hold in Sri Lanka.

Divergence in India Sri Lanka Relations

India and Sri Lanka are separated by the narrow and shallow Palk Straits. However, Indo-Sri Lanka bilateral relations need not be a mirror image of this geographic reality.[8] The two nations share cultural, religious and social affinity that could help to foster goodwill and friendship among the peoples of the two countries,[9] yet the relations have seen a roller coaster ride and somehow it has not been robust which could eliminate insecurities and vulnerabilities arising out of the internal, regional or from extra regional powers and events. Asymmetry between the countries will pose a threat to bilateral relations and lead to periodic mistrust and conflict.[10] India's relationship with Sri Lanka has to be seen with the prism of cultural affinity, political stability, economic ties, regional and bilateral security, fishing rights and prevention of organized crimes. It is a tall order, but all the issues mentioned above have significance for both nations.

- Sri Lanka–India relations have been shrouded in distrust and scepticism. First Prime Minister of Sri Lanka DS Senanayake had termed India as 'feared and not trustworthy.' According to Ivor Jennings, India was looked upon as; 'a mountain which might at any time, send down destructive avalanche.' To make matters worse, Sri Lanka allowed refuelling of planes and ships carrying war like material and troops during the run up to the 1971 Indo-Pak war. It was construed by India as an act of defiance. In spite of such acts of unfriendly behaviour, India still consented to hand over sovereign rights over Kachativu Island for which the Indian government had to face the wrath of Tamil population and political parties of the southern states.
- Disastrous intervention by Indian government was indeed a miscalculation and misreading of the capabilities of LTTE. It created animosity with Tamils and Sri Lankan government alike. The problem in the relationship is that Sri Lanka does not want to remain in the shadow of India, especially with regard to strategic autonomy and vital national interests. 'Self-restraint and reassurance'[11] to each other is must in building strong bilateral relations.
- Relationship with India also hinges on acceptance of Tamils as equal citizens alongside ethnic Sinhalese in Sri Lanka.[12] India desires that Sri Lanka should allow smooth execution of Indian developmental projects[13] in Sri Lanka, which are focused on rehabilitation of the

displaced Tamils. Construction of dwelling units for those who lost their houses during the war, reconstruction of the rail link Omanthai-Pallai and Kankesanthurai and rebuilding of Kankesanthurai harbour[14] remains a priority for India and it seeks the support of the Sri Lankan government to complete these projects at the earliest.

- Developing cooperation between China and Pakistan is viewed by India as defiance and betrayal of mutual friendship. Strategic divergence is the biggest thorn in bilateral relations and this manifests itself from the perception in Sri Lanka that India did not do enough to rein in the LTTE. Whereas China and Pakistan did seize this opportunity to make inroads in to Sri Lanka. India did not take timely action to build Humbantota Port which ultimately went to China. The China watchers do admit that it was a cardinal mistake for India to give a toe hold to China and that too so close to India. Grant of $100 million for construction of army camps in North and East[15] is seen as an unfriendly act because of close proximity to India and intended militarization of Tamil dominated areas of the North and East. Incidentally, China has emerged as the largest aid giver to Sri Lanka in 2012 with a commitment of $1.05 billion, while India is providing over $700 million.[16] This is also one of the factors of Sri Lanka tilting towards China. India is upset about the fact that Colombo allowed Chinese submarines and war ships to dock in Sri Lankan ports. It is in complete disregard to India's sensitivities on matters relating to its maritime strategic interests.
- The fishing rights issue is a sore point between two nations. India feels that it is very difficult to identify the maritime boundary especially in Gulf of Munnar/Palk Straits. More than Sri Lanka, it is the Indian fisher folk who are vulnerable because in search of a good catch Indian fishermen do venture close to Sri Lankan waters. Dichotomy has emerged because India interpreted the agreement of handing over of Kachativu Island to Sri Lanka which stated that the vessels of India and Sri Lanka will enjoy in each other's waters such rights as they have traditionally enjoyed therein. There was an apparent ambiguity in this statement, because the two countries interpreted the phrase 'traditional rights' differently. Tamil Nadu claims that traditional rights include fishing while Sri Lanka claims it doesn't.[17] The Government of India has sought a permanent solution to this perceived transgression by Indian fishermen in Sri Lankan waters and does reinforce the view that historical rights of fishermen must be respected.

Convergence of Interests

India and Sri Lanka are linked together by culture, demography, religion and geographical proximity. It will be unwise to allow any other nation or organization to cause fissures between the two neighbours. There are common interests, values and vulnerabilities which the two nations share with each other. Some of the issues of convergence which need to be nurtured and strengthened are as under:

- Internal instability in Sri Lanka has the potential to destabilize both nations and has become a priority area to work together. The pragmatic solution to this challenge is to work in coordination with each other so as to engage with the vulnerable minority population.
- Proliferation of small arms and drugs is indeed a threat to India and Sri Lanka. LTTE was known to have one of the largest commercial maritime infrastructures in South Asia which was primarily used for drugs and gun running. LTTE may no more be potent enough to create instability, but elements sympathetic to LTTE or non-state actors may still be continuing with the organized crime. The demand for weapons and war like stores from the non-state and state sponsored non-state actors in and around the Indian periphery is increasing by the day. Al-Qaeda cargo freighters unloaded supplies on Kenyan coast for the suicide bombers who weeks later destroyed the US embassies in Kenya and Tanzania.[18] Cargo freighters sympathetic to LTTE or JVP can repeat what Al-Qaeda did on the Kenyan coast. Thus, Sri Lanka plays an important role in the region to prevent use of Sri Lankan waters and coast by organized crime syndicates.
- Consensus to deal with rising incidents of organized crime on the high seas. Therefore, there is a case for a joint task force to deal with organized crime on high seas and prevention of rising incidences of piracy in areas of common interests.
- Maritime pollution and regulated fishing in the region impacts the maritime ecology. Therefore, both nations have convergence on this vital issue of protection of environment.
- Economic Cooperation and infrastructure development.

Pitfalls of Chinese Investment in Sri Lanka

Sri Lanka has realized that to do trade and business with China, it will cost them control of land, wealth, fortune and even their future. True manifestation came when the current government declared in their manifesto that, 'The land that the White Man took over by means of military strength is now being obtained by foreigners by paying ransom to a handful of persons. This robbery is taking place before everybody in broad daylight... If this trend continues for another six years our country would become a colony and we would become slaves.'[19] India must take advantage of this situation and slowly replace China in Sri Lanka.

Sri Lanka's *Sunday Times* newspaper claimed in 2010 that there were 30,000 Chinese working in the country. It certainly is bothersome and more so because the overall profiling of these men has not been undertaken by the Sri Lankan authorities. Some of these men have come on tourist visas and not on work permit and continue to stay back as technical support or workforce. Many projects including Hambantota are financially unaffordable to Sri Lanka since repayment is very heavy and it appears that the infrastructure created by China is not likely to be self-sustaining. There are reports that China has arbitrarily increased the interest rates to close to 6% which is abnormally high. Sri Lankan authorities have realized that the future investment from China has to be carefully planned and wetted. A case in point is the development of Colombo Port City at the cost of $1.34 billion. The deal is shrouded in controversy since the Chinese firm has demanded 100 hectares of land in Colombo's high security area in return for their investments. It has forced the new government to rethink the entire plan of development of the Port City. Acceptance of the proposal of China would mean willy nilly trading territorial rights of their own land. It appears a complete sell out and unlikely to go down well with the people of Sri Lanka.

Long Term Policy Options to Build Partnership with Sri Lanka

What India expects out of the relationship with Sri Lanka is a big question? Should India make Sri Lanka an ally, partner or a relationship strategic in nature. What Chanakya said in Arthashastra was that, first make a non-ally nation neutral so that it is pulled out of the sphere of influence of an adversary. Second, develop relations as a partner in areas of common interest. Here the common interests between India and Sri Lanka are economic growth and common threat to internal security. The next question will come up, how Sri Lanka will gain by developing relations with India that it has not gained from the relationship with China or any other country. It has historically been proven that India can be a net security provider to an internal or maritime crisis to Sri Lanka. Third aspect is what gains India will have by investing in relations with Sri Lanka? The answer to this vital question is, that India would like Sri Lanka to respect their security concerns by not allowing China or any other inimical force to gain a foothold so close to Indian territory, thus Sri Lanka should not allow their land to be used by inimical forces/adversaries for military or non-military purposes, which compromises Indian security and economic interests in the region. India cannot wait and allow the building of relationship at a leisurely pace. Case in point is Hambantota, no matter what India does in future to build ports and communication networks, but it will be difficult to uproot China from Hambantota. Effective leadership means never to relinquish your command[20] of influence and territory. Thus, a nation must do whatever possible to preserve its strategic domain, because if it abdicates its position, it may not be possible to regain it.

Way Ahead

Frank dialogues, confidence building measures and building consensus over the vital strategic interests is imperative to make a beginning to take bilateral relations to the next level. India as a larger economic and national power could become a bridge for mutual development and growth. India and Sri Lanka can make the beginning by being partners in following areas of mutual interests:

- In the last century 70% disasters had taken place in the region due to density of population, fragile ecology and poor infrastructure. India has the wherewithal to provide assistance to deal with natural disasters.[21] India and Sri Lanka are ideal partners to undertake disaster relief operation on the high seas and in the archipelagos of IOR. The tsunami had caused widespread destruction and it certainly needed cooperative and coordinated effort to mitigate the impact of disaster. India is better equipped to deal with large scale disasters and Sri Lanka can count on India during a crisis. The citizens of the regional countries were dependent on India for evacuation of their Diaspora from war torn Syria and Yemen. It signifies the role of India as a net security provider during natural and manmade crisis.
- Historically, India and Sri Lanka are natural trading partners of each other. There is huge potential to implement free trade agreement to accommodate growth of business, investment and development of infrastructure. Sri Lanka has the potential for development of the services sector, communication, tourism (including religious tourism)

and market for Indian industrial produce. Similarly, Indian markets are large enough to absorb the Sri Lankan industrial produce.

- India has become a global destination for education sector and development of soft skills. These facilities should be ideally shared with Sri Lanka and other neighbouring nations to build a regional bonhomie. It will empower the youth and help in engaging them in the nation building process. India should look at becoming a regional education, sports, cultural and scientific study centre for collective development of youth of the regional countries. Over a period of time, the strength of Sri Lankan students studying in south Indian Universities has declined, attributed to the ethnic conflict in Sri Lanka and expected animosity against Sinhala students. Whereas it is through education that a lasting relationship with future leaders can be made. India could consider opening of a subsidiary of Nalanda University in Sri Lanka to foster closer ties with the tomorrow's leaders. India could offer scholarship to bright and meritorious students for education at premium institutes of India such as IITs, IIM and medical institutes.
- Deep sea mining, oil and gas exploration is an area with a huge potential. India has the technical knowhow and financial capability to develop this sector. This will assist both nations in cost reduction and availability of energy resource to give impetus to economic growth. India has some of the biggest oil refineries in Asia which are being utilized for converting crude into finished product. At the cost of Rs20,000 crores, Indian Oil is in the process of establishing an oil refinery in Sri Lanka.[22]
- Sea Food processing and marketing is an area which can assist India and Sri Lanka economically. India has the market for absorbing the sea food production and can assist in setting up food processing industries in Sri Lanka for export.
- People are at the heart of the relationship with a country. Visa on arrival and sea and air link is vital to improve people to people contact. Exchange programmes in the fields of culture, sports, education, media and arts will further strengthen the bond between the two nations. Ramayana trail in Lanka and the Buddhist circuit in India should be established[23] to increase the flow of tourists.
- Military-to-military cooperation for training, joint patrolling of disputed maritime boundary and exchange of citizen apprehended

for transgression in territorial water is required to prevent bilateral standoffs.

- It is true that Sri Lanka has autonomy to choose friends and allies. Therefore, it will be in correct to expect that Sri Lanka-China relationship should be through Delhi. But there is also a need to accommodate Indian sensitivities as well.

Political activities of a nation are its internal business. A nation should ideally refrain from building strategic relations on the basis of political ideology of a prospective ally. President Sirisena is perceived to be pro India, but politics is fickle, whereas national interests are permanent in nature. Long term vision suggests that diplomatic and business partnership nurtured by the choice of political ideology/regime is unlikely to be resilient. India should focus on developing relations with Sri Lanka as a nation and not with a political party in power. It will be a fatal mistake to allow the long term relations to be prisoner of a political ideology. Can India afford turbulent relations with Sri Lanka if Rajapaksa has to return as Prime Minister? The answer is No. Thus, relations with a nation should ideally be unaffected by the political dispensation of the time.

Conclusion

Sri Lanka is a natural ally and can assist in consolidation of position of India in the IOR. Considering the geographical proximity, culture, historical economic interdependence, people to people contact and maritime security, the only way ahead is to form resilient partnership. Over a period of time, there is divergence of views and interests, which has allowed both the nations to drift apart. The convergence of interests needs to be strengthened so that they act as a bridge to reset the pace of building partnership and also to iron out the irritants with regard to the developing relations of Sri Lanka with India's adversaries. To make the relationship robust, it is mandatory to consider Sri Lanka as co-equal in bilateral relations. There is a need to lay down a road map for building a resilient relationship without encumbrances to serve the respective mutual interests. Economic ties are a key pillar to relationships[24] and should ideally become a cornerstone of developing a strong and resilient partnership. The relationship should be strong enough to withstand challenges to address irritants in a pragmatic manner, not through emotions, but through statesmanship, thereby further strengthening the traditionally close relationship.[25] Cooperation between India and Sri Lanka in the IOR is essential to safeguard peace, stability and containing crisis in the region. The coup in the Maldives and natural disasters in the region have proved that if there is any country which can respond to the crisis in time, it is India and no other nation. Therefore, logically India is irreplaceable as a reliable and long term partner of Sri Lanka.

NOTES

1. Samaranayake, N. (2014), "The Indian Ocean: A Great-Power Danger Zone?", *The National Interests*, May 30.
2. See http://atimes.com/2016/03/sri-lanka-will-not-allow-military-base-for-china-port-city-project-given-green-light/ for details
3. Burke, J. (2014), "UN takes step towards Sri Lanka war crimes inquiry", The *Guardian*, 27 March.
4. Ibid.
5. SRW De A Samarasinghe, (2003), "Political Economy of Internal Conflict In Sri Lanka", Netherland Institute of International Relations 'Clingendael' Conflict research Unit, July3, p. 14.
6. S. Thampapilla, (2010), "Sri Lanka's bitter peace one year on", The Sunday Morning *Herald*, May 20,Australia.
7. World Report 2015,(2015), "Sri Lanka, Human Rights Watch", [Online: web] Accessed 25 24 June 2015,http://www.hrw.org/world-report/2015/country-chapters/sri-lanka.
8. "Re-setting India-Sri Lanka Relations" (2014), Joint Study Group Report under a joint initiative of the Manipal Global Education, *Asian Tribune*, March, 04, New Delhi.
9. Ibid.
10. Dr. M. Samatha (2015), "India, Sri Lanka and Maldives Trilateral Maritime Security Cooperation: Political and Economic, Constraints in Implementation", Indian Council of World Affairs, 8 July.
11. D. Brewster (2014), "India's Ocean: The Story of India's Bid for Regional Leadership", Rutledge Publication, New York.
12. K. Mukherjee (2015), "Rajapaksa defeat: 5 things likely to change in India-Sri Lanka relations", *Hindustan Times*, 9 January, New Delhi.
13. Ibid.
14. Ibid.
15. R. Hariharan (2013), "China's Strategic Presence in Sri Lanka", *Scholar Warrior*, Autumn:37.
16. Ibid., p. 38.
17. V. Kailash (2015), "Why did India cede the Katchatheevu Island to Sri Lanka in 1974?", [Online: web] Accessed 09 July 2015, http://www.quora.com.
18. V. Sakhuja, (2006), "The Dynamics of LTTE's Commercial Maritime Infrastructure", Observers Research Foundation, Occasional Paper, April, New Delhi.
19. H. Cox (2015), "New Sri Lankan government hobbled by old Chinese debts?" A Blog on beyond brics.
20. R. Greene (2006), "The 36 Strategies of War", Viva Books, New Delhi.
21. G.S. Khurana (2005), "Indian Ocean In India's Security Calculus", in "Emerging India: Security and Foreign Policy Perspectives", edited by N. S. Sisodia and Chitrapu Uday Bhaskar, IDSA, New Delhi, p. 209.

22. Bussiness Standard (2012), "Indian Oil to set up refinery in Sri Lanka for Rs 20,000 cr", July 30, New Delhi.
23. "Economic Ties a Key Pillar in India-Sri Lanka Relationship", Says PM Narendra Modi in Colombo: Highlights, NDTV, March 13, 2015
24. Ibid.
25. "Re-setting India-Sri Lanka Relations" (2014), Joint Study Group Report under a joint initiative of the Manipal Global Education, Asian Tribune, March 04, New Delhi.

13

Armed Conflict in Sri Lanka and International Humanitarian Law: A Critical Study

Mayur Dumaniya and Saurabh Sharma

Introduction

Conflicts in the 21st century are very different from conflicts during the cold war and before that era.[1] Today, there is an absence of any major international war in the world between and among nation-states (one country fighting another or several fighting each other). If we look at the conflicts in the 21st century, the international conflicts have been replaced by the non-international conflicts. Non-international conflicts are armed conflicts occurring within the territory of a single state in which two or more armed groups either fight amongst themselves or against the state armed forces. According to common Article 3 of the Geneva Convention, non-international or internal armed conflicts are 'armed conflicts that are non-international in nature occurring in one of the high contracting parties.'[2]

According to the Amnesty International, the majority of today's armed conflicts are internal in nature. These conflicts are often caused by issues of identity, ethnicity, religion and competition for resources, particularly oil and mineral wealth. If we review the Afghanistan conflict, it has resulted in the death and injury to thousands of innocent civilians. War crimes have been committed by all parties to the conflict, including international as well as Afghan security forces and the Taliban. Similarly, in the Iraq conflict, security forces had committed crimes rather than preventing sectarian violence.[3] At least a dozen or more countries in Africa have been affected by armed conflict in the 21st century, despite numerous peace and international mediation processes. In all of these conflicts, civilians have suffered and human rights have been violated. The most affected have been women, children and elderly people.[4] No matter, whether the conflict is international or domestic in nature, civilians always suffer and become the victims of the armed conflicts.

In Sri Lanka's armed conflict, thousands of civilians lost their lives, suffered greatly, had a disruptive life and were forced to flee their homes. Though, civilians were protected under international humanitarian and human rights law, still they became the main victims during armed conflicts.[5]

Background of the Conflict

Before going into the details of the armed conflict in Sri Lanka and violation of international humanitarian laws, it is important to understand the causes of this conflict. What were the responsible factors behind this conflict? Why did this conflict become an armed conflict? The answer to these questions will help to understand the conflict in depth. Conflict in Sri Lanka was an ethnic conflict[6] between two ethnic groups the majority Sinhalese and minority Tamils. Whenever people of different race, religion, language and different groups disagree on several issues, it leads to a conflict. These issues may be social, political and economic.

There were numerous factors[7] responsible for this conflict in Sri Lanka and these factors can be split into two parts. The first part deals with pre-independence era of Sri Lanka; as during that time the majority Sinhalese believed that the minority Tamil's enjoyed higher status in society under British rule. They played a greater role in every sector of life like an influential role in bureaucracy, economy and also in society and due to this the Sinhalese felt discriminated against. The second part deals with the post-independence era during which time the Sinhalese government came into power, and this resulted in the formation of discriminative policies towards the Tamil's leading to the conflict. These policies included the citizenship rights policy of 1948, Sinhala only policy of 1956, other factors like racial discrimination, university education, issue of land, issue of employment, etc. The burning of Jaffna public library,[8] which was a symbol of Tamil culture and important source of original texts relating to the origins of the Tamils, was a turning point in the Sri Lankan conflict. This led to a formation of a separatist Tamil group, the Liberation Tigers of Tamil Elam (LTTE), also known as Tamil Tigers. The main objective of the LTTE was to create a separate Tamil state. LTTE waged a violent, brutal and separatist campaign to create an independent state in Sri Lanka's north and east for the Tamil people.

During the 1980s, the international community including India played a crucial role and made an attempt in resolving the conflict and in accordance with that effort certain measures to establish peace were undertaken. India signed the Indo-Sri Lankan Peace Accord in 1987 and sent the Indian Peace-keeping Force (IPKF) on the island. The mission failed to establish peace and by 1990 all of the IPKF had left Sri Lanka.[9] The conflict escalated further and became violent. The following period has been divided into Eelam War II (June 1990–January 1995) and Eelam War III (April 1995-February 2002).[10] Both these wars ended with a ceasefire agreement between the government and the rebels. However, in both cases the agreements were violated which led to further turmoil in the country. In 2000, at the request of the Sri Lankan government, headed by President Chandrika Kumartanga, and Tamil Tigers, Norway was initiated as an international mediator and successfully established a ceasefire between LTTE and government of Sri Lanka in 2002. This agreement was more successful compared to previous attempts, but in 2005 violence re-escalated and in 2006 both parties withdrew from this ceasefire agreement.[11] Various attempts were made to establish peace but they could not stop the conflict. Gradually, fighting reached to its extreme resulting in numerous civilian causalities. Finally, in 2009, the Sri Lankan government defeated the LTTE after killing its leader Velupillai Prabhakaran, and ended the war.

The real problem started after the elimination of LTTE. The way the Sri Lankan military had crushed the LTTE resulted in the violation of human rights and international humanitarian laws. There were huge expressions of concern over human rights issues from the international community. David Miliband, foreign minister of Britain, and Bernard Kouchner, foreign minister of France, visited Sri Lanka in April 2009, with the intention of drawing the government's attention 'to the human suffering, and to call for the fighting to stop.'[12] Apart from this visit, various peace efforts by the international community took place.

Introduction to the International Humanitarian Law (IHL)

The idea of rules to regulate armed conflict is almost as old as conflict itself, and the beginning of modern international humanitarian law to codify and develop customary international law dates back to the middle of the nineteenth century. The process of drafting and adopting rules has mainly taken place in Hague and in Geneva.[13] The Hague law is concerned with the means and methods of warfare, whereas the Geneva Convention is concerned with the protection of individuals.

In the mid-1850s, Henri Dunant,[14] founder of the International Red Cross, helped to establish the first universally applicable organization of international humanitarian law: the Geneva Convention of 1864. From these roots, international humanitarian law evolved. The Hague Convention of 1899 and 1904 limited the means by which belligerent states could conduct warfare. The Charter of the United Nations specifies that the threat or use of force against other states is unlawful, except in the case of self-defence. Following World War II, the Geneva Convention of 1949, as well as its two additional protocols of 1977, further limited the means of warfare and provided protection to non-combatant civilians and prisoners of war. In the aftermath of the atrocities of the holocaust, the Genocide Convention of 1948[15] forbids acts that were carried out with the intention of destroying a particular group. In addition to these conventions, IHL has been developed and refined through several statutes and precedents laid down by international tribunals to try war criminals, as well as advisory opinions of the International Court of Justice.

Sri Lanka and International Humanitarian Law

After understanding the international humanitarian law, it is necessary to probe how it has been applied in Sri Lanka's armed conflict. According to the common Article 3[16] of the Geneva Convention, every nation who is party to the IHL is obliged to the IHL. It is the prime responsibility of the governments to take care of the international human rights and international law. According to Article 2 of the International Convention on Civil and Political Rights (ICCPR), governments are principally responsible for the implementation of international human rights and humanitarian law during periods of armed conflict.[17] According to the Common Article 3 of the Geneva Convention, during non-international armed conflicts, governments and armed opposition groups may each bear responsibility for their obedience to these norms.

In the case of Sri Lanka, 'it is party to the Geneva Convention of 1949 and, therefore, it is legally bound to implement the human rights safeguards.'[18]

It is also signatory to other major international human rights treaties.[19] In addition to its treaty obligations, Sri Lanka is also obliged to respect the applicable rules of customary international law, particularly those concerning the 'elementary consideration of humanity' in times of armed conflict as well as in times of peace. When the state involved in the conflict is not a party to Protocol 2, belligerents must rely on the rules of customary international law for their obligations during military operations, besides the common Article 3. Not only the legitimate governments but also opposing parties involved in the armed conflict are equally responsible for the respect of the minimum humanitarian principle. According to the common Article 3 'each party to the conflict shall be bound to apply.'[20]

According to the various Security Council resolutions, both states and non-state armed groups have to abide by international humanitarian law and international human rights obligations. In its resolution 1894 (2009),[21] which was on *protection of civilians in armed conflict*, the Security Council, said that 'it is the main responsibility of the state to respect and safeguard the human rights of their citizens as well as all individuals within its territory.' It also said, 'All parties to armed conflict bear the primary responsibility to take all possible steps to ensure the protection of civilians.' It also demanded that all parties to the armed conflict comply strictly with the obligations applicable to them under international humanitarian and human rights law. For example, special reporter[22] Chaloka Beyani on extrajudicial summary or arbitrary executions said in the context of its mission to Sri Lanka, 'A non-State actor, the LTTE, does not have legal obligations under it [the International Covenant on Civil and Political Rights], but it remains subject to the demand of the international community, to respect the international humanitarian law and human rights law.' According to the Universal Declaration of Human Rights (UDHR), every organ of society should respect and promote human rights. Finally, not only states and non-state actors, but even individuals who are linked neither to the state nor to an armed group are subject to international criminal law, precisely regarding war crimes, if a connection exists between their conduct and the armed conflict.

Violation of International Humanitarian Law and Human Rights in Sri Lanka: Allegations by the International Community

Grave violations of international humanitarian law, especially in internal armed conflicts, is a growing phenomenon,. Internal armed conflicts cause a huge loss, and the magnitude of losses caused by internal armed conflicts is immeasurable. According to the Bassiouni, since Second World War alone, it is estimated that more than 250 conflicts of a purely internal character have occurred and it has resulted in an estimated 85 million military casualties over the same period of time.[23] During the prolonged conflict in Sri Lanka more than 100,000 people have lost their lives. The Sri Lankan armed conflict brought about enormous human suffering, economic loss, and socio-political and moral degradation. According to the Rajasinghe, 'The losses caused by this civil war were really immeasurable. The human losses caused by this war are very difficult to quantify, it contains the death and injury of armed personal, combatants, civilians, the suffering of widows, orphans, the displacement of people, and homelessness.'[24]

During the final phase of the Sri Lankan conflict (January 2009 to 19 May 2009) credible allegations of IHL and human rights violations were found. There were allegations that war crimes were committed by both the Sri Lankan army as well as the rebellious LTTE during the final months of the Sri Lankan conflict in 2009. Shahnewaz noted that, alleged war crimes involved 'attacks on civilians and civilian buildings by both sides; execution of combatants and prisoners by both sides; enforced disappearances by the Sri Lankan military and paramilitary groups backed by them; acute shortages of food, medicine, and clean water for civilians trapped in the war zone; and recruitment of young boys and girls as a child soldiers by the Tamil Tigers.'[25]

According to an estimate by the United Nations Human Rights Council (UNHRC), the death toll intensified in the final days of the conflict in May 2009 which resulted in the death of thousands of civilians. As of 19 June 2009, the number of internally displaced Tamils was 5,50,000. The panel of experts[26] appointed by United Nations Secretary-General (UNSG) Ban Ki-moon, found credible allegations regarding war crimes and crimes against humanity committed by the Sri Lankan military and the rebellious LTTE. The panel also found that as many as 40,000 civilians may have been killed in the final months of the civil war, most as a result of indiscriminate shooting by the Sri Lankan military. The panel concluded that 'the conduct of the war represented a grave assault on the entire regime of international law designed to protect individual dignity during both war and peace.'

Protecting civilians during armed conflict is an important humanitarian issue in every conflict. But during the long civil war in Sri Lanka, there have been number of instances in which IHL has been violated. Both the government and LTTE were responsible for these violations. According to

Rajasinghe,[27] millions of innocent civilians became the victims of this conflict. The day to day activities and the lives of the civilians, mainly of those living in the war-affected areas, were crippled by the war. The fundamental requirements of life were denied to Tamils, they were forcibly evacuated from their native places and their lives were restricted to refugee camps. Due to this ruthless war, most of the victims completely lost their living. European Centre for Constitution and Human Rights noted that, during Sri Lanka's conflict, both the Sri Lankan government forces and the LTTE forces have violated the international humanitarian law, and human rights law.

Other major human rights groups like, Amnesty International, International Crisis Group (ICG) and Human Rights Watch (HRW), as well as the United States Department of State and the European Union (EU), expressed great concern about the violations of human rights and IHL during the final phase of the war in Sri Lanka by both the government of Sri Lanka and the separatist LTTE. Reports from these organizations claimed that during 2009, thousands of Tamil civilians were killed, countless wounded and many more deprived of basic food and medical care which resulted in unnecessary deaths. These reports concluded that war crimes were committed by both the Sri Lankan armed forces and the Tamil Tigers. During the final phase of the conflict, most of the atrocities were committed by the government forces. According to the report by Permanent People's Tribunal, government's decision in September 2008 to order humanitarian agencies out of the LTTE controlled area greatly worsened their difficulty. Ongoing fighting, lack of oversight and the manipulation of aid delivery by the government and LTTE forces contributed to the deepening humanitarian crisis.[28] The report further described the atrocities of the last weeks of the war as:

> *The atrocities carried out by the military relate particularly to civilians, and there is evidence of cluster weaponries being dropped by warplanes. Some witnesses reported that white phosphorous was used in violation of international law. Several witnesses had seen burn marks on wounded civilians. Others believed that indications of napalm were apparent, and evidence of other incendiary devices has been confirmed by doctors who had cared for hundreds of Tamil civilians wounded in this manner* (PPT 2010).

According to the Gordon Weiss,[29] war crimes were committed during the final stages of the civil war and up to 40,000 civilians may have been killed in the final stages of the civil war. Weiss in his book, *The Cage*, reports about the final stages of the civil war in detail, the way in which Sri Lankan military achieved victory and the price paid for peace by all of Sri Lanka's ethnic communities. Further, Weiss highlights the pathetic condition of the civilians and how they were sandwiched between the armed forces and LTTE.

Frances Harrison[30] claimed that human catastrophe and crimes against humanity were committed by both sides, the Sri Lankan army as well as LTTE. According to Harrison, A UN panel of experts found credible allegations of war crimes and crime against humanity by the Sri Lankan government in its widespread shelling, extrajudicial killings and disappearance, deprivation of food, medicine and mass detention. The panel also found crimes by the LTTE ranging from widespread or systematic attacks on civilian population, holding civilians against their will and killing whoever tried to leave. LTTE also deployed suicide bombers against civilians during the war. Ashoka Bandarage[31] noted that until the Sri Lankan government militarily defeated LTTE in May 2009, Sri Lanka was the home to what was considered one of the world's most intractable war and the longest running conflict in Asia.

The UN High Commissioner of Human Rights, Navi Pillay, described the level of civilian deaths as 'truly shocking,' and warned it could reach 'catastrophic' level.[32] Noam Chomsky[33] said, "What happened in Sri Lanka was a major Rwanda-like atrocity, in a different scale, where the West didn't care. There was plenty of early warning. This conflict has been going on for years and decades. Plenty of things could have been done to prevent it. But there was not enough interest.' According to the investigations conducted by *The Times* and *The Sunday Times* in late May 2009, more than 20,000 Tamil civilians were killed in the final phase of the Sri Lankan civil war, most of them as a result of government shelling.[34] The UN estimated that up to 7,000 people had died by the end of April. In late May 2009, the French newspaper, *Le Monde*, accused the UN of deliberately hiding facts about civilian deaths during the last months of the war in order to protect possible involvement in crimes committed in Vanni. There were no perfect figures of civilian deaths during the last phase of the conflict but according to the report of the UNSGs panel of experts, thousands of civilians were killed in the final stage of the conflict, adding that most civilian casualties in the final phases of the war were caused by government shelling. Roughly, as many as 100,000 people were killed during 26 years of war.[35]

The documentaries, *No Fire Zones: The Killing Fields of Sri Lanka* directed by Macrae Callum,[36] and *Sri Lanka's Killing Fields* directed by Jon Snow,[37] found some of the most shocking allegations. Both the documentaries claimed that the government of Sri Lanka has gathered thousands of civilian in what it called No Fire Zones (NFZs) during the final months of the conflict for their safety. But the reverse has happened. Instead of providing security to them government forces were found shelling in these NFZs. The documentaries provide some of the most horrific video footage of the extra-judicial executions of prisoners, targeted shelling of civilian camps, hospitals, and NFZs. The soldiers of the government forces committed rape and sexual violence as well as killed innocent people and children. The Documentaries also provide evidences of some of the horrific atrocities carried out by the Tamil Tigers, who used civilians as human shields. These crimes are considered as war crimes and crimes against humanity, and these are the worst form of crimes in recent history. The documentaries also pointed out that the international community including the UN, ICRC, other humanitarian agencies, and international journalists were not allowed to enter in NFZs during the final months. Finally, according to the Jon Snow most of the atrocities were committed by the government forces.

According to the allegation by the international community, widespread human rights abuses took place during the 26-year civil war in Sri Lanka. Especially, the final months of the conflict saw a brutal escalation of violence as displaced civilians were trapped between the warring parties. There were credible allegations that both sides committed crimes under international law. The LTTE used civilians as human shields and conscripted child soldiers while the Sri Lankan army shelled densely populated areas as well as hospitals. The documentaries prepared by Jon Snow and Macrae Callum highlight the events of the final days of war. All the above mentioned reports found credible allegations of war crimes and crimes against humanity from both sides and especially by the Sri Lankan army.

After going through the reports, various newspaper articles and statements by global personalities, it is clear that credible human rights violation and war crimes were committed during the conflict by both parties to the conflict. The study further probes how the government of Sri Lanka has managed and responded to the allegations and criticism regarding war crimes and human rights violations made by the international community.

Government of Sri Lanka's Response to the International Community

The Government of Sri Lanka has condemned and rejected all the allegations made by the international community against it regarding human rights violations and war crimes. It replied that there were no such violations which the international community and media had highlighted. In response to the demand for an independent international investigation during the final months of the conflict, the Government of Sri Lanka (GoSL) stated that an independent investigation was an unnecessary infringement on its sovereignty.[38] Despite overwhelming evidences, President Mahinda Rajapaksc said no civilian had been killed deliberately. Furthermore, GoSL criticized all reports claiming that human rights and international humanitarian law had been violated by the GoSL and, therefore, it required no international probe and investigations. In response to the UNSGs panel of expert's report which claimed war crimes and crimes against humanity were committed by the Sri Lankan military and LTTE, the GoSL said that UN panel of experts was unwarranted and unnecessary interference in sovereign state and denied that its forces committed war crimes while strongly opposing any international investigation. Further, the GoSL condemned the UN report as 'fundamentally flawed in many respects' and based on deliberately biased material which has been presented without any verification.[39]

President Mahinda Rajapakse, in an interview with the *Times of India*,[40] published on 28 June 2010, said the international community was making unnecessary interference in Sri Lanka without understanding the situation of Sri Lanka. Earlier, they said that the LTTE was world's most dangerous terrorist organization and Prabhakaran was the world's most ruthless terrorist. But after LTTEs defeat, they started talking differently. He further added that international community could advise them but cannot direct the Sri Lankan government what to do and what not to do.

Sri Lankan Government's Response to the US

The international community not only criticized the GoSL and made allegations, it also made several recommendations. But the government of Sri Lanka has not followed the basic recommendations which were made by the international community against it, which shows that GoSL is lacking in its commitment on accountability, justice and equality. For instance, 'the government of Sri Lanka has rejected a call from the US to end immunity for human rights violations and fulfil its legal obligations regarding accountability. It has also rejected Thailand's recommendation to strengthen the relevant legislative and administrative measures to ensure transparency and non-immunity in the judicial process.'[41]

In response to the US argument, GoSL said that[42] the US is playing a dual game. United States, since 1997 had declared LTTE as a Foreign Terrorist Organization (FTO), it had also pressurized the European Union and West to declare LTTE as a Global Terrorist Organization. Indeed, the US ambassador to Sri Lanka, Robert O. Blake, delivered a statement on 21 May 2009[43] that to achieve peace and to ensure a long-lasting end to terrorism, bold actions were needed. It would help to share power and to assure all of Sri Lanka's communities a future of hope, respect and dignity. Only through such actions could Sri Lanka truly unite and emerge as a peaceful country.

But later on, the US has changed its stand and made increasingly critical noises against Sri Lankan army's final action. The US has demanded the protection of civilians and called for international investigation and access to them. After the conflict was over, the US criticized the GoSL and held it responsible for violations of human rights and international humanitarian law, and for war crimes and crimes against humanity. According to John Whitesides,[44] 'Obama has issued his first statement on the Sri Lankan government's final action on 14 May 2009, expressing concern regarding civilian casualties, and calling for Sri Lanka to conclude a peace that is grounded in respect for all of its citizens.' Furthermore, the US has also pressurized the UN to pass two resolutions against the Sri Lankan army's final action, demanding an independent international probe.

According to the United States Senate Committee on Foreign Relations (2009) report,[45] chaired by US Secretary of State, John Kerry, 'The Sri Lankan Government said America's such attitude and military restriction is responsible for the Sri Lanka's close relationships with China, Burma, Iran, and Libya.' The Minister of Science and Technology and All-Party Representative Committee Chairman, TissaVitarana told committee staff, 'We have the United States to thank for pushing us closer to China.' According to Vitarana President Rajapaksa was forced to reach out to other countries because the West refused to help Sri Lanka to finish the war against the LTTE.[46]

Government of Sri Lanka's Response to the Channel 4

The documentary called *Sri Lanka's Killing Fields*[47] presented by UK's channel 4 found some of the most shocking allegations of war crimes and crimes against humanity committed by the Sri Lankan army during the final stage of the conflict. In response to these allegations, GoSL criticized it and said that the allegations in the documentary regarding the conduct of the Sri Lankan army during the final months of the conflict were in striking contrast to the standards maintained by the Sri Lankan army. Furthermore, GoSL said,[48] 'This is an exercise which is carried out by a small section of international media at the request of certain parties with vested interest and it satisfies the interest of only separatist forces living outside Sri Lanka. The final objective of which is to push Sri Lanka back to war, by way of lacerating the wounds that the country is attempting to restore.' GoSL also said, 'This documentary has the potential to spread hatred amongst the people of different communities in Sri Lanka, it would have a bad effect on future generation, and it also adversely affects the ongoing process of the reconciliation.'

GoSLs Response to the Allegations Regarding Threatening of Media and Journalists

The international community including many international organizations have claimed that during the conflict, media persons were threatened and killed. According to Amnesty International's (2013) report,[49] *Sri Lanka's Assault on Dissent*, the media community said that, during the conflict especially during the last phase of the conflict, the government of Sri Lanka has restricted the media's access to war affected areas. The freedom of expression was restricted, the journalists were threatened, pressurized, and even some media persons have been killed, detained and put into the custody, particularly Tamil journalists. Further, the report found that the GoSL has issued the guidelines for journalists which said, 'All reporting related to the national security and defence, should be first submitted to the defence ministry's media centre for national security before publication, telecast or broadcast.'

International Press Freedom and Freedom of Expression Mission (2008), to Sri Lanka in its report, *Media Under Fire: Press Freedom Locked in Sri Lanka 2008*,[50] noted the media persons were not allowed to visit the war affected areas. They had no access to the field of operations for a year and the authority refused to give the real casualty figures. They even banned some of the media from covering the military parade. The report noted, 'There were no proper safety regulations for the media persons in war zones during conflict.'

Despite sufficient evidence of threatening, kidnapping and killing of journalist, the GoSL has rejected those allegations and said that the safety of the media was the priority for the government forces. Journalists were safe in Sri Lanka. They were not kidnapped or killed. They were allowed to visit the war affected areas. The defence ministry delivered the statement in 2009 which said:

> *Those who are 'pretending to be humanitarian and aid agencies' are prolonging the conflict 'to secure their income'. It says a 'vicious coalition' that has 'been pretending to be humanitarian agencies, aid agencies, free media, civil rights movements, etc.,...has made the continued bloodshed on Sri Lankan soil a lucrative business.*[51]

After going through the allegations by the international community and the response by the GoSL, it is clear that there is lack of accountability for human rights in Sri Lanka. Therefore, there is a need to establish independent international investigation to ensure accountability. Hence, the GoSL should allow independent international investigation and cooperate with them. It is also important to observe how President Mahinda Rajapakse defended and justified GoSL's war against LTTE.

Conclusion

The GoSL has denied all the allegations and the facts represented by the international community, which claimed that thousands of civilians were killed during the war. In addition, the GoSL appointed a Lesson Learnt and Reconciliation Commission (LCRC)[52] to inquire into these allegations. The Report of the LLRC stated that the Sri Lanka's army had not targeted civilians deliberately, instead the key focus of the army was protection of civilian life and property during its military operation. In addition, the LLRC commission blamed the LTTE for its violent tactics and civilian causalities, which established a distinct disregard for human rights and international humanitarian law.

Hence, from the above mentioned responses by the government of Sri Lanka it is clear that, the GoSL justified its armed conflict by denying all the allegations made against it by the international community. It is also clear that the way the government of Sri Lanka has defeated terrorism on its soil has now become a learning exercise for many countries facing the problem of internal conflict. For Sri Lanka, it has become a historic event which is being celebrated in the form of defence seminars. It is difficult to say whether the action GoSL had taken to defeat the LTTE in the name of terrorism was justifiable or not. It is also difficult to predict what the international actors are going to learn from the Sri Lankan experience.

Finally, it is quite challenging to make any judgmental conclusion on the subject studied in this work. Since the subject of this study involves a complex field, the conclusion cannot be simple and close-ended. The nature of the research also poses a serious question to the researchers that whether the States have shifted their attention from the primary objectives of welfare (to deliver food, education, security, peace, etc.) and are becoming more obsessed with the concern of sovereignty, for which they can even go to extent of killing their own citizens. Here, the authors would like to ask one natural question and to put it forward for further debate, that what is more important for states, is it humanity or sovereignty?

NOTES

1. There are mainly two types of armed conflict, International Armed Conflict (IAC) and Non-International Armed Conflict (NIAC). IAC occurs between two or more opposing states while NIAC occurs between two or more armed groups or between armed group and states armed forces within the territory of the state. How is the term 'Armed Conflict' defined in the International Humanitarian Law? ICRC opinion paper 2008.
2. See the ISIL, Year Book of International Humanitarian and Refugee Law, *Common Article 3 of Geneva Convention 1949 in the Era of International Criminal Tribunals*, by M.Gandhi to know more about the relevance and implication of the Article 3.
3. According to Geneive Abdo, traditionally, sectarianism can be understood as an institutional set of arrangements determining familial, local, regional, and even broader kinds of loyalty and affiliation. *The New Sectarianism: The Arab uprisings and the rebirth of the Shia-Sunni divide*, analysis paper, 29th April, 2013.
4. See Amnesty International Report 2007, *The State of the world's Human Rights.*
5. United Nations Human Rights Office of the High Commissioner, (2011), "*International Legal Protection of Human Rights in Armed Conflict*".
6. Ethnic conflict is a conflict in which organized ethnic groups confront each other and/or with the State in which they live. Karl Cordell & Stefan Wolff, "*Ethnic Conflict: Causes, Consequences, and Response*",. *Cambridge: Polity.*
7. "Identity Conflict in Sri Lanka: A case of Tamil Tigers", International Journal of Humanities and Social Science, 2012.
8. The Jaffna public library has emotional significance for the Sri Lanka's Tamil minority. This library consisted documents related to the emergence of the Tamils, their culture, and traditions. Jaffna is considered the cultural capital of the Tamils. The library was attacked and burnt by the Sinhalese mob in 1981. This attack is considered as a one of the most important factors responsible for the Sri Lanka's armed conflict. *BBC news*, 1st November, 2010. http://www.bbc.co.uk/news/world-south-asia-11668352
9. P.A. Ghos (1999), "Ethnic Conflict in Sri Lanka and Role of Indian Peace Keeping Force (IPKF)", APH Publishing, New Delhi.
10. The Sri Lankan armed conflict has been divided in four phase, Elam War I (July 23, 1983-July 29, 1987), Elam War II (June 1990-1995 January), Elam War III (April 1995-February 2002) and Elam War IV (July 2009-May 2009). "*History of Civil War in Sri Lanka*", the article is available online at: http://www.zum.de/whkmla/sp/0809/kyungmook/kyungmook1.html
11. MR Narayan Swamy (2011), "Sri Lanka and Peace Makers: A story of Norway and India", IPCS, New Delhi.
12. David Miliband, and Bernard Kouchner, visited Sri Lanka and delivered a statement that

government forces have killed innocent civilians and also violated the ceasefire agreement. See, "French, British ministers in Sri Lanka for talks" available online at: http://www.unhcr.org/cgi-bin/texis/vtx/refdaily?pass=463ef21123&id=49f7f0528

13. Rikke Ishoy (2008), "Handbook on the practical use of International Humanitarian Law", Danish Red Cross.
14. Jean Henri Dunant also known as Henry Dunant was a Swiss citizen. He had experienced the battle of Solferino when he was on a business trip, the battle was ending and people were dying. With the help of local women he did what he could to care for them. That trip affected him a lot and after returning to Geneva, Dunant wrote 'A Memory of Solferino.' He was a founder of the ICRC.
15. On December 9, 1948, UN General Assembly adopted Convention on the Prevention and Punishment of Crime of Genocide. It consists of 19 Articles.
16. Common Article 3 is a special Article for the Non International Armed Conflict (NIAC) and it applies in the case of NIAC occurring in the territory of one of the high contracting parties.
17. ICCPR was adopted on 19th December, 1966 by the UN General Assembly. After sufficient number of States became party to ICCPR, it came into effect in 1976. For more detail see, http://www.cirp.org/library/ethics/UN-covenant/
18. Rajasinghe Tushara (2007), "*International humanitarian Law In Conflict Situations-A Sri Lankan Case Study*", Handbook of International humanitarian Law In South Asia.
19. Sri Lanka is party to the major international human rights treaties, including the International Covenant on Civil and Political Rights (ICCPR) and the Convention against Torture and Other Cruel, Inhuman or Degrading Treatment or Punishment. Sri Lanka acceded International Covenant on Civil and Political Rights in 1996 (G.A. res. 2200A (XXI), U.N. Doc. A/6316 (1966), which entered into force in March 23, 1976. Sri Lanka acceded to the ICCPR on June 11, 1980. Convention against Torture and other Cruel, Inhuman or Degrading Treatment or Punishment, G.A. Res. 39/46, U.N. Doc. A/39/51, entered into force June 26, 1987. Sri Lanka ratified the Convention against Torture on February 2, 1994. Sri Lanka has also ratified the four Geneva Convention in 1959.
20. Ibid.
21. United Nations have passed many resolutions regarding armed conflict, children's right, women's protection etc...For further information on various security Council Resolutions look into the UNSCs resolutions here: http://www.un.org/en/sc/documents/resolutions/
22. A special rapporteur is an independent expert appointed by the Human Rights Council (HRC) to examine and report back on a country situation or human rights specific theme. UN has appointed Chaloka Beyani as a special rapporteur on Sri Lanka to examine the situations of the Internally Displaced Persons (IDPs). UN Human Rights country page on Sri Lanka: http://www.ohchr.org/EN/Countries/AsiaRegion/Pages/LKIndex.aspx
22. "Accountability for Violations of International Humanitarian Law and Other Serious Violations of Human Rights", Bassiouni, M. Cherif, the article is available online at: http://www.soattentats.org/publications/bassiouni.violations.pdf
23. Tushara Rajasinghe (2007), "*International humanitarian Law In Conflict Situations-A Sri Lankan Case Study*", in V.S. Mani (ed.)*Handbook of International humanitarian Law In South Asia*", Oxford University Press, New Delhi.
24. Shahnewaz Abdullah (2012), "Military Solutions of Political Crisis," URL: http://www.biliabd.org/bwps.php
25. United Nations Secretary-General (UNSG) Ban Ki-moon, appointed a panel of expert to review the Human Rights situation in Sri Lanka. The panel published report titled "Secretary-

General's Internal Review Panel on United Nations Action in Sri Lanka in 2012. The panel found credible allegation of the violation of human rights and international humanitarian law by the both side GoSL as well as LTTE. The panel found that most of the causalities were committed by the government forces.

26. See note 28.
27. Permanent People's Tribunal. *Tribunal on Sri Lanka*, Dublin: Trinity College, 2010.
28. Gorden Weiss is a founding adviser and consultant expert to the *International Crimes Evidence Project*, currently he is investigating war crimes. *The Cage* is his first published book. http://www.gordonweissauthor.com/
29. Francis Harrison is a British Journalist. She has worked in Sri Lanka during conflict. She has written a book titled, "Still Counting the Dead: Survivors of Sri Lanka's Hidden War". The book tells the story of what happened during the Sri Lanka's conflict in the last phase (Five month, January to May). According to her, Sri Lanka's conflict was a worst conflict of the century in which thousands of innocent people were killed.
30. Bandarage, Ashoka (2008), "*The Separatist Conflict in Sri Lanka: Terrorism, Ethnicity, Political Economy*", Routledge.
31. BBC News South Asia, "Sri Lanka 'War Crimes': Main Allegations", available online at:http://www.bbc.co.uk/news/world-south-asia-13158916
32. Noam Chomsky said that what happened in Sri Lanka was a Rwanda-like atrocity, where west didn't care. http://www.tamilnet.com/art.html?catid=13&artid=29846
33. *The Times*, UK, "Sri Lanka's sacrifice of life may sow seeds of a new conflict", available online at: https://groups.google.com/forum/#!topic/worldtamil/ZsfqkJ-4zAw
34. Report of the Secretary General's panel of Experts on Accountability in Sri Lanka. The report is available online at:http://www.un.org/News/dh/infocus/Sri_Lanka/POE_Report_Full.pdf
35. Both documentaries, *No Fire Zones: The Killing Fieldsof Sri Lanka* prepared by Macrae Callumand *Sri Lanka's Killing Fields* directed by Jon Snow, have found some of the most shocking and horrific video footage of civilian killings.
36. See note 41.
37. Sri Lanka Campaign for Peace and Justice, "The Current Situation", available online at: http://www.srilankacampaign.org/currentsituation.htm
38. "Sri Lanka Forces Committed War Crimes Says, UN", available at: http://www.independent.co.uk/news/world/asia/sri-lanka-forces-committed-war-crimes-says-un-2269021.html
39. Sri Lanka's President, Mahinda Rajapakse, gave an interview to the Times of India in 2009. In his interview he rejected all the allegations made by the international community against GoSL and its forces. Indeed, Rajapaksa said that they have defeated the terrorism and now Sri Lanka is free from terrorism. The President has criticized the international community, he said that the international community is unnecessarily interfering in a Sovereign country.
40. Rupeindia's (2013), "Whose Agenda? US Strategic Interests, India, and Sri Lankan War Crimes", URL: http://rupeindia.wordpress.com/2013/03/13/whose-agenda-us-strategic interests india-and-sri-lankan-war-crimes/
41. Ibid.
42. Report of the U.S. Department of State, titled *Report to Congress on Incidents During the Recent Conflict in Sri Lanka,* 2013.
43. Whitesides, John,(2009), "Obama urges action to avert Sri Lanka catastrophe", URL:http://www.reuters.com/article/2009/05/14/us-srilanka-idUSN1343603620090514
44. US Senate Committee Report 2009.
45. Ibid.

46. See note 41.
47. Sri Lanka's Defence Minister, Gotabaya Rajapaksa delivered speech on 5th May 2011, at the military conference 'Defeating Terrorism Sri Lankan Experience', Colombo: Sri Lanka.
48. The Amnesty International alleged that in Sri Lanka's brutal conflict human rights and international humanitarian law violated by both sides. The media persons were threatened, they were not allowed to access the war affected areas and many journalists were killed, especially in the last phase of the conflict from January to May 2009. Still, today, the fair and independent investigation has been not allowed by the GoSL. http://www.amnesty.org/en/sri-lanka
49. "*Media Under Fire: Press Freedom Locked in Sri Lanka in 2008*". The report found that, there was a lack of safety and security for the media person and the safety regulations were not followed by the both sides, especially by the GoSL. http://www.mediasupport.org/publication/media-under-fire-press-freedom-lockdown-in-sri-lanka/
50. Sri Lanka's Defence Minister, Gotabaya Rajapaksa delivered speech on 5th May 2011, at the military conference 'Defeating Terrorism Sri Lankan Experience', Colombo: Sri Lanka.
51. For further information look into the report of the LLRC is available at: http://www.priu.gov.lk/news_update/Current_Affairs/ca201112/FINAL%20LLRC%20REPORT.pdf

14

India-US Defence Cooperation in the Post Cold War Era: From Strategic Distancing to Strategic Partnership

Sanjeev Kumar Shrivastav

> *"As we Americans consider our future role in the world, the rise of a democratic and increasingly powerful India represents a singularly positive opportunity to advance our global interests. There is a tremendous strategic upside to our growing engagement with India. It is a unique opportunity with real promise for the global balance of power."*[1]
>
> —R. Nicholas Burns

Introduction

Defence cooperation encompasses multiple dimensions which include the sale, purchase, joint production and development of military equipments, transfer of military technologies, joint military exercises, cooperation for counter-terrorism and intelligence sharing, cooperation in protecting sea lanes of communication against piracy as well as cooperation for counter-proliferation and anti-drug trafficking activities. India and the United States are in the process of developing close defence ties in the post-Cold War period. After the 9/11 terror attacks on the United States, the pace of defence cooperation gained significantly between both sides because of convergence of interests as well as the emergence of common threats.[2]

A brief of India United States Defence Cooperation during the Cold War years

India and the United States entered into a reimbursable military aid agreement in 1951.[3] During the period of the Cold War, India's non-alignment policy was not welcomed by the United States. The US policy makers were of the view that in the face of evil communism, non-alignment was immoral.[4] However, despite these differences, few other initiatives were taken during the Cold War years between India and the United States in the sphere of defence. The US policy makers viewed India as the 'pivotal' state of the region and Pakistan as a useful place to base long range US bombers as well as a potential ally to best serve US interest in the tense Persian Gulf region.[5] The reflection of this view can be seen as US approved the sale of 200 Sherman tanks worth $19 million, S-55 helicopters for the Indian Air Force and 54c-119 Fairchild military transport aircraft.[6] During the early years of a young Indian nation, India's defence equipments imports from the United States were extremely limited. During the India-China war in 1962, the United States provided military supplies to India in the form of small arms, ammunition and communication systems for mountain warfare. United States also provided transport aircraft in order to assist Indian troops in the Himalayan bases.[7] But given the difference in world views as well as goals of both sides during the Cold War era, defence ties failed to develop further.

India-US defence co-operation began showing the signs of change during 1980s after the Soviet intervention in Afghanistan. The US made offers to sell American military hardware to India. Responding to this offer, an Indian team of experts paid visit to the United States in 1980 to explore the possibility of buying TOW anti-tank missiles and long range howitzers. The Carter administration overturned its policy of disapproving the use of an advanced American electronic guidance system in India's Jaguar aircraft. With this move, it appeared that the United States is attempting to prevent India from moving any closer to the Soviet Union in the wake of Afghan crises apart from improving Sino-US ties as well as rearming Pakistan with US weapons. On the other side, India too appeared willing to diversify its sources of military acquisitions. To achieve this, upgrading of relations with the United States was considered to be a significant step forward. In 1984, a Memorandum of Understanding (MoU) was signed between the United States and India on technology transfer and based on that some sensitive technology transfer took place.[8] India could receive Super Computers, General Electric F-404 engines for the LCA program,[9] LM-2500 gas turbine engine, night vision devices as well as co-production of TF-5 aircraft in India.[10] However, during the period of 1984-88, US administration's approval of civilian technology exports to India rose by five times.[11]

Defence Cooperation in the post-Cold War period

With the disintegration of the Soviet Union in 1991, the Cold War era ended. This changed the strategic outlook of both India and the United States and opened up new opportunities for closer cooperation. This development coincided with the economic liberalization program which began in India in 1991 and which hugely attracted US investments in India. These two major developments paved the way for closer ties between India and the United States including in the defence sector. The United States first proposed closer military-to-military cooperation with India in 1991 when Lt. Gen. Claude M. Kicklighter, Commander, US Army Pacific, came up with a comprehensive set of proposals. These proposals included reciprocal visits of army chief of staff, creation of executive steering groups at the service level, symposia on security and strategy, and joint exercises.[12] The Indian government positively reacted to these proposals. It was believed in India that the United States would be a moderating influence on Pakistan and also such cooperation would facilitate technology transfers. At that time, there were growing concerns as well difficulties in defence equipment supplies from Russia. This was the result of the crisis in the Russian military–industrial complex following the disintegration of the Soviet Union. So clearly, a need for further diversification of sources was felt in India.[13]

Agreed Minutes on India-United States Defence Cooperation

India and the United States signed the 'Agreed Minutes on Defence Cooperation' during the visit of the US Secretary of Defence, William J. Perry, on 12 January 1995. This agreement was termed as the 'beginning of new era' in bilateral defence cooperation. It was agreed to set up three separate groups to foster more interaction and facilitate deliberations:[14] These three groups are the following:

- A joint Defence Policy Group (DPG), to review the issues of joint concerns such as post-Cold War security planning and policy perspectives on both sides and to provide policy guidance to the Joint Technical Group and Joint Steering Committee.[15]

- A Joint Technical Group (JTG), to develop the scope and content of further expansion of cooperative defence research and production activities. However this was to be within the laws, policies and treaty commitments of each country.
- A Joint Steering Committee (JSC), to increase the frequency and scope of service to service cooperation. It was agreed upon that emphasis of such cooperation would be on professional/technical training and joint exercises at progressively higher levels of scale and sophistication.[16]

Agreed Minutes on Defence Cooperation, promoted mutual understanding, familiarization and confidence-building through exercises, exchange of doctrines, high-level visits, courses, seminars and a focus on areas of mutual interest. However, the Defence Policy Group (DPG) appeared as the primary mechanism to guide India-US defence ties. It was decided that DPG will be led by the Defence Secretary on the Indian side and the Under Secretary of Defence for Policy on the US side. Sub-groups such as the Defence Production and Procurement Group, the Military Cooperation Group, the Joint Technology Group and the Senior Technology Security Group will report to and provide inputs to the DPG.[17]

Underlining the significance of Defence Policy Group (DPG), US Secretary of Defence, William J. Perry said, 'The agreement would open a new era in our security relations.' The accord provides for consultations between the Pentagon and India's Defence Ministry, as well as joint military exercises, military training, defence research and weapons production.[18] Furthermore, according to Ambassador J.N. Dixit, the above agreement has three parts, first one provides for civilian contacts between the US Department of Defence and Indian ministry of Defence. The second part provides for cooperation in the field of Defence production and research. The third part consolidates the Kirklighter suggestions on military to military cooperation. The agreement was the result of continuing high level political and military contacts between Indian and US defence establishments. Ambassador Dixit believed that this agreement was the first defence agreement between India and the USA at the political level and, therefore, is significant, in the sphere of defence cooperation. However, these beginnings remain subject to certain overall limitations, based on the larger orientation of US policies. [19]

On 11 and 13 May 1998, India conducted a series of nuclear tests. After which Clinton administration imposed sanctions on India. But merely four months after the tests and the subsequent sanctions, the then India's Prime

Minister Atal Bihari Vajpayee visited the United States and declared that India and the United States were 'natural allies' though he meant it in a figurative sense rather than in its traditional military connotation.[20] Though nothing much could be developed in the defence sphere between India and the United States, these sanctions were gradually withdrawn by the Clinton administration. In this process, talks between the then US Deputy Secretary of State, Strobe Talbot, and the then Indian Foreign Minister, Jaswant Singh, began on 11 June 1998 and continued over a period of 26 months, helped in clearing away misconceptions and developing an understanding between both the sides. A joint statement issued at the conclusion of the London talks in January 2000 between Jaswant Singh and Strobe Talbot stated that purpose of these talks was to lay a foundation of a broad-based forward looking relationship between the United States and India. Among the issues covered on a regular basis at these talks were control over exports of sensitive products and technologies and issues related to defence posture. On the issues of terrorism also, a mutual understanding was reached between both the sides during these talks.[21] A Joint Working Group on Terrorism was established in January 2000.

The Bush Administration and the Vajpayee Government

As a fallout of the 9/11 terrorist attack on the United States in 2001, a new age began in United States foreign policy making. In the wake of the 9/11 attacks on America, US National Security Strategy, 2002, noted that 'U.S. interests require a strong relationship with India.'[22] This was most visibly evident in the changed military-to-military ties, which is believed as the most 'conspicuous example of the improved bilateral relationship between the two nations.'[23]

According to changed perceptions of India during the Bush administration, the US Department of Defence (DoD) redefined defence cooperation with India. India was perceived as a potential partner who may provide peace and stability in the Indian Ocean and could shape a new Asian balance of power. Bush administration also viewed India as a partner which could counter China in Asia. In May 2001, the US Deputy Secretary of State Richard Armitage visited India to explain the Bush administration's strategic framework which included Missile Defence Program. He also indicated at a new beginning with India and countering of rogue states by naming Iran, Iraq, Libya, North Korea and some in India's neighbourhood.[24]

Similarly, in July 2003, the then US Ambassador to India Robert Blackwill noted that India's support for the missile defence system and full cooperation to the United States after 9/11 were seen positively by the Pentagon. In fact, since September 2001, and despite a concurrent US rapprochement with Pakistan in its War on Terrorism, India-US security cooperation and the military to military cooperation increased extraordinarily in the scale, scope, range and frequency of joint exercises and both the nations had at least one joint military exercise or engagement each month which focused on improving their combined capacity for combined military operations across the board by Special Forces against terrorists, maritime interdiction, search and rescue, air lift support, logistics transport and airborne assaults. The India-U.S. Defence Policy Group (DPG)—moribund since India's 1998 nuclear tests and ensuing U.S. sanctions—was revived in late 2001 and began to meet frequently. Chiefs of Defence Services as well as political leaders visited each other's capitals more frequently.[25]

Commenting upon the impact of 9/11 on India-United States relations, prominent author on the subject Dennis Kux wrote that the war on terrorism has 'transformed' US-India relations. Although the claim may be overstated, ties between Washington and New Delhi since September 11 have become closer than at any time since President John F. Kennedy came to India's aid during its 1962 border war with China. The war on terrorism has greatly strengthened political dialogue between the United States and India and enhanced cooperation on sensitive issues such as Afghanistan and Pakistan.[26] Kux further noted, 'The "transformation" has been most visible in security relations, where Washington and New Delhi have had few dealings for nearly four decades. This change became possible when the United States lifted nuclear sanctions in the wake of September 11. With less publicity but perhaps equal significance, it also eased export controls on so-called dual-use technology, which can serve both civilian and military purposes. Nuclear non-proliferation supporters fought a stiff rear-guard action to limit the scope of this loosening but lost out to those in the Bush administration who wanted a broader security relationship with India.[27] The Bush administration made early breakthroughs in arms sales to India at the end of 2002 with measures and decisions such as simplification of the Congressional notification of arms sale to India, sale and lease of Fire Finder radars, fast track delivery of spares of Sea King helicopters, consideration of the sale of Special Forces' equipment and the sale of GE engines and avionics for the Indian LCA. Since October 24, 2002, only those Major Defence Equipment (MDE) items above $14 million now require Congressional notification. This change puts India in a category with American Treaty Allies such as South Korea and Japan.[28]

A joint statement issued by Prime Minister Vajpayee and President Bush in January 2004 declared that India-United States 'strategic partnership' includes expanding cooperation in the areas of easing restrictions on dual use technology export to India, increase in civil nuclear and civil space cooperation, as well as expanding dialogue on missile defence. These steps were known as 'Next Steps in Strategic Partnership' (NSSP).[29]

Next Steps in Strategic Partnership (NSSP)

The NSSP was launched in January 2004 by President Bush and then India's Prime Minister Vajpayee. India and the United States agreed to expand cooperation in three specific areas: civilian nuclear activities, civilian space programs, and high-technology trade. In addition, the two countries agreed to expand dialogue on missile defence. These areas of cooperation were designed to progress through a series of reciprocal steps that build on each other.[30]

As the then India's Foreign Secretary Shyam Saran pointed out that the progress made through NSSP[31] enabled India to put in place a regulatory framework for promoting strategic trade and high-technology commerce by addressing concerns of liberal and predictable licensing on the one hand, and technology security and export controls on the other. Among the various results of the NSSP were the removal of many Indian organizations such as Indian Space Research Organization (ISRO) Headquarters from the Department of Commerce Entity List, de-licensing of certain categories of dual-use items, institution of a presumption of approval policy in other categories and direct cooperation in developing, producing, marketing and operating commercial satellites. These policy changes were facilitated through the upgradation of India's export controls, reflected in the passage of legislation on that subject in May 2005 that underlined India's credentials as a secure and responsible destination. India and the United States have improved preventive enforcement capabilities, conducted outreach programs and embarked on technical exchanges in support of their export control goals.[32]

New Framework for the India-US Defence Relationship

On 28 June 2005, India's Defence Minister Pranab Mukherjee and the US Defence Secretary Donald Rumsfeld signed a ten-year defence partnership agreement known as 'New Framework for the India-US Defence Relationship.'[33]

Under the New Framework, India and USA agreed to:

- Conduct joint and combined exercises and exchanges;
- Collaborate in multinational operations if it is in common interest;
- Strengthen capabilities of militaries to promote security and defeat terrorism;
- Promote regional and global peace and stability;
- Enhance capabilities to combat the proliferation of weapons of mass destruction;
- Increase opportunities for technology transfer, collaboration, co-production, and research and development;
- Expand collaboration relating to missile defence;
- Strengthen abilities of the Armed Forces to respond quickly to disasters, including in combined operations;
- Conduct successful peacekeeping operations;
- Conduct and increase exchanges of intelligence.

Under the New Framework, the institutionalized framework for cooperation was further strengthened with the establishment of Defence Procurement and Production Group and the Defence Joint Working Group, under the comprehensive bilateral mechanism of the Defence Policy Group.[34] Furthermore, India-United States partnership reached a major milestone when the historic India-United States civil nuclear cooperation agreement was signed in October 2008, marking the end of India's 34 year isolation from the global mainstream in the sphere of civil nuclear energy technology.[35]

Military exercises between India and the United States were restarted in 2002. US has since conducted more joint military exercises with India than with any other country. [36]

Joint Military Exercises

The Malabar series of joint naval exercises are the most significant annual naval exercise between India and the United States and have evolved over the years. In 2002, the Malabar exercises included basic passing manoeuvres as well as naval vessels, anti-submarine exercises and replenishment-at-sea drills. In 2003 and 2004, Malabar exercises included advanced assets such as the USS Alexandria, and US Navy P-3C Orion maritime patrol aircraft. With this the navies of India and United States could engage in submarine familiarization exercises, a key capability for anti-submarine warfare collaboration. Malabar 2005 exercises featured the participation of the aircraft carriers USS Nimitz and INS Viraat. In Malabar 2006, a US expeditionary strike group, which was comprised of amphibious ships, cruisers, destroyers and submarines, participated in the exercise for the first time. However, while organizing Malabar-2007 naval exercises, surface and anti-submarine warfare, maritime interdiction and VBSS (visit, board, search and seizure) operations to counter piracy and terrorist activities at sea were also included besides interception and air combat exercises.[37] Malabar 2008 was strictly a bilateral exercise. However in the Malabar 2009 exercises, the Indian Navy, the Japan Maritime Self Defense Force (JMSDF) and the US Navy participated. This exercise was conducted in the Pacific Ocean in Sasebo, Japan. Commenting on the importance of Malabar Exercises 2009, Lieutenant Aaron Kakiel, 7th Fleet South Asia Policy & Exercise officer, stated, 'MALABAR 2009 is significant because it is the second time the Indian, US, and Japanese have operated together in the Western Pacific.'[38] MALABAR 2010 was conducted in the Arabian Sea in which thrust was on Anti-Submarine Warfare (ASW), Surface Firings, Maritime Interdiction Operations (MIO), Visit Board Search and Seizure (VBSS) and Submarine Operations. The US Navy`s frontline units of 7th fleet and Indian Navy`s Western Fleet participated in this exercise.[39]

The Indian Air Force (IAF) has been conducting Joint Air Exercises with the US Air Force (USAF), named as Cope India series of air exercises since 2002. The first exercises were carried out in Agra 2002 which focused on air transport functions and airlift interoperability.[40] Exercise Cope India 04 marked a beginning of a new chapter in Indo-US bilateral defence cooperation since it was the first opportunity since 1963, when USAF fighters operated from Indian soil.[41] 'Cope India 05' was conducted at the Kalaikunda airforce station in West Bengal on 7 November 2005. From the USAF side, F-16 Fighting Falcons and E-3 Sentry Airborne Warning System and Control aircraft took part for the first time in the massive two-week joint exercise, while from the IAF side, Sukhoi-Mk-30I, MiG-29, MiG-27 and MiG-21 BIS took part.[42] While in the last Cope India 2009 exercises, which took place from October 19-23, 2009 the USAF team was comprised of three C-130H Hercules, one C-17 Globemaster III, and one C-130J aircraft while the IAF was comprised of by one IL-76 Gajraj, four AN-32 Sutlej, two MI-17 Pratap, and one Chetak Alouette III aircraft for the exercise.[43]

India took part in Cope Thunder series of exercises held in Alaska in 2004. This series of exercises are now known as Red Flag-Alaska Exercises. India has also been invited to observe and participate in the multinational Air Exercise 'Red Flag-Alaska' in 2007 and 2008 as well.[44]

India and the United States conducted the first joint army exercise in May 2002. The US Special Operations Command (SOCOM) coordinated this joint exercise with Indian armed forces in Agra. This exercise was part of a series of such engagements named as 'Balance Iroquois' which is also known as 'Vajra Prahar.' It was the first occasion in 39 years when Indian and US Special Forces conducted joint training.[45] After a few months in September 2002, American and Indian troops participated in exercise 'Geronimo Thrust 02' at Fort Richardson and Elemendorf Air Force Base in Alaska.[46] In April 2003, combined Indian and US Special Operations Forces staged a raid on a mock terrorist hideout in the jungle terrain of Mizoram in Northeast India.[47] This exercise was followed by Operation 'Vector Iroquois' in Guam in May and June of 2003.[48] In September 2003, 'Balance Iroquois' was held in Leh (on the Tibetan plateau in India) and offered US forces terrain which is not available in the United States. In addition to these exercises, three Shatrujeet exercises had also been conducted with US marines up to March 2008.[49] However from October 12-19, 2009, Indo-US Joint Exercise 'YUDH ABHYAS 09' was conducted under the aegis of HQ Southern Command. The scope of the exercise is to conduct Indo–US joint training exercise with CI/CT focus in a semi urban scenario.[50]

Commenting critically on the India-United States Defence ties, Professor Stephen Cohen stated, 'Developments have not proceeded at the pace many had envisioned.'[51] However, while writing the appraisal on India-US joint exercises, a Naval officer and Defence analyst Gurpreet S. Khurana pointed out that joint exercises help in many ways such as: [52]

- Self-Assessment through 'Exposure'
- Training Value, Motivation, and Morale
- Introduction to Operational Concepts
- Assessment of Hardware and Technologies
- Operational Compatibility
- Politico-diplomatic Considerations
- Symbolic Dividends
- Strategic Imperatives

The rationales behind these exercises were to develop '*inter-operability*', the ability of the two forces to communicate, coordinate and fight together and enhance the cooperative security relationship between the two countries.

Counter-Terrorism Cooperation

In the post-9/11 scenario, India and the United States have been closely cooperating on counter terrorism strategies and their implementation. At a bilateral level, the India-US Counter Terrorism Joint Working Group, which was formed in 2000, has proved to be a useful mechanism for exchange of information, intelligence sharing, anti-terrorism training programs as well as for strengthening institutional links between crime prevention agencies between the two democracies.[53]

Now the main emphasis is being given on greater intelligence sharing, an upgraded Anti-terrorism Training Assistance Programme (ATAP) for Indian law enforcement officials, improving border monitoring, counter terrorism equipment sales, counter-narcotics, money laundering, and the ratification and implementation of the Treaty on Mutual Legal Assistance in order to enhance counter terrorism cooperation between India and the United States.[54] India-US Cyber Security Forum was also launched in 2002 with a focus on cyber security, cyber forensics and related research towards enhancing cooperation among law enforcement agencies on both sides in dealing with cyber crime.[55]

United States International Military Education and Training (IMET) Assistance to India

Following the revival of military relations in 2002, United States International Military Education and Training (IMET) assistance to India has been going up consistently. IMET budget allocation for India was US$ 0.5 million in 2001 where as in 2009, it was increased up to US$ 1.4 million.[56]

The United States-India Nuclear Cooperation Approval and Non-proliferation Enhancement Act was signed by President Bush on 8 October 2008. Since then onwards, defence ties have also grown further. India's defence equipment imports from the United States, in terms of contracts signed since 2008, stands at US$ 3.1 billion.[57] During the US Secretary of State, Hillary Clinton's visit to India in July 2009, India and the United States agreed to enter into an End User Monitoring Agreement (EUMA) aimed at paving the way for greater defence cooperation.[58] EUMA pertains to the 'end-use monitoring' (EUM) commitments that United States law requires from foreign purchasers of US defence articles and services. In the past, India was reluctant to agree to standard EUM verification commitments in military sales contracts. Now this changed perception and practice marks a change in the US-India defence relationship which should make India-US defence cooperation even better.[59] It is expected that the recently signed EUMA will provide a boost for US defence technology transfer to India.[60]

In early June 2010, on the eve of the inauguration of the first strategic dialogue between India and United States at Washington DC, the US Congress approved the sale of ten C-17 Globemaster III strategic lift aircraft for India through the Foreign Military Sales (FMS) route, with a maximum package value of $5.8 billion. It was an unprecedented growth in defence trade between India and United States.[61] On the invitation of the US Secretary of Defence, Mr Robert Gates, India's Defence Minister A.K. Antony paid an official visit to Washington DC from September 26-28, 2010. The visit was part of the intensive ongoing bilateral dialogue on strategic partnership including defence cooperation.[62]

Reports noted that during the meeting, Secretary of State Hillary Clinton urged Antony to buy American military hardware.[63] However Antony expressed India's concerns about US restrictions on export of dual use high-technology items as well as the rise in US military aid to Pakistan. Furthermore, the Defence minister noted that such high level interactions had successfully served to develop deeper mutual understanding on defence and security issues of shared interest and played an important role in the process of unlocking the full potential of defence cooperation in the overall context of the strategic partnership between India and the United States.[64]

Obama Administration and India-US Defence Cooperation

President Obama paid a landmark visit to India in November 2010. Before the Obama visit, the total defence trade between India and the US since 2008 in terms of contracts signed stood at $ 3.1 billion. As one of the significant outcomes of this visit, both nations have finalized agreements on two defence deals worth nearly $5 billion which includes ten C-17 Globemaster III military transport aircraft worth $4.1 billion and General Electric engines for Tejas light combat aircraft (LCA) worth $820 million. After the formal signing of these two contracts, the total defence trade volume between the two countries since 2008 has reached nearly $ 8.1 billion in terms of contracts signed, which is an unprecedented growth level in the history of defence trade between the India and the United States. This growing defence cooperation between India and the United States clearly indicates the growing confidence of the two nations in jointly dealing with future security challenges in whichever form they might arise.[65]

Similarly, during the Obama visit, building upon the Counter Terrorism Initiative which was signed in July 2010, India and United States have also announced a new Homeland Security Dialogue between India's Ministry of Home Affairs and the US Department of Homeland Security aimed at further deepening the operational cooperation, counter terrorism technology transfers and capacity building. It is hoped that growing intelligence sharing and anti-terror cooperation between India and the United States will act as a stronger deterrence against agencies in Pakistan and will discourage them from webbing any evil designs against the two democracies and their freedom loving societies and peoples.[66]

In 2013, a Joint Declaration on Defence Cooperation was issued which highlighted the deepening of the India US defence ties. For the first time, an Indian Navy ship participated in Rim of the Pacific (RIMPAC) exercise in 2014. During Prime Minister Modi's visit to the US in September 2014, it was decided to renew the 2005 'New Framework for India-US Defence Relationship' in 2015. Aggregate worth of defence acquisition from United States has crossed over US$ 10 billion. India and the United States have set up a Defence Trade and Technology Initiative (DTTI) which is aimed at simplifying technology transfer policies. Considering the fact the Prime Minister Modi has a launched a Make in India programme, DTTI is more about co-development and co-production of defence equipments in India. The first working group meeting was held in September 2014. A Task Force under the DTTI has been established by both sides to identify unique projects and technologies which would have a transformative impact on bilateral defence ties and upgrade India's military capabilities. India-US Counter Terrorism Cooperation Initiative was signed in 2010 to enhance counter terrorism cooperation, information sharing and capacity building. A Homeland Security Dialogue was announced during the President Obama's first visit to India in November 2010. It was aimed at further deepening of operational cooperation, counter terrorism technology transfers as well as capacity building.[67]

A joint statement issued after the first Strategic and Commercial dialogue between India and the United States in Washington DC on 22 September

2015, both sides noted that 'building on the conclusion of their 10-year Defence Framework Agreement, both sides expressed satisfaction with progress on defence technology and trade initiative pathfinder projects, including the establishment of the working groups on aircraft carrier technology and jet engines, and the growing cooperation between US and Indian defence industries through the Make in India initiative.[68]

Conclusion

India-United States defence cooperation has been transformed substantially in the post cold war era, especially after 9/11. This has been possible because of the growing nature of India-United States strategic partnership. In this regard, it must be worth noting that India and the United States not only share values such as democracy, freedom of expression and individual liberty but also have shared interests. This partnership has been further boosted by massive substance which has been generated with the developments over the past two decades in India. India is a trillion dollars economy and now the second fastest growing economy in the world. It also has more than one billion population of which 60 percent are youth. Shared interests related to counter terrorism, and protecting sea lanes of communications have brought India-United States closer in their defence and security partnership. Rise of China is certainly a factor which is at the back of the minds of policy makers both in New Delhi and Washington DC, which they may not express openly.

As Former India's Ambassador to the United States, Lalit Man Singh notes that Defence cooperation, which was of a token nature during the five decades of the Cold War, has now moved to the centre of the relationship, as India is now being offered almost the entire range of advanced US military technology: from F-16 and F-18 aircraft to the futuristic PAC-3 anti-missile system, the F/A-22 and F-35 fighters and the P-8A multi-mission maritime aircraft. From the Indian pint of view, this has provided a new and positive perspective to the Indian defence forces.[69]

However, India's steps towards future defence cooperation with the United States must be cautious and well thought off. In Ambassador J.N. Dixit's words, 'There is no doubt that nurturing a close working relationship with the US should be a matter of very high priority in our foreign policy. But it should not be at the cost of ignoring its multi-dimensional strategic and tactical requirements.'[70] India-US defence ties must fulfil India's long term goal of capacity to design, manufacture and develop arms including economic viability of transfer of technology and its applicability to India's requirements. In fact, increased US investment in the Indian defence sector, dual use technology transfer and a partnership of equals is going to be the hallmark of military cooperation between these two democracies.

NOTES

1. R. Nicholas Burns (2007), "America's Strategic Opportunity with India: The New U.S.-India Partnership" Foreign Affairs, November/December.
2. G. Kanwal (2007), "Indo-US Defence Co-operation: Forging Ahead" Asian Tribune,30 October, New Delhi.
3. "Department of State Policy Statement on India" (2006), in Rashmi Jain, "The United States and India 1947–2006: A Documentary Study", Radiant Publishers, New Delhi.
4. K. Santhanam (2008), "A Perspective on the Indo-US Defence Interactions" in N.S. Sisodia, P.R. Lavoy, C. Samuel and R. Walker (edited), "India-US Relations: Addressing the challenges of the 21st century", Magnum Books Pvt. Ltd., New Delhi.
5. Ibid.
6. Dinesh Kumar (1997), "Defence in Indo-US Relations," Strategic Analysis, 20: 5, August: 751.
7. U.S. Department of State (1961-1963), "*South Asia", Office of the Historian,* FRUS, Vol. XIX.
8. C. Mahapatra (1998), "Indo-US Relations into the 21st Century", Knowledge World, New Delhi.
9. R.T. Cupitt and S. Gahlaut (1999), "Non-Proliferation Export Controls: US and Indian Perspectives," in *Engaging India: US Strategic Relations with the World's Largest Democracy,* ed. Gary K. Bertsch, S. Gahlaut, and A. Srivastava, Routledge, New York.
10. J. Saksena and S. Grillot (1999), "The Emergence of Indo-US Defence Cooperation: From Specific to Diffuse Reciprocity", in *Engaging India,* edited by Gary K. Bertsch, Seema Gahlaut & Anupam Srivastava, Routledge, New York.
11. B. Chellaney (1993), "Nuclear Proliferation: The US-India Conflict", Orient Longman, New Delhi.
12. J. Saksena and S. Grillot (1999), "The Emergence of Indo-US Defence Cooperation: From Specific to Diffuse Reciprocity", in *Engaging India,* edited by Gary K. Bertsch, Seema Gahlaut & Anupam Srivastava, Routledge, New York quoted in C. Samuel (2007), "Indo-US Defence Cooperation and the Emerging Strategic Relationship", Strategic Analysis, Vol. 31, No. 2:216.
13. C. Samuel, "Indo-US Defence Cooperation and the Emerging Strategic Relationship", Strategic Analysis, Vol. 31, No. 2, March 2007, p.216
14. D. Kumar (1997), "Defence in Indo-US Relations", *Occasional Paper Series,* Institute of Defence Studies and Analyses, August, New Delhi.
15. Ibid.
16. J. Saksena and S. Grillot (1999), "The Emergence of Indo-US Defence Cooperation: From Specific to Diffuse Reciprocity", in *Engaging India,* edited by Gary K. Bertsch, Seema Gahlaut & Anupam Srivastava, Routledge, New York.
17. India-U.S. Relations: A General Overview Indian Embassy in Washington D.C., [Online: web] Accessed 19 September 2015 URL: http://www.indianembassy.org/newsite/induspolAug06.asp

18. "U.S.-India Pact on Military Cooperation", Friday, *New York Times*, January 13, 1995.
19. J.N. Dixit (2002), "India's Foreign Policy: Challenges of Terrorism, Fashioning New Interstate Equations", Gyan Publishing House, 2002, New Delhi.
20. Cherian Samuel (2007), "Indo-US Defence Cooperation and the Emerging Strategic Relationship", Strategic Analysis, Vol. 31, No. 2, March:217.
21. Ibid.
22. S.K. Shrivastav (2009), "Contours of the India-United States Strategic Partnership", IDSA Strategic Comment, September 29, [Online: web] Accessed 19 September 2015 URL: at http://www.idsa.in/idsastrategiccomments/ContoursoftheIndia-UnitedStatesStrategicPartnership_skshrivastav_290909
23. Christine C. Fair (2005), "US-Indian Army-to-Army Relations: Prospects for Future Coalition Operations", Asian Security, vol. 1, no. 2, April:164.
24. S. Trikha (2001), "We have questions about Pakistan": Armitage", *Indian Express*, 12 May, New Delhi.
25. "Text of Ambassador Robert Blackwill's speech" at the Confederation of Indian Industry, New Delhi, July 17, 2003, [Online: web] Accessed 19 September 2015 URL:http://www.rediff.com/news/2003/jul/17black1.htm?zcc=rl.
26. D. Kux (2002), "India's Fine Balance", Foreign Affairs, May/June:3.
27. Ibid.
28. R.D. Blackwill (2002), "The Quality and Durability of the US-India Relationship," November 27, Kolkata, [Online: web] Accessed 19 September 2015 URL: at http://www.mtholyoke.edu/acad/intrel/bush/blackwill.htm
29. S.K. Shrivastav (2009), "Contours of the India-United States Strategic Partnership", IDSA Strategic Comment, September 29 [Online: web] Accessed 11 Nov 2015 URL: at http://www.idsa.in/idsastrategiccomments/ContoursoftheIndia-UnitedStatesStrategicPartnership_skshrivastav_290909
30. "The American Vision of U.S.-India Economic Cooperation" (2004), *Press Release,* by US Embassy, [Online: web] Accessed 11 Nov 2015 URL: *http://chennai.usconsulate.gov/wwwhprind.html*
31. U.S. (2004), "India Announce Progress in Strategic Trade Talks", US Embassy in India, *Press Releases,* 17 September, New Delhi.
32. Shri Shyam Saran at the Opening Session of Fourth India-US High-Technology Cooperation Group Meeting, [Online: web] Accessed 19 September 2015 URL: available at *http://www.mea.gov.in/*
33. "India-US Defense Relations", Embassy of India, Washington D.C. [Online: web] Accessed 1 Nov 2015 URL: at http://www.indianembassy.org/india-us-defense-relations.php
34. Ibid.
35. S.K. Shrivastav (2009), "Contours of the India-United States Strategic Partnership", IDSA Strategic Comment, September 29 [Online: web] Accessed 11 Nov 2015 URL: at http://www.idsa.in/idsastrategiccomments/ContoursoftheIndia-UnitedStatesStrategicPartnership_skshrivastav_290909
36. S.K. Shrivastav (2010), "Inherent values and substance bind India and the United States", IDSA Strategic Comment, August 24,[Online: web] Accessed 19 September 2015 URL: at http://www.idsa.in/idsacomments/InherentvaluesandsubstancebindIndiaandtheUnitedStates_skshrivastava_240810
37. "Malabar 2007: India, United States, Japan, Australia, Singapore Begin Massive 5-Day Naval Exercises", India Defence, September 9. [Online: web] Accessed 19 September 2015 URL: at http://www.india-defence.com/reports-3519

38. "India, Japan, U.S. foster relationships during MALABAR" (2009), Bharat Rakshak, May 5, [Online: web] Accessed 2 Oct 2015 URL: http://www.bharat-rakshak.com/NAVY/Galleries/Bridges/2009/Malabar/
39. "Indo-US naval war-games begin in Arabian Sea" (2010), Thaindian, April 23, [Online: web] Accessed 2 Oct 2015 URL: at http://www.thaindian.com/newsportal/india-news/indo-us-naval-wargames-begin-in-arabian-sea_100352605.html
40. Cherian Samuel (2007), "Indo-US Defence Cooperation and the Emerging Strategic Relationship", Strategic Analysis, Vol. 31, No. 2, March: 219.
41. "Cope India 04", Indian Air Force, [Online: web] Accessed 19 September 2015 URL: http://indianairforce.nic.in/show_page.php?pg_id=144
42. "Cope India 05 takes-off, Marxists demonstrate" (2009), *Outlook,* November 7, [Online: web] Accessed 25 March 2009 URL: http://www.outlookindia.com/pti_news.asp?id=333559.
43. "India-US air force exercise begins in Agra", The Times of India, October 19, 2009
44. C. Samuel (2007), "Indo-US Defence Cooperation and the Emerging Strategic Relationship", *Strategic Analysis,* Vol. 31, No. 2, March:219.
45. "Balance Iroquois" actually dates back to the 1960s, when the United States and India had relatively strong military cooperative engagement, mostly motivated by a joint threat perception concerning China. Christine C. Fair(2005), "US-Indian Army-to-Army Relations: Prospects for Future Coalition Operations", Asian Security, vol. 1, no. 2, April:164.
46. S. Ganguly (2003), "The Start of a Beautiful Friendship? The United States and India," *World Policy Journal,* Volume XX, No 1, Spring.
47. C.C. Fair (2005), "US-Indian Army-to-Army Relations: Prospects for Future Coalition Operations", *Asian Security,* vol. 1, no. 2, April: 164.
48. No publicly available information exists about this exercise. The author spoke with officials within the US Special Operations Command Pacific and with the Defence Attaché, Embassy of India, Washington DC, in February 2005. See also Christine C. Fair(2005), "US-Indian Army-to-Army Relations: Prospects for Future Coalition Operations", *Asian Security,* vol. 1, no. 2, April:164.
49. G.S. Khurana (2008), "India-US Combined Defence Exercises: An Appraisal", Strategic Analysis, Vol. 32, No. 6, November: 1049.
50. "Exercise Yudh Abhyas 09" (2009), Press Information Bureau Release, October 12,[Online: web] Accessed 2 Oct 2015 URL: http://www.pib.nic.in/release/release.asp?relid=53143
51. S.P. Cohen (2008), "More Than Just the 123 Agreement: The Future of U.S.-India Relations," House Committee on Foreign Affairs, Subcommittee on the Middle East and South Asia June 25, Brookings Institutions [Online: web] Accessed 2 Oct 2015 URL: http://www.brookings.edu/testimony/2008/0625_india_cohen.aspx
52. G.S. Khurana (2008), "India-US Combined Defence Exercises: An Appraisal", *Strategic Analysis,* Vol. 32, No. 6, November: 1049-58.
53. 'People, Progress and Partnership: The Transformation of US–India Relations', Embassy of the United States of America, New Delhi, September 23, 2004, cited in B. Mishra, 'India–US Relations: A Paradigm Shift', *Strategic Analysis,* 29(1), 2005, p. 90.
54. The intricate details of the workings and dynamics of the Indo-US CTJWG have not been easy to capture because of the diplomatic norms that prohibit US and Indian officials from divulging details of the meetings and discussions. For further details of the CTJWG, see S. M. D'Souza(2008), "Indo-US Counter-Terrorism Cooperation: Rhetoric Versus Substance", *Strategic Analysis,* Vol. 32, No. 6, November:1071.
55. Ibid.

56. C. Samuel (2007), "Indo-US Defence Cooperation and the Emerging Strategic Relationship", *Strategic Analysis*, Vol. 31, No. 2, March: 220.
57. S.K. Shrivastav (2009), "Contours of the India-United States Strategic Partnership", IDSA Strategic Comment, September 29, [Online: web] Accessed 19 September 2015 URL: http://www.idsa.in/idsastrategiccomments/ContoursoftheIndia-UnitedStatesStrategicPartnership_skshrivastav_290909
58. "India, US agree on end user monitoring pact" (2009), *The Times of India*, July 20, [Online: web] Accessed 19 September 2015 URL: http://timesofindia.indiatimes.com/india/India-US-agree-on-end-user-monitoring-pact-/articleshow/4800054.cms
59. "U.S.-India defense trade expected to increase" (2010), *Association of Corporate Council*, March 31, [Online: web] Accessed 24 September 2015 URL: at http://www.lexology.com/library/detail.aspx?g=c42df5d8-54c6-4aba-a275-8ea638b8e4b7
60. S.K. Shrivastav (2009) "Contours of the India-United States Strategic Partnership", IDSA Strategic Comment, September 29, [Online: web] Accessed 19 September 2015 URL: http://www.idsa.in/idsastrategiccomments/ContoursoftheIndia-UnitedStatesStrategicPartnership_skshrivastav_290909
61. S.K. Shrivastav (2010), "Inherent values and substance bind India and the United States", IDSA Strategic Comment, August 24, [Online: web] Accessed 19 September 2015 URL: http://www.idsa.in/idsacomments/InherentvaluesandsubstancebindIndiaandtheUnitedStates_skshrivastava_240810
62. "Press release on the visit of the Defence Minister of India, Mr. A.K. Antony to the United States", India Embassy in the United States, Washigton D.C., September 28, 2010[Online: web] Accessed 24 September 2015 URL: http://www.indianembassy.org/prdetail1592/press-release-on-the-visit-of-the-defence-minister-of-india,-mr.-a.k.-antony-to-the-united-states
63. "US asks India to buy American arms" (2010), *The Economic Times*, September 29,New Delhi.
64. "Press release on the visit of the Defence Minister of India, Mr. A.K. Antony to the United States", India Embassy in the United States, Washigton D.C., September 28, 2010 at [Online: web] Accessed 19 September 2015 URL: http://www.indianembassy.org/prdetail1592/press-release-on-the-visit-of-the-defence-minister-of-india,-mr.-a.k.-antony-to-the-united-states
65. Sanjeev K Shrivastav (2011), "An Impact Assessment of President Obama's Visit on the India-US Strategic Partnership" IDSA Issue Brief, December 9[Online: web] Accessed 24 September 2015 URL: at www.idsa.in/issuebrief/AnImpactAssessmentofPresident Obamas VisitontheIndia USStrategicPartnership+ impact+india+us+strategic&cd=1&hl=en&
66. Ibid.
67. "Brief on India-U.S. Relations", Embassy of India, Washington DC.
68. "Joint Statement on the First India-U.S. Strategic and Commercial Dialogue" (2015), Washington, DC, Ministetry of External Affairs, September 22, [Online: web] Accessed 19 September 2015 URL: http://myemail.constantcontact.com/Joint-Statement-on-the-First-India-U-S—Strategic-and-Commercial-Dialogue.html?soid=1115496907910&aid=ey-W1KA5e9s
69. L.M. Singh (2006), "The nuclear deal and beyond", India Seminar, [Online: web] Accessed 19 September 2015 URL: http://www.india-seminar.com/2006/560/560%20lalit%20man singh.htm.
70. J.N. Dixit (2002), "India's Foreign Policy: Challenges of Terrorism, Fashioning New Interstate Equations", Gyan Publishing House, New Delhi.

SECTION II

Internal Dimensions

15

Quest for Energy Security within and Beyond Borders

P.L. Dash

Posing the Problem

Energy is the locomotive of economic growth. From this vantage, India's energy needs are apparent. In post-1991, when India began embarking on the growth path and the economy picked up to look bright, India looked towards energy rich countries of the world in various regions to ensure her energy security as much as it looked within to garner indigenous resources. The farther it looked to procure oil and gas from distant shores, the more inward it was driven to look for indigenous ways to be self-sufficient. The efforts of the past two decades have driven India to Sakhalin in the Russian Far East, to Central Asia and the Caspian regions to seek and build collaborative pipelines from the neighbourhood, famously known as TAPI and IPI. Both have not materialized, but hopes have not been entirely dashed.

Energy resources are unevenly distributed worldwide. The richest regions are Russian Siberia, the Persian Gulf and West Asia. With both the regions, India traditionally has had a good channel of procuring energy for its consumption. The same year, in 1991, as India began economic reforms, the West Asia, particularly Iraq, ran into troubled waters. Saddam Hussein's annexation of Basra elicited US anger and the first Gulf War that the US waged on Iraq, shattered one of India's established channels of energy supply.

It was not only Iraq's energy supply to India that stopped, but the Soviet supply also ceased. Then in the political turmoil leading to the precipice of its collapse, the Soviet Union did not have the wherewithal to take up cudgels with the US and ensure that oil flowed from Iraq to India. All through the years, leading up to 1991, the Soviet Union had a swap deal with Iraq to which it supplied arms, and in payment for those arms, Iraq supplied oil to India. People knew it as Soviet oil supply, but indeed it was Iraqi oil coming to India. The first Gulf War partially severed this supply channel, and the second Gulf War, when the US dethroned Saddam, the Iraqi source entirely dried up.

India then endeavoured to explore possibilities of its energy engagement with Russia in the Far Eastern sector, particularly in Sakhalin. The initial success of importing oil and gas from Sakhalin I, prodded India to venture into other fields westward in Siberia from where Russia has been implementing two major pipelines: Angarsk-Daqing in the Chinese direction and Angarsk-Nakhodka in the Japanese and Korean directions. ONGC Videsh's big oil deal in 2015 with Russia was its decision to buy 15 percent in to the Rosneft oil field in Siberia for $ 1.2 billion.[1] From 2001 onwards, India's efforts in this direction have been consistent. That year itself, India invested $1.7 billion in Sakhalin I oil and gas field. In 2009, it further invested $2.1 billion for taking over the London listed, but Russia focused Imperial Energy. In addition, India has been in the quest for expanding the activities of ONGC Videsh in other areas of the world. In 2013, it had put a further investment of $4.12 billion for a 16 percent stake in Mozambique's Rovuma offshore area I, which holds as much as 75 trillion cubic feet of gas reserves.[2]

The quest for alternative sources of energy supply was equally pursued as India's economic growth became discernible worldwide post 1991. As needs for ensuring energy security rapidly grew year after year, India began profiling in the neighbourhood and seeking energy supply from wherever it could. Aside from the traditional sources of Persian Gulf and the Russian Federation, new areas such the Caspian and Central Asian regions assumed importance. This papers critically looks at these new regions, their capability to meet the growing needs of India's energy demand, their positioning in the Asian and world energy market and, finally, whether and how far India could rely on these emergent energy markets with plenitude of political instability and economic volatility surrounding energy supply from the Caspian and Central Asian region. It also looks at indigenous renewable sources of clean energy generation.

Caspian Flank Mired in Geopolitics

As independent countries of Eurasia assert their legitimate right to their natural and mineral resources across the post-Soviet space, hydrocarbon resources can be singled out as the most important aspects of their versatile cooperation with countries in all directions. Further, with the sway of globalization, countries are looking forward to future cooperation in the energy sector. However, the countries endowed with significant resources are not technologically equipped to tap opportunities which the market economy has thrown open at their doorsteps. Precisely, the challenge before them is the lag in technology and expertise to lay pipeline outlets in various directions to market their crude, gas and related petrochemical products. And they do not know how to turn these challenges into opportunities. Therefore, there is an urgent need to focus on pipelines stemming from various regions of the Caspian and Central Asia. The Caspian region is one such rich region with potential energy reserves that requires outlets to outside markets.

For all through the Soviet years what the Soviets had thought to be their reserves for the future suddenly became exclusive properties of independent Caspian states and the discovery and exploitation of new oil and gas fields became the order of the day. Many of these deposits are of trans-boundary in nature, thereby meaning that they need intraregional efforts to connect the source of energy production with viable markets. For the past over two decades, all five Caspian countries, Turkmenistan, Kazakhstan, Iran, Azerbaijan and Russia, have been making strenuous efforts to resolve many a bilateral and trilateral conflicts plaguing their region. Transporting oil and gas from this energy rich region is posing a real problem primarily because the region is mountainous or desert and landlocked sans access to the open sea or ocean. Any new pipelines have to be cross-country outlets to pass through many transit points and for that cordial relations with neighbours is a necessary prerequisite that is largely absent across the region. Added to this, the region has become an arena of a new great game between Russia on the one hand and the US on the other, frequently interloped by a visibly growing China. What Russia visualizes as its natural sphere of influence, the US contends that the area is of its vital national interests and the Chinese emphasize on the proximity of resources to their benefit. In any case, several pipelines are mooted from the region; some have already materialized and others are yet awaiting fruition.

1. The Baku-Tbilisi Ceyhan or BTC oil pipeline and a parallel Baku-Irzhurum gas connectivity were the pet western projects from the

region. It is for the first time that Caspian oil and gas have flowed to Turkey and beyond bypassing Russia. It is for the first time that political astuteness and geo-political considerations have overwhelmed economic realities of cost effectiveness and sustainability. In any case, the lines are operational and would serve the region for ages to come. In the second half of 2007, Kazakhstan and Azerbaijan have signed a deal by which Kazakh oil would be transported via BTC.

2. Baku-Novorussisk or the Northern Pipeline and the Baku Supsa southern pipeline are two more traditional directions of sea-surface-sea that has seen Caspian oil flow to Eastern Europe and beyond. The lines are operational and continue to serve the region.
3. The Russian pipeline from Atyrau to Samara is an existing outlet that runs to its full capacity.
4. The construction of Kazakhstan-China pipeline took place in two phases. The partners launched the Atasu-Alashankou section in 2006 and the Kenkiyak-Kumkol section in 2009. The initial capacity of the pipeline estimated at 10 million tons per year (mt/y) was increased up to 20 mt/y in 2013. However, due to the delays in the commercial oil production at the Kashagan field, Kazakhstan still has no enough hydrocarbons to ensure full utilization of the pipeline capacity. At the moment Kazakhstan is able to transport over 12 mt/y of oil to China on average.[3]
5. The Caspian Pipeline Consortium connects Kazakh oil fields with the Russian port of Novorosiiski. Owned by private western companies and state owned companies of Russia, Kazakhstan and Oman, the route can transport 560 thousand barrels of oil per day.[4] The major shareholders of CPC are Russia with 24 percent, Kazakhstan with 20.75 percent and Chevron with 15 percent. The pipeline boosted oil supplies to 42.759 million tonnes (927,466 barrels per day) from 39.958 million tonnes (858,315 barrels per day) in 2014. The pipeline connects the Tengiz field in Kazakhstan, and a number of other fields, to the sea terminal near Novorossiisk in Russia. The consortium plans to boost its capacity to 67 million tonnes this year after reaching 52 million tonnes in 2015.[5]
6. While these efforts are afoot in the northern tier of the India's neighbourhood, southward looking pipelines are envisaged through Iran, Afghanistan and Pakistan from the oil and gas rich fields of Turkmenistan and Kazakhstan. Thus, Turkmenistan-Pakistan-

Afghanistan-India pipeline popularly known as TAPI is an indicator of an insidious desire to connect concerned countries with one another through a permanent pipeline. Although prevailing security realities defy this strong desire, the inevitability of economic growth in India will precipitate an urgency to be realpolitik rather than maverick in intrastate approach to pipelines.

Recent Initiatives

Two incidents could be singled out as the most prominent political and diplomatic developments in recent times in the arena of energy diplomacy concerning Turkmenistan. Instead of talking for decades, action on the TAPI project and finding out ways of exporting Turkmen gas in the westerly direction to Europe. As a result, what was lagging behind for years has suddenly sprung a surprise, when India's Prime Minister, Narendra Modi convinced the Turkmenistan President about the viability and mutual profitability of TAPI during his maiden official visit to Ashgabat in July 2015. Indian Minister for Petroleum, Dharmendra Pradhan has been assiduously pursuing TAPI to flow gas to India, albeit with all constraints. Pradhan's Personal Secretary, another Pradhan, an IFS officer who served in Ashgabat in the past as Indian Deputy Chief of Mission to Turkmenistan, has surely been instrumental in forging inroads in materializing the talks.

During these numerous powwows, the nitty-gritty of how to overcome the impediments was discussed and now it has been decided that instead of having buyer seller relations, the concerned countries would become stakeholders. A consortium is to be formed, the share holding pattern of which has been largely sketched out. Turkmenistan, the seller country, would invest 51 percent in the gas fields and pipelines whereas India, Pakistan and Afghanistan would possibly share the 49 percent investment all by themselves. They have to share the cost and assure that political volatility in Afghanistan and Pakistan stay away from pragmatic pipelines, which are essential for the country's growth and development. The $10 billion and 1800 km long TAPI was thus discussed threadbare on 18-19 August 2015 in Dubai by representatives of all four countries including gas field management, laying of pipelines, controlling it through the treacherous terrain in the mountainous segments of Afghanistan and Pakistan before it reaches India, the transit and tariff issues, safety of gas passage and pipelines.[6] Since all countries have become stakeholders in the consortium, hopefully, hurdles will prove hollow to block it anymore.

Besides, this time around, Turkmenistan has taken the leadership initiative of the project, thereby reassuring the buyers of its gas about implementation of the project. Turkmenistan, that was earlier reluctant to accept foreign participation, has conceived a new idea to accommodate Japanese investment in TAPI, thus making it a five-stakeholder project, revealed Pradhan, who took part in the 22nd steering committee meet held in Ashgabat in the first week of August 2015.[7]

In another concrete area where Caspian spreads its pipeline wing is Nabucco. Way back in February 2002, the Austrian firm OMV and Turkish firm BOTAS began preparing a gas pipeline project that became the genesis of Nabucco. Three months later, in 2002, three other oil companies, that is, MOL of Hungary, Bulgargas of Bulgaria and Transgas of Romania expressed their desire to join the former duo and in October 2002 signed a cooperation agreement in Vienna that laid the foundation of Nabucco. In December 2003, the European Commission was ready with an unspecified award of 50 percent of the total cost of feasibility study of Nabucco that included technical details, market analysis, economic and financial implications, and so on, After a gap of one and half years, on 28 June 2008, the five partners signed a joint venture agreement that they had been formalized earlier on 26 June 2006 with a ministerial statement on the Nabucco pipeline, which was finally inked.[8]

Turkmenistan in recent years has been trying to internationalize its efforts to obtain access for its gas in the wider European market, which has largely been overshadowed by predominant Russian influence. Pursuing a polyphonic approach, Ashgabat also wishes to involve the UN to protect its pipelines in various directions from the Caspian to EU countries. That would minimize Russian influence and provide as much access to the EU to play a role in Turkmen gas as it would allow international peacekeepers to oversee the safety of gas supply through pipelines in various directions, including TAPI. Here the role of the UN, as a universal global framework in which it is possible to achieve a broad international consensus on the formation of a new architecture of energy security, is quite vital. This clearly implies that Turkmenistan has been making all-out efforts to reach out to the markets where it could sell its gas without Russian help.

India's Energy Requirements

Given that India is into an upswing in the growth process for over two decades and poised to grow further, the demand for energy is likely to continue in the foreseeable future. Roughly, if the growth process would be pegged at 8 percent per annum for the next five years, the demand would proportionately soar by 8 percent. It is a huge surge in demand for which India has to diversify her indigenous energy generation basket plus look to tangible sources of supply. Currently, India's energy basket is coal dependent, which is not a source of clean energy. Rough estimates suggest that coal in India's energy consumption basket is roughly around 60 percent. The dependence on hydroelectric and hydrocarbon put together are 33 percent and nuclear energy 3-4 percent and the rest constitutes all other forms of alternative energy sources such as solar, wind, etc. If India's growth trajectory is designed to development and development, in turn, is aimed at reducing the number of 'persons living on less than one dollar a day', energy requirement is an essential prerequisite because one third of India's population, largely in rural pockets, live below subsistence level.

Former Energy Minister, Sushilkumar Shinde, while speaking in Istanbul at the World energy leaders meet had said that India is projected to be the third largest energy consumer by 2020, next to the US and China. He further said that a two-pronged strategy has been adopted to meet this challenge: augmenting domestic supply sources including renewable energy and focusing on demand-side management and energy efficiency measures. Domestic capacities for building power plants with super critical and ultra-super critical technologies are also being established to reduce dependency on coal for power generation. International players such as Mitsubishi, Toshiba, Hitachi, Alstom and Ansaldo have already started the process of partnering with Indian manufacturers to set up super critical manufacturing facilities in India. While the fast-growing Indian economy has been grappling with acute shortage of power, estimates show that India's energy supply would need to rise by 6.5 percent annually if it intends to achieve an economic growth of 9 percent.[9] This is by far a sober assessment, while the actual requirements are far more urgent. Many parts of our urban pockets go without electricity for hours in summer months. The rural pockets are still using dried cow dung cakes for cooking and water heating. In fact from end winter to end summer that is the fuel available to villagers.

Despite this acute situation, the cleanest nuclear energy component in India's consumption basket is not more than 3 percent. For the country's sustainable development, this segment must be upped and dependence on coal component has to reduce. With this clean energy in view, India has signed 123 agreements that has enabled India to join the nuclear club—the first country that refused to sign the NPT but was taken as a member. This has enabled India to sign nuclear energy cooperation treaty alone with Russia to build 12 nuclear reactors for energy production in upcoming years. The second reactor at Kudankulam in Tamil Nadu is up into production this year and other reactors are likely to be built in West Bengal and Maharashtra. In any case, dependence on coal will prod the quest for clean energy and difficult availability of indigenous hydrocarbons will lead to research in unexplored areas to obtain alternative sources of energy production and supply in which hydroelectricity production, wind mills and nuclear power plants and solar units will augment their share in the years to come.

North East as Energy Anchor

Water is life and it has no substitute. No human activity is possible without water. The north east part of India, comprising of seven sister states, is a distinct part of the country with enormous endowment of water resources. One third of India's usable water resources in the northeast are untapped. The following are some plain facts to ponder over and act.

- The Brahmaputra and Barak river systems passing through the north east possess 34% of India's total water resources. This constitutes more than one third of the country's freshwater availability.
- The north east has only 7.9% of India's land mass and availability of 34% water resources on 7.9% of the territory makes the north east one of highest in terms of per capita and per hector availability of water for use.
- The north east region has 37% of hydropower potential of the country of which only 3-4% have been tapped. Thus, there is enormous untapped potential for generation of hydropower.
- Irrigation potential of the north east river system is 4.26 million hectors, whereas only 0.85 million hectors are under coverage.
- The ground water potential of the north east region is enormous. Within a shallow depth of just 20 meters, plenty of water is available in the Brahmaputra and Barak basin. However, only 4.3% of the ground water potential is put to use.
- 890 km stretch of river navigation system in Water Way 2 between Sadiya to Bangladesh border is lying either unused or underused.
- India's northeast is one of the most flood prone areas of the country. The Brahmaputra is a furious river when in spate. Brahmaputra and

Barak are trans-boundary and cross-country rivers flowing through the territories of China, India, Bangladesh and Bhutan, besides affecting four of the seven states in the north east—Arunachal Pradesh, Assam, Manipur and Meghalaya. Flood control mechanism and disaster management system is woefully inadequate.

- How and where we could utilize the available river water is a burning issue that requires a coordinated action plan. It requires not only regional and national planning, but a cross-country approach, which is mostly disputed.
- The government of India has identified some 226 sites in the north east for building big and medium hydro power systems, mostly along Brahmaputra and Barak flows.
- Upper and lower Subansiri, upper, middle and lower Siang, Kameng and Ranganadi are some prominent sites where the work for building hydropower stations has started and which are in various stages of development. Much remains to be done in this area.[10]
- Thus, there is a potential mismatch between the available water resources and their optimal utilization. Adequate attention needs to be paid to this.

Sun Comes to Help

Many summers ago, this author was visiting Betab Valley away from Pehelgaon in the Indian state of Jammu and Kashmir. A typically Taliban looking man, aged around 55, was standing near his house, where a signboard in Urdu displayed that he owned a tea stall inside. My friend, wife and I decided to have tea there and requested the man to make necessary arrangement. He immediately complied with. The interior of that tea stall took us by surprise. There was a small kitchen, an electric bulb, burning feebly and tik-tik sound coming from a grinding mill he was running. Upon asking he replied that he was making his own flour because he did not like the taste of flour available in the market. The grinding mill was powered by electricity he generated by blocking the flow of a small waterfall. Everything was rudimentary and indigenous, inherited and traditional. The lamp was lighted by that power. The household needs were met neatly by rural entrepreneurship by a semi-literate herd owner, who had a dozen cattle to graze. If a single individual could meet his electricity requirement by his own efforts, the situation could certainly change with collective support of the government and private sector.

Public–private partnership is what is required to tap the numerous cascading falls in the Himalayan terrain to be self-sufficient in power generation and supply. If properly harnessed, the surplus could be used elsewhere. While this could be a viable method of power generation in the mountainous areas, where rivulets cascade, the valley and plains could rely on solar power.

India's enormous solar potential is a unique source of power. 100,000 villages across the country do not have access to electricity till this day. They live in the dark age of yore away from the glee and glamour of 21st century. All those Indians who live on less than one dollar a day can benefit by putting solar panels atop their homes and generate electricity for their consumption. India's Prime Minister, Narendra Modi, has initiated an ambitious solar project for installing solar panels to generate 100 Giga watt of power by 2022, which could make India the largest solar power producer in the world.[11] Villages unconnected to the grid system could be lighted and their lifestyle could change. In order to set up photovoltaic panels on isolated rooftops may initially prove costly, but done in a bulk manner, cost reduces and efficiency improves. As more and more villages would opt for solar energy, generation of energy from this natural, clean source would gain popularity.

The Map below shows the state wise distribution of solar energy potential in India, which could be exploited in future. Ironically, industrially less developed states Rajasthan and Jammu and Kashmir have the highest solar energy potential. India's National Institute of Solar Energy, headquartered in Gurgaon, has done considerable research on availability of solar energy across the country and charted out a roadmap on how to exploit this clean energy potential. The map itself is an indicator of where to go from here and where to focus on.

Some more progressive states in farming such as Punjab and Maharashtra have been exploring the possibility of how solar energy would replace the use of diesel for farm activities. Incentives are doled out to farmers to set up solar panels for generating power to be used in farm activities. Studies reveal that Punjab received accolades for raising solar power generation capacity from 9 MW in 2012 to 235 MW in 2014. The state's future target is to increase the solar power generation to 4200 MW by 2020.[12] There are two primary ways of generating solar energy: The photovoltaic method that converts sunlight directly into electricity and the thermal method where a thermal plant uses heat to generate electricity. Maharashtra has 250 to 300 clear days of sunshine with an available average radiation of 4 to 6 kWh/square meter over a day. This implies that there is potential to generate 1.5 million MW a year through

State-wise Breakup of Solar Energy Potential in India

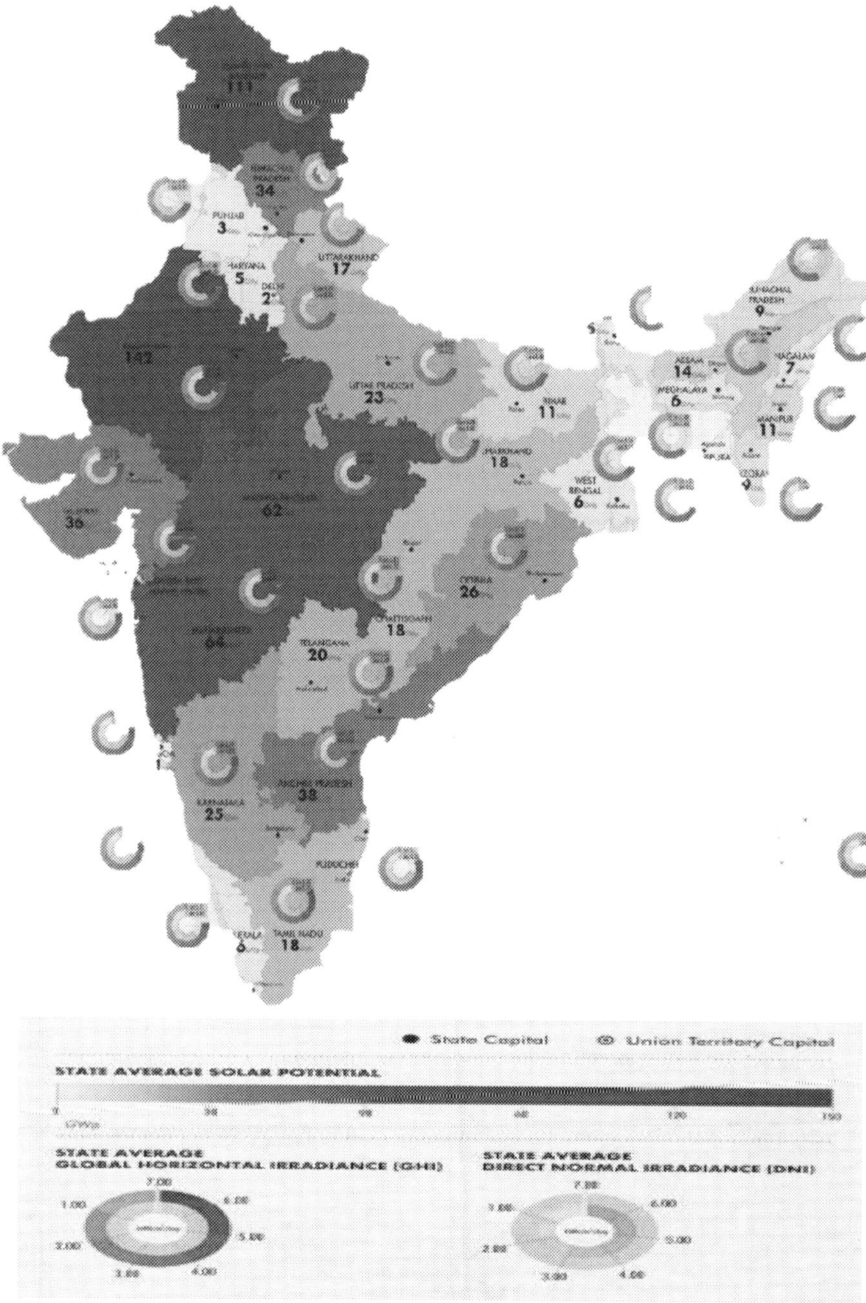

Source: National Institute of Solar Energy.

solar photovoltaic method and up to 2.5 MW through the solar thermal system.

Conclusion

In the years to come India's energy consumption pattern is going to change from coal and hydrocarbon based energy sources to renewable clean energy sources such as wind, solar and nuclear. As economic growth is likely to surge, energy consumption would move northward too. In order to meet the demand-supply asymmetry, the country would look within and beyond borders to ensure its energy security. Shale gas, natural gas and thorium based nuclear plants to generate electricity would balance out the present coal based energy industry. With oil prices dropping by a third from the record high a few years ago, this may tell a tale in favour of hydrocarbons for the time being. However, in India's long term interests, many changes are likely to occur and further research in all directions may open up new vistas of renewable and clean energy that India essentially requires.

NOTES

1. "OVL to buy 15% in Rosneft's oilfield in Siberia for $1.2 billion", The Times of India, September 5, Mumbai, [Online: web] Accessed 9 September 2015 URL: http://timesofindia.indiatimes.com/business/india-business/OVL-to-buy-15-in-Rosnefts-oilfield-in-Siberia-for-1-2-billion/articleshow/48831686.cms?
2. Ibid.
3. http://www.ayu.edu.tr/static/aae_haftalik/aae_bulten_en_48.pdf.
4. Eurasia Today, Moscow, 2007, p.58.
5. http://www.reuters.com/article/oil-cpc-idUSL8N14V1OG20160111
6. "Step on Gas over TAPI pipeline" (2015), The Times of India, 11 August, Chandigarh, [Online: web] Accessed 19 September 2015 URL: http://timesofindia.indiatimes.com/business/india-business/Modi-Pradhan-step-on-gas-over-TAPI-pipeline/articleshow/48429723.cms
7. Ibid.
8. Bayram Balci et al. (2010), "China and India in Central Asia A new great game—Basingstoke", Palgrave Macmillan US.
9. http://articles.economictimes.indiatimes.com/2012-04-21/news/31379071_1_energy-consumer-renewable-energy-power-minister-sushilkumar-shinde
10. Water Vision: North East 2050, Report of the Brahmaputra Board, Ministry of Water Resources, Government of India, New Delhi, 2000.
11. D. Pinner and M. Rogers (2015), "Solar Power Comes off Age", Foreign Affairs, March-April: 114.
12. S. Singh and S.S. Gill (2014), "Punjab's Energy Sector: Growth, Structure and Strategic Policy Issues", Policy Brief No.3, Centre for Research in Rural and Industrial Development.

16

Galvanizing India's Nuclear Doctrine in the Changing Strategic Milieu: Pros and Cons

Rajendra Prasad

Contemplating unconventionally about the nuclear issues in contemporary politico-strategic milieu of South Asia, especially revisiting India's Nuclear Doctrine, is replete with certain quandaries and uncertainties, particularly due to the uncertain posture of an unstable Pakistan towards emerging India as a major power, along with China's nuclear deterrent capabilities and military modernization programme and an overriding ambition to become a super power in the changing global scenarios. Consequently, Indian policy-makers are inclined to scrutinize prevailing apprehensions, with a sense of indispensability to do a timely strategic review of India's Nuclear Doctrine and nuclear policy moving towards new realities in the 21st Century. This paper deals in detail with various issues intertwined with India's current Nuclear Doctrine and suggests certain possible options to meet the nuclear challenges likely to be posed by nuclear-armed adversaries for Modi's government.

Introduction

Given the historical legacy and geo-strategic manifestations, India's main political parties, the Congress party and the BJP, along with their respective allies in the United Progressive Alliance (UPA) and the National Democratic

Alliance (NDA) cannot discard the historical facts and action-reaction based harsh realities of the nuclearization of South Asia. Notably, one of the cornerstones of India's nuclear policy and doctrine, 'No-First Use' pledge, was originally pronounced by the Indian government after it conducted the May 1998 nuclear tests and, in a consequent reaction, followed by Pakistani tests. The then Indian Prime Minister Atal Behari Vajpayee asserted thereafter that India would adhere to a policy of 'No-First Use' of nuclear weapons vis-à-vis other nuclear weapons states (NWS) and would not use these weapons against non-nuclear weapons states (NNWS). This self-discipline was also implanted in the draft nuclear doctrine declared in August 1999 and officially promulgated in January 2003.

Viewed in retrospect, India's prior experiences after its 'peaceful nuclear explosion (PNE)' in May 1974 was based on some sort of strategic presumption that further nuclear tests would not prompt India's entry into the realm of Nuclear Non-Proliferation Treaty as a nuclear weapons state (NWS), mainly due to the obligation of more harsh sanctions.

Despite the claims of some decision makers that sanctions helped indigenous research and development, it remained crystal-clear, however, that despite some degree of accomplishments, India relied heavily on outside support to create its nuclear infrastructure and facilities. This reality gained more prominence in the Indian government's raison d'être for entering into the Indo-US civil nuclear deal in 2008, predominantly to save India from foreign technology denial and facilitate it with the alternative courses for imports of nuclear materials and technology from supplier countries. In these changing circumstances, India's rise as a major responsible power in the world, in general, and Asia, in particular, would need to revisit almost all vital determinants of India's nuclear policy as well as its Nuclear Doctrine to meet its foreseeable needs and probable challenges.

Necessity for Revisiting India's Nuclear Doctrine

There are timely and strong arguments to revisit India's nuclear doctrine as much has occurred over the prevailing circumstances that override the past formulations made by the past governments during their consecutive terms in power. On the theoretical plane, the limitations and quandaries of nuclear deterrence have become more evident. In probable scenarios and situations, India's acquisition of nuclear weapons hasn't emboldened its security imperatives.

It is worth-recalling that in the beginning of April 2014, in a conference on *A Nuclear Weapon-Free World: From Conception to Reality* the then Indian Prime Minister Dr Manmohan Singh proposed for the creation of a global convention to give up the first use of nuclear weapons.[1] Why the Indian Prime Minister Dr Singh resorted to initiate this major policy pronouncement in the final stints of his tenure in office is to be reasoned with a sense of speculation. Having realized the primacy of outgoing PM Dr. Singh's assertion, Bhartiya Janata Party (BJP) had instantly issued a rejoinder in its election manifesto and pledged to 'study in detail India's nuclear doctrine, and revise and update it, to make it relevant to [the] challenges of current times.'[2] This germinated a mysterious anxiety in some domestic and outside politico-strategic circles that the BJP would renounce No-First Use (NFU) pledge, which has remained an essential facet of India's nuclear doctrine since the country conducted a series of nuclear tests in 1998 and emerged as a de facto nuclear weapons state (NWS).

Shortly after assuming office as Prime Minister, in response to an audience in Japan in August 2014, Mr Narendra Modi admitted that 'there is a tradition of national consensus and continuity on such issues. I can tell you that currently, we are not taking any initiative for a review of our nuclear doctrine.'[3] This would have eased speculators as it reflected that Modi's self-possessed farsightedness towards foreign and security policy probably would find a cautious revalidation or fresh initiative in the nuclear field, despite the fact that his party's election manifesto 2014 was blatantly indicative of a new course of critical judgement on India's nuclear doctrine, however, was only a pre-election rhetoric. But the critical problem that remains and will warrant serious attention of the government of Narendra Modi is how India contemplates to convincingly engage Pakistan in the wider interests of nuclear stability in South Asia.

Following the aftermath of its 1998 nuclear tests, India was humbled by the US predicament and declared a draft nuclear doctrine that denied first use of nuclear weapons and endorsed 'Credible Minimum Deterrence' while appreciating that the latter was 'a dynamic concept related to the strategic environment, technological imperatives and the needs of national security.'[4] That flexibility was imbibed in the next exposition of the nuclear doctrine as an official statement issued publicly in 2003.[5] By that stage, India's nuclear doctrine was firmly based on an essential specification, signifying that India would not use nuclear weapons first, but if its enemies did so, then India's response would be devastating.

This might imply that the inclination to modify the No-First Use (NFU) policy, like the interest of others, arose largely from a widespread yearning for political assertiveness as a response to the perceived change in India's security and nuclear milieu, rather than from a belief in some specific deterrent benefits of potential first use. In 2012, P.R. Chari, a noted strategic analyst, had presented 'an alternative blueprint' of India's nuclear doctrine,[6] and declared that 'India will not initiate a nuclear strike.' By implication, 'Initiation' encompasses the course of action culminating into the actual use of a nuclear weapon by an enemy. This would include mating component systems and deploying nuclear warheads with the intention of using them if obligatory. This sort of justification of nuclear initiation could create a situation to admit that in a nuclear contingency, if Pakistan were simply to mate warheads to missiles or even co-locate formerly isolated nuclear pits and warheads to enhance the weapons' alertness and therefore survivability, this might be understood in India as Pakistan having formally 'initiated' a nuclear attack. This, in turn, would allow India to use nuclear weapons first while claiming that it had adhered to its No-First Use (NFU) policy.

Significantly, such assertions are not on the extreme. In June 2014, Lieutenant General B.S. Nagal, head of India's Strategic Forces Command (SFC) between 2008 and 2011, stated that India under a NFU posture 'cannot conduct a first strike on the adversary's counterforce targets, thus allowing the adversary full capability to attrite [India's] own capability.'[7] Gen. Nagal's contention is that a NFU obligates India to potentially take up a nuclear aggression on its own nuclear weapons, leaving New Delhi's nuclear weapons stockpiles depleted and therefore unable of launching a second strike to destroy the enemy's residual nuclear forces. This, in turn, can compel India to resort to counter-value/counter-city attacks—that is, strikes against population centres—something involving ethical issues and a 'Moral Dilemma.'[8] As a consequence, Gen. Nagal asserts in support of substituting the NFU policy with a policy of 'ambiguity'[9] as 'ambiguity provides a better range of options to launch decapitating and/or disarming strikes to deal with the adversary leadership/arsenal.'[10] These are remarkable arguments, coming from individuals who have served in important capacities in India's nuclear command structure.

The arguments such as the above are likely to characterize the nature and essence of the public discourse on India's nuclear policy and posture in the foreseeable future, weighing doctrinal alternatives of future Indian governments. For the critical theorists, one of the primary rationales of attenuating the NFU pledge might be to carry on India's enemies visualizing about the nuclear threshold in the anticipation that the consequential ambiguity deters a greater range of threats.[11]

The Pakistani Factor and Limitations of India's Nuclear Deterrence

While nuclear weapons have evident weight as a currency of power for the external dimensions of national security, they cannot avert threats and overt challenges to India's territorial integrity that emanate from domestic unrest or cross-border militancy and transnational terrorism germinating from Pakistani sponsorship or direct support, especially after 9/11 terrorism.[12] Simplistically speaking, nuclear weapons cannot offer any protection against the sub-conventional threats and challenges to India's national security posed by extremist elements within its own territory or particularly by those non-state actors or terrorist groups who get moral and material support from across the border. Moreover, the South Asian Region is a hideout to a large number of terrorists groups like Lashkar-e-Tayyiba (LeT), Al-Qaeda and a host of others, who want to provoke war between India and Pakistan. Al-Qaeda and other militant groups have been desperate to get their hands on fissile material or an assembled warhead. Terrorists also long to get direct control of Pakistan's nuclear weapons. Surgical strikes of militant camps and 'hot pursuits' of them could be potent strategies to eliminate them in many cases.[13]

However, nukes can't provide any guarantee of internal security and safety to any country having them. Notably, after Pakistan reacted with its own nuclear tests in May 1998, India's supremacy in conventional forces was evidently battered and diminished. This can be further observed in India's inconsistent and sporadic responses to violent onslaughts perpetrated by Pakistan-sponsored cross-border terrorism and its uncertain willingness to provide primacy to its *Cold Start* strategy and removal of impediments in establishing the forces' structure irrevocably essential to operationalize it.[14] Credibly, nuclear deterrence can only afford security against the use of nuclear weapons or a major conventional offensive. These inescapable realities elude India's strategic community and its armed forces to a large extent.[15]

In a greater hope, nuclear deterrence can promote a peaceful state of affairs to be observed. However, given the situation in South Asia and India-Pakistan distancing, a domineering array of security threats and challenges may also germinate and persist, stretching from border intrusions to sub-conventional warfare and cross-border terrorism and insurgency, coupled with emerging transnational terrorist threats from organizations like al-Qaeda and ISIS. Nuclear weapons give no security guarantee to nuclear armed States like India and Pakistan against this sort of existential security threats looming on the horizon.

Thus, practically, the primacy of nuclear deterrence vis-à-vis Pakistan had only restricted value for India's overall national security considerations. As evidenced, it did not deter Pakistan's cross-border intrusions in winter 1998 and spring 1999 into the Kargil sector of Jammu and Kashmir, which culminated into a small but fierce fight compelling the expulsion of Pakistan's regular and irregular forces. Pakistan was distressed by its call to uphold the 'invented story' that militants had conducted these intrusions and, therefore, it could not overtly position its regular forces to defend them. Appreciably, these events evidenced that a nuclearized Pakistan had confined Indian forces from directing a counter offensive elsewhere along the Line of Control or into Pakistan and nuclear weapons encouraged it to do so.[16] Political leverage was supposed to be at its demonstrative play, as India intended to demonstrate that it was a responsible nuclear power by not pushing or enabling 'the escalation of the operations' beyond control.

The similar momentum of occurrences reserved India's initiative during its border confrontation impasse with Pakistan following the attack by Pakistan-sponsored terrorists on the Indian parliament in December 2001. Again in November 2008, India remained reticent in retaliating against blatant attacks by Pakistan-sponsored terrorists on several high-profile targets in Mumbai. By and large, it would give the impression that Pakistan has secured a clear-cut resolve in perpetrating terrorist attacks against India through radical terrorist organizations that get its sponsorship as well as material and moral support. Despite open provocations by these Pak-backed terror groups, India has not mounted any retaliatory strike and remained restrained by exposing Pakistan's religious extremist ambit, and branding it as a patron of transnational terrorism within the international system.

Some have argued that the possession of nuclear weapons by India and Pakistan now has produced a more or less stable balance of terror that will preclude Armageddon in South Asia. This argument may prove true over time, but that is an 'uncertain bet.' However, deterrence continues to remain a significant factor in the India-Pakistan context. But, as noted by the four Cold War warriors, George Shultz, Henry Kissinger, Sam Nunn, and William Perry, reliance on nuclear weapons for this intention is becoming more and more risky and decreasingly effectual.[17] Particularly, the irresponsible behaviour of nuclear-armed Pakistan in South Asia might prove cataclysmic. As Pakistan is enlarging its nuclear arsenal, the risks are mounting. That some terrorist organizations may get access to nuclear weapons as they have repeatedly attacked military installations where the country's nuclear weapons are stockpiled.[18]

Furthermore, Hans M. Kristensen and Robert Norris, identified Pakistan and China as either having or developing non-strategic nuclear weapons.[19] As Kristensen told, Pakistan had made obvious that it was developing its nuclear-capable Nasr or Hatf IX (60-kilometer range) missile 'for use against invading Indian troop formations that Pakistan doesn't have the conventional capabilities to defeat.'[20]

These strides, on the other side, have unfolded the deficiencies of India's NFU pledge to deter Pakistan's destabilising strategy against India. For one reason, this policy pronunciation relieves Pakistan from the ambiguity and worry that India might consider the pre-emptive use of nuclear weapons to meet the terrorist attacks or sub-conventional offensives by Pakistan. Pakistan could also move to the level of deploying its short-range Nasr missile without being alarmed that India would aim it with its own nuclear missiles. For another reason, the belief is in-built in India's nuclear doctrine that any level of nuclear aggression will provoke massive retaliation is too extreme to add much credibility.[21]

Furthermore, in an inimical confrontation between two nuclear armed adversaries, the choice of massive retaliation by one side would unhesitatingly prompt a counter strike with a similar blow. How would the mutual annihilation, that would follow, fulfil the ends of national security? This is an open question that must stimulate greater manifestation on how to formulate a more suitable Indian strategy to meet Pakistan's threat of using tactical nuclear weapons in crises situations along the India-Pakistan border or across the Line of Control (LoC).[22]

Nuclear armed Pakistan, for its part, has not tolerated India's NFU policy on the ground that as a conventionally weaker nation-state, it has to rely on nuclear weapons to guarantee its security. However, a common sense forewarns that deployment of tactical nuclear weapons along the border leaves these arms susceptible to attack which, in turn, could breed a 'use or lose' mindset on the part of Pakistan, the deployer country, and the onus would be on India to prevent escalation.[23] Pakistan holds the view that positioning tactical nuclear weapons along the India-Pakistan border in a state of battle-readiness would qualify it to counter India's Cold Start doctrine, which foresees locating offensive, battle-ready forces along the India-Pakistan border to prevent any cross-border offensive.

Following this kind of modus operandi and modus vivendi, Pakistan has upped the nuclear ante in South Asia by choosing to adopt tactical nuclear weapons because they lower the nuclear threshold, the point at which nuclear weapons are brought into use.[24] As such, they are straining South Asia's deterrence stability, the idea that roughly equal nuclear capabilities will deter adversaries from using these weapons.[25] Pakistan asserts that deploying its tactical nukes would facilitate it with 'full spectrum deterrence' against India. It would also be enabled to respond to any offensive operations India might think of against Pakistan in reaction to another Mumbai-type terrorist hit.

The fussy risk of this deployment blueprint is that it generates stress to pass on to field commanders the right to employ these missiles in an emergency situation. In addition, the domestic circumstances in Pakistan have been speedily worsening over the last few decades. How far this ever dysfunctional system can sustain a viable nuclear strategy is an alarming jigsaw-puzzle.

India's current Nuclear Doctrine is faced with an in-built dilemma of acquiring a 'credible minimum deterrent.' But India is attempting to build a force structure that would almost be identical in quality, if not in quantity, to that developed by the United States or Russia in due course of time. In this way, India is in search of a strategic triad consisting of land-based, air-borne, and underwater nuclear weapon systems that will consume huge material and financial resources, along with human capital.

It is obviously arguable whether India's strategic circumstances necessitate a naval constituent for its deterrent capability or whether the country needs only a submarine-based deterrent force on the conjecture that the nuclear deterrent position eventually relies on the survivability of the nuclear stockpiles. Land-based and air-borne systems are more exposed to counter-strikes and devastation than submarine-based missile systems are. This issue has not been sincerely addressed in India, thus culminating into a strident demand from the three services that the government should admit to create some constituent of the nuclear deterrent to strengthen each of them.

Indeed, critical appreciation is all-pervasive that there is a trivial notion about the size and composition of India's nuclear forces and what its 'credible minimum deterrent' encompasses in terms of quality and quantity of weapons systems. Contrary to discussing these subjects, official spokespersons have contended that it is not viable to define what a 'credible minimum deterrent' necessitates, since there can be no rigidity in this connection. This implies that the emerging shape of the 'credible minimum deterrent' is a moving bench-mark.

Stress on the 'No-First Use' Pledge

The 'No-First Use (NFU)' pledge engrossed in India's nuclear doctrine encompasses certain notable shortcomings. Initially, a NFU is identical to a pronouncement of non-use against nation-states that do not possess nuclear weapons. However, in its 1998 policy initiative, a modification was introduced by marking that nation-states that do not possess nuclear weapons but are 'aligned with' nuclear-weapon states (NWS) were not covered.[26] The repercussion would be that non-nuclear-weapon states (NNWS) allied with India's nuclear-armed enemies—evidently, China or Pakistan—could be hit with Indian nuclear warheads, if the ally or both together were to have launched a nuclear strike against India first.

In 2003, when the Nuclear Doctrine was promulgated, India further extended the doctrinal reality by warning that it might use nuclear weapons in response to a 'major attack' with chemical or biological weapons, admittedly indicating the calculated uncertainty of a nuclear posture in relation to attacks with non-conventional arms other than nuclear ones.[27] This exposition of India's No-First Use (NFU) pledge made through the policy and posture encapsulated in its Nuclear Doctrine is inconsistent due to many astounding factors and underlying limitations, which can be enumerated as under:

- The NFU pledge does not count the probable scenarios of an offensive by transnational terrorists and their outfits, which is currently an imminent challenge looming large on the horizon.
- How would a 'major attack' with biological or chemical weapons be detected? Non-state actors or transnational terrorist organizations might be attracted to use these weapons due to the comparatively cost-effectiveness as well as their low-cost production, storage, camouflage, and portability.
- Technically, it is hard to identify the doer in a biological or chemical weapons offensive that could be perpetrated by a nation-state or transnational non-state actors or, not unthinkably, by a non-state actor supported by a nation-state.

- It is also suggestible that emerging India should uphold a nuclear posture, which is not 'weaker' than those of nuclear weapon states like the United States or China.[28] For example, when China was unreliably seen as having modified its own No-First Use pledge in 2013, some Indian observers started pleading that India should follow suit.[29]
- If India's nuclear rivals are initiating assertive ventures, it should do so too even if a response, with a structure of a more formidable doctrine, would take for granted a totally distinct shape. For example, India should counter to a nuclear rival's triad build-up as a form a 'change in posture' by modifying its No-First Use policy, requiring a 'change in its doctrine.'
- As a necessity to strengthen the nuclear deterrence, a threat of first use can implant larger improbability in India's nuclear rivals and thereby deter them from even non-nuclear conventional/sub-conventional provocative adventurism.
- As a desire to retain the pre-emption option on its part, arguably, first use would enable India to counter an enemy's imminent nuclear use, reducing the probable collateral destruction on the Indian side, providing India's comparatively small nuclear-armed forces with a better opportunity or survivability, or both.

India's NFU pledge cannot be isolated from its overall calculus of Nuclear Doctrine as it has evolved ever since 1999. Having realized the inadequacies as discernible, this doctrine warrants to be revisited in the light of adjustments, readjustments and transformations over the preceding one and half decade's vis-à-vis its nuclear enemies. On the other hand, Pakistan relies heavily on its first strike doctrine to deter conventional conflict with India and, under the shadow of its nuclear umbrella, it continues to wage low intensity 'proxy war' against India in Jammu & Kashmir and elsewhere. It is obviously for this reason that Pakistan is not ready to accept India's no-first use offer of a bilateral treaty as a nuclear Confidence Building Measure.[30]

Avoiding Rather than Risking Armageddon

The choice of nuclear-armed India and Pakistan lies between risking Armageddon and creating Nirvana.[31] India's Nuclear Doctrine in its present form entails that nuclear retaliation against a first strike would be 'massive' and intended to inflict 'unacceptable damage' upon the attacking country. This is a complicated idea because, ethically, killing or maiming a large part of the non-combatant population violates the laws of war, along with the limits on the means and methods of warfare. Besides, threatening massive retaliatory response against any form of nuclear offensive, which would indispensably prompt assured nuclear devastation in the mutually inimical circumstances, is almost not a credible alternative. Undoubtedly, it generates a complicated situation and asks: Would India then resort to either a counterforce or counter-city/counter-value strategy? Having learnt from the experiences of the two Super Powers during the Mutually Assured Destruction situation, we must admit to accept that it makes 'more strategic sense to slide over from a retaliatory targeting doctrine to one based more on counter-force targeting of military and political assets. This would actually enhance the credibility of deterrence by making it more likely that the threat of a nuclear response would be credible to a potential aggressor.'[32]

In a nuclear confrontation scenario, moreover, the inescapability of mutual annihilation must also be well-thought out. Is a counter-force strike on the enemy's military forces and installations the alternative? The ticklish problem of uncontainable escalation then surfaces, for which there is no comforting response. Keeping the initiative of how India should retaliate to a nuclear first strike at the prudence of the prime minister would give larger flexibility to launch the counter-attack instead of threatening assured nuclear annihilation, which is just not be credible.

It is very often elapsed that 'massive retaliation' was not always a component of India's doctrine. India's 1999 draft doctrine promised only 'punitive' retaliation, a workable phrase compatible with both limited and higher-level nuclear strike. It was mentioned three times in the document, signifying that substantial concern was observed into its practice. Yet, four years later, the précis of India's 2003 promulgated doctrine emphasized that 'nuclear retaliation to a first strike will be massive and designed to inflict unacceptable damage.'[33] Indian worries over the credibility of massive retaliation have been long-standing and have intensified in recent years, mainly because of Pakistan's reported development of tactical nuclear weapons and their deployment, which themselves can be found under the broader grouping of limited nuclear options.[34]

As debated, Pakistani tactical nuclear weapons are supposed to hold back India's capability to conduct limited conventional war in retaliation for terrorist attacks certified by the Pakistani patrons, including ISI. This is because if Pakistan used tactical nuclear weapons while refraining from striking Indian population centres in the onslaught, a massive Indian nuclear counter-strike would not be a relatively credible response. Adding together, Pakistan's strategic nuclear weapons would provide the guarantee that it could then launch a new round of nuclear retaliation against Indian population centres, were India to have first launched an attack on Pakistani population centres, thereby constituting a further cover of deterrence against India.

Whereas India itself is progressively more prepared to fight a limited war, 'massive retaliation' presupposes a war with unlimited means for unlimited ends.[35] If wars are limited, the sense of punishment must be subsidiary to the sense of war termination.[36] Limited objectives necessitate that a country terminates a war at the first probable chance attuned with these objectives. Because, given a chance, 'massive retaliation' can escalate a conflict to a higher level of annihilation, favouring 'highly calibrated Indian counter-response to terminate war at the lowest possible level of nuclear exchange.'[37]

As seen from an official angle, India's decision-making elites have openly asserted that, despite restraints, they will not be self-deterred from resorting to the letter and spirit of their doctrinal posture on 'massive retaliation.' Former Foreign Secretary Shyam Saran, shielded India's nuclear doctrine and posture from a range of vitriolic denigrations. According to him, '[If India] is attacked with such weapons, it would engage in nuclear retaliation which will be massive and designed to inflict unacceptable damage on the adversary.' As I have pointed out earlier, the label on a nuclear weapon used for attacking India, strategic or tactical, is irrelevant from the Indian perspective. According to Rear Admiral Raja Menon, 'The ideational systems that will ensure the 'massive' retaliation promised in [India's] doctrine are being increasingly questioned by scholars and analysts worldwide'[38] and lamented that India should replace 'massive' with 'punitive,' as was the case in India's 1999 draft doctrine, with the aim of signalling India's 'readiness to fight an escalatory nuclear war.'[39] Similarly, Brig. (retd.) Gurmeet Kanwal, fostered the view that the word 'massive'...should be substituted with 'punitive' as massive is not credible and limits retaliatory options.[40]

Many other strategic analysts and informed minds have argued likewise.[41] Looking at future challenges, India will have to bring together its nuclear flexibility with outstandingly strong and constructive civilian control authority. It is noteworthy that India's existing chain of command with regard to nuclear weapons works under the rubric of a Nuclear Command Authority (NCA) and a Strategic Forces Command (SFC). The Prime Minister has been designated as the 'release authority.' He has the indisputable authority to make a decision whether, when, and how to use nuclear weapons.

The Strategic Forces Command (SFC) is headed by a commander-in-chief, coming from one of the three services of the Indian Armed Forces, on a rotational basis. The SFC is located within the Integrated Defence Headquarters in the Ministry of Defence. But it also functions under the Chiefs of Staff Committee. Its chairman is the most senior service chief, which ensures that the post rotates among the three services, without any fixed tenure. A conscious arrangement is evidently required, however, to affirm the primacy of civilian control over the military at all levels of the nuclear command arrangement.

The point of difficulty emanating from this arrangement is that a tri-service command like the Strategic Forces Command (SFC) should, sensibly, function under a single line of authority representing the tri-services, like a Chief of Defence Staff (CDS), who would be a singular advice-giver to the government on sensitive security matters, including nuclear contingency. The option of a CDS has been recommended by numerous inquiry committees, it must not remain in limbo and unimplemented.[42]

Conclusion and Recommendations

Keeping in view the fragile politico-strategic variables of the nuclear calculus, a meticulous review of India's Nuclear Doctrine is irrevocably required to concentrate on all the pertinent issues in their entirety. Obviously, none of the core issues that strain India's Nuclear Doctrine inherits trouble-free responses in letter and spirit. For example, centrally, the historical realities and arguments on India's 'Credible Minimum Deterrence' and the 'NFU' pledge are to be revisited to agree and devise viable options for the foreseeable future.

The matter of whether the retaliatory nuclear counter-strike should resort to a counter-force or counter-value/counter-city strategy can be discussed at length. However, a rational discourse on this and other contentious issues is an irrevocable need of the hour. The major issues that call themselves for reappraisal include India's command-and-control preparations with a sense of higher degree of transparency, the perils seized within guaranteed 'massive retaliation' and 'punitive' riposte, which foreshadow self-annihilation, adding superior substance to the idea of 'credible minimum deterrence,' and revisiting or renouncing the No-First Use (NFU) pledge in view of its various considered lapses and fallibilities.

It would also be sensible to realize that India's main nuclear security tribulations crop up not from the calculated formulations of its Nuclear Doctrine but from the nuances and intricacies of its highly fragile geo-strategic circumstances. India confronts two nuclear rivals—Pakistan and China—that have the benefit of close nexus with each other. It is crystal-clear that Pakistan's nuclear weapons are undeniably aimed at Indian targets and are under the command and control of the Pakistan's military organ. But the talks on nuclear problems and confidence and security building measures (CSBMs) have been assigned to Pakistan's civilian establishment, which is evidently deficient in authority and operates under the close direction of the military. How, then, should India hold talks on ticklish nuclear quandaries and questions in a fragile situation in South Asia?

There is a larger unanimity that the actual threats from Pakistan's nuclear weapons germinate from extremists' thinking to gain trigger-hunt control over them. The ingenuity with which terrorists had attacked Pakistani military installations and headquarters clearly indicated the failure of its military to protect its critical infrastructures of command and control, as well as the complexities of possible survival during any conspiracy hatched with support of transnational terrorist organizations or non-state actors. In addition, the growing potency of suicidal terrorists along with their technical capabilities might enable them to use rudimentary-type radiological or 'dirty bombs.' Prevailing domestic compulsions and disorganized management and direction in the Pakistani establishments have added fresh fuel to fire in this situation. On the other hand, India should be readied to make a sustained quest for viable options, coupled with the realizations that 'if you wish for peace, understand war.'

NOTES

1. Dr. Manmohan Singh's Inaugural Speech at IDSA, New Delhi, April 2, 2014, [Online: web] Accessed 22 July 2012; URL: http://idsa.in/keyspeeches/InauguralAddressShri ManmohanSingh.html.
2. Bharatiya Janata Party, Election Manifesto 2014, March 26, 2014, p. 39, [Online: web] Accessed 22 July 2012; URL: http://www.bjp.org/images/pdf_2014/full_manifesto_english_07.04.2014.pdf.
3. I. Bagchi (2014), "India Not Revisiting Its Nuclear Doctrine, Modi Assures Japan," The Times of India, August 30, [Online: web] Accessed 2 June 2012; URL: http://timesofindia.indiatimes.com/india/India-not-revisiting-its-nuclear-doctrine-Modi-assures-Japan/articleshow/41231521.cms.
4. GOI (1999), "Doctrin," MEA, New Delhi, August 17, clause 2.3, [Online: web] Accessed 22 July 2012; URL:http://mea.gov.in/in-focus-article.htm?18916/Draft+Report+of+National+ Security+Advisory+Board+on+Indian
5. S.D. Sagan (2009), "The Evolution of Pakistani and Indian Nuclear Doctrines," in Scott

Douglas Sagan (ed,), "Inside Nuclear South Asia," Stanford Security Studies, Stanford, CA, p. 245-251.

6. P.R.Chari (2012), "India's Nuclear Doctrine: An Alternative Blueprint" Institute of Peace and Conflict Studies, New Delhi, [Online: web] Accessed 12 December 2012; URL: http:/ /www.ipcs.org/Indias-Nuclear-Doctrine.pdf.
7. B.S. Nagal (2014), "Checks and Balances", Force Magazine, [Online: web] Accessed 12 December 2012; URL: http://www.forceindia.net/Checks_and_Balances.aspx. Ibid
8. Ibid.
9. Ibid.
10. Ibid.
11. Bruno Tertrais (2009), "The Trouble with No First Use," *Survival*, Vol. 51, No. 5:24-25.
12. Rajendra Prasad (2011), "Global War on Terror: The Role Reversal", *Defence and Security Alert*, Vol. 2, Issue 7:80-82.
13. Rajendra Prasad (2012), "Preventing Armageddon: Search for a New Strategy," *Defence and Security Alert*, Vol 3, Issue 4, January: 50-54.
14. Nitin Gokhale (2012), "Execise Sudarshan Shakti: Validating Doctrine", *Defence and Security Alert*, Vol. 3, Issue 4, January: 86-88.
15. Rajendra Prasad (1988), India's Civil Defence in the Nuclear Age", Prakash Book Depot, Bareilly, 1988, also, see: Ron Rosenbaum(2011), How The End Begins, The Road To A Nuclear World War III, Simon &Schuster: London.
16. Pakistani PM Nawaz Sharif said, "...They (People of Pakistan) are confidant for the first time in history that in the eventuality of an armed attack, they will be able to meet it on equal terms." Quoted in Rajendra Prasad (2012), "Preventing Armageddon: Search for a New Strategy", *Defence and Security Alert*, Vol.4, Issue 4, January:54.
17. G. Shultz, H. Kissinger, S. Nunn, and W. Perry (2007), "The Global Zero" *Wall Street Journal*, January 4, [Online: web] Accessed 12 December 2012; URL: http://online.wsj.com/ news/articles/SB116787515251566636.
18. Banyan (2012), "Nuclear Profusion", *The Economist*, August 25, 2012, For a justification of terrorists' effort to acquire nuclear devices or fissile material, see: G. Tenet, At the Center of the Storm: My Years at the CIA, Harper Collins, New York, 2007.
19. There is no agreed upon definition on what constitutes a non-strategic nuclear weapon. In addition to "non-strategic," frequent terms used to describe this category of weapons include "battlefield," "short-range", "tactical" and "theater" nuclear weapons. For a description, see: Hans M. Kristensen (2011), "Pakistan's 'Shoot and Scoot' Nukes: FAS Nukes in Newsweek," FAS Strategic Security Blog, May 17, [Online: web] Accessed 12 December 2012; URL: http://www.fas.org/blog/ssp/2011/05/pakistan.php.
20. Ibid.
21. P.R. Chari (2014), "India's Nuclear Doctrine: Stirrings of Change," Carnegie Endowment for International Peace, June 4, [Online: web] Accessed 22 November 2015; URL: http:/ /carnegieendowment.org/2014/06/04/india-s-nuclear-doctrine-stirrings-of-change/hcks.
22. S. Thapiyal (2012), "Subcontinental Dilemma", *Defence and Security Alert*, Vol.3, Issue $, January:89-90.
23. Ibid.
24. M. Chansoria (2014), "Pak nukes upping nuclear ante in South Asia", *The Nation*, May7, [Online: web] Accessed 22 November 2015; URL: http://nation.com.pk/national/07-May-2014/pak-nukes-upping-nuclear-ante-in-south-asia-indian-expert.
25. Ibid
26. GOI "Doctrine," MEA, New Delhi, August 17, 1999, clause 2.5.

27. S. D. Sagan, "Evolution of Pakistani and Indian Nuclear Doctrine," in Scott D. Sagan (ed.), op.cit., p. 249; Also see: Scott D. Sagan, "The Commitment Trap: Why the United States Should Not Use Nuclear Threats to Deter Biological and Chemical Weapons Attacks," *International Security*, Vol. 24, No. 4, April 1, 2000, p. 85.
28. T. Farrell (2005), "World Culture and Military Power," *Security Studies*, Vol. 14, No. 3, p. 454.
29. Adityanjee (2013), "No First Use Nuclear Doctrine with 'Chinese Characteristics' ", Vivekananda International Foundation, May 2, [Online: web] Accessed 22 November 2014; URL: http://www.vifindia.org/article/2013/may/02/no-first-use-nuclear-doctrine-with-chinese-characteristics.
30. G. Kanwal (2004), "Pakistan's Nuclear Threshold and India's Options", Air Power Journal, Vol.1. No.1.
31. B. Riedel (2013), "Avoiding Armageddon", Harper Collins Publishing India, Noida, p.202.
32. B.S. Klein (1994), "Strategic Studies and World Order, The Global Politics of Deterrence", Cambridge University Press, New York.
33. Indian Prime Minister's Office, "Cabinet Committee on Security Reviews Progress in Operationalizing India's Nuclear Doctrine," January 4, 2003. [Online: web] Accessed 5 November 2015; URL: http://pib.nic.in/archieve/lreleng/lyr2003/rjan2003/04012003/r040120033.html.
34. Pakistan prefers the term "battlefield weapon system" to replace "tactical nuclear weapon." Shashank Joshi (2013), "Pakistan's Tactical Nuclear Nightmare: Déjà Vu?" The Washington Quarterly, Vol. 36, No. 3, Summer:161.
35. Gaurav Kampani (2013), "India: The Challenges of Nuclear Operationalization and Strategic Stability," in A. J. Tellis, A. M. Denmark, and T. Tanner (eds.), *Strategic Asia 2013-14: Asia in the Second Nuclear Age*, Washington: National Bureau of Asian Research, p. 118.
36. A. J. Tellis (2011), "India's Emerging Nuclear Posture: Between Recessed Deterrent and Ready Arsenal", RAND, Santa Monica, CA, pp. 364-366.
37. Kampani, "India," p. 119.
38. R. Menon (2014), "A Mismatch of Nuclear Doctrines," *The Hindu*, January 22.
39. R. Menon (2014), "Boxed In by Pakistan," *Indian Express*, September 8.
40. G. Kanwal (2015), "India's Nuclear Doctrine: Reviewing NFU and Massive Retaliation," Institute of Peace and Conflict Studies, January 7. [Online: web] Accessed 2 December 2015; URL: http://www.ipcs.org/article/india/indias-nuclear-doctrine-reviewing-nfu-and-massive-retaliation-4798.html.
41. J. Prasad (2014), "For a Clear Nuclear Doctrine," *The Hindu*, May 6; Also, see: R. Sood, "Should India Revise Its Nuclear Doctrine?" Policy Brief, No. 18, (Asia Pacific Leadership Network for Nuclear Non-Proliferation, Canberra, December 2014), p.11;
42. G. Kanwal (2013), "Chief of Defence Staff Must Be Appointed Immediately", IDSA Comment, [Online: web] Accessed 22 July 2015; URL:http://www.idsa.in/idsacomments/ChiefofDefenceStaffmustbeAppointedImmediately_gkanwal_121213.html.

17

State, Violence and Maoists: Elusive Peace?

Uddipan Mukherjee

"Violence is an irresistible instrument for the insurgents—more so for the Maoists as their philosophy, strategy and methodology compel them to tread the path of violence. Violence could be cathartic to the protestors, at the same time it challenges the edifice of state-structure. In this complex matrix, the paper attempts to discern the chequered path of peace."

"Francis Fukuyama asserts that the monopoly of legitimate power that states exercise allows individuals to escape what Hobbes labelled the 'war of every man against every man'—that is, the rudderless state of anarchy. As if to buttress the argument of Fukuyama, comes in to the rescue the sociologist Max Weber's definition of the state as 'a human community that (successfully) claims the monopoly of the legitimate use of physical force within a given territory.' Friedrich and Brzezinski (1965) described the 'totalitarian' state—which tried to abolish the whole of civil society and subordinate the individuals to its own political ends. It had both right as well as left wing expressions—Nazism, Fascism and Stalinism being the representative variants."[1]

As explicitly stressed by Fukuyama, the essence of stateness is enforcement: the ultimate ability to send someone with a uniform and a gun to force people to comply with the laws enunciated by the state.[2] Beyond all reasonable doubt, be it a lathi-wielding Daroga in colonized India or an upgraded version of a policeman in post-colonial India, is there any wonder why both are symbols of authority—reasons being manifold.

Partha Chatterjee writes that the basic apparatus of governmental administration in independent India was inherited from the colonial period. Indeed, the administration consists of a small cadre of Indian Administrative Service (IAS) aided by the Indian Police Service (IPS) specifically for law and order: both as All India Services (the personnel are allotted a 'cadre' or a province); with provincial civil services working under IAS, and Central Civil Services for specialized functions like railways, defence sectors and the like.[3] To say that the working of the High Courts and district courts, as Chatterjee claims, 'maintained an unbroken history from colonised times, continuing the same practices of legal tradition and precedent,' would surely be close to exaggeration, but nevertheless the assertion is hard to negate on all fronts even now; and not at all may be, at least in the first two decades till 1967. State and politics in India from 1947 to 1967 was a period of the formation of a developmental state. It implied significant intervention of the government in the economy through the progressive taxation of personal and corporate incomes and the consequent provision by the state of public services such as education, health and transport. And Chatterjee exonerates the Indian state thus: 'This was perhaps the principal governmental function that legitimized the post-colonial state.'

But a sad fact remains that the 1960s saw an acute food shortage in the country. There was also a severe foreign exchange crisis, exacerbated by the hugely increased defence expenditures in the wake of the wars with China and Pakistan in 1962 and 1965, respectively. With high food prices and slowing down of growth, as a natural corollary, economic hardship skyrocketed. Data too corroborates the affirmation—the CPI Inflation in India was 17 per cent and 14 per cent in 1964 and 1966, respectively. Pockets of the hoi polloi were cut and this was reflected in massive and often violent agitations all over the country. Marxist accounts/narratives, according to Chatterjee, explained these conflicts and the repressive use of state power as systematic features of Indian democracy. The effect of inflation and the 'Hindu rate of growth' were ostensible in the political lanes too. Indian National Congress [INC] lost control in six provinces and for the first time in post-colonial India it lost in West Bengal. The United Front – Left Front [UF-LF] coalition emerged victorious.[4]

Land was the crux of the problem in the then West Bengal.[5] The UF-LF government pledged to bring about the long overdue land reforms—a contentious issue which the communists were championing since the 1940s. Incidentally, a veteran CPM peasant leader Harekrishna Konar donned the role of Minister in charge of land and land revenue. He announced a policy of quick distribution of surplus land among the landless and prohibiting the eviction of sharecroppers. However, as Banerjee lets us understand, that CPM was unsure of the modus operandi of recovering the land transferred by landlords under the 'benami' head.

Violence

The late 1960s and especially 1966-68 is a period which modern history so peculiarly boasts of revolutions, cutting across regions and continents and a phase when student agitation gained unprecedented ground. Whether it was Berlin or Paris or Calcutta, intellectual stimulus had engineered student movements, highly radicalized in thought and action. Blame it on the zealot-philosophers Frantz Fanon, Herbert Marcuse or Jean-Paul Sartre! Fanon passed away due to leukaemia in 1961, but before that his firebrand writing achieved what it could. In his monograph 'The Wretched of the Earth', he wrote: '...this same violence will be vindicated and appropriated when, taking history into their own hands, the colonized swarm into the forbidden cities.' Fanon believed, as Peter Reed illuminates, that society had to be changed and could only be changed through violence, and violence was a personal cathartic—an individual could only find true expression and release in violence. It was a period of the rise of the 'New Left.' Marcuse believed that man in Western capitalist society was every bit as enslaved as his counterpart in the totalitarian societies of the Soviet bloc. The New Left rejected both Western capitalism and Soviet-esque communism. According to the New Left, the state maintained a dominant class interest through violence, psychological as well as physical. Hence, it was 'just' to use violence against the state as an instrument of emancipation.[6]

Nevertheless, violence was glamorous and in the post-1967 world, as Reed opines, rugged good looks and violence came together in the ideal poster: Che Guevara. Heroic failure was more potent than success.[7] 1967 was an eventful year—death of a student in Berlin in a fracas with the police which later on assumed deadly proportions in the rise of the Baader-Meinhoff gang and its series of abductions and highjackings, the death of Che Guevara in a Bolivian ravine and the commencement of the historic Naxalbari uprising in India's eastern province of West Bengal.

On 18 March 1967, 16 days after the formation of the UF-LF government, a peasants' conference was held under the auspices of CPM's

Siliguri sub-division in the Darjeeling district of West Bengal. The conference called for the ending of monopoly ownership of land by the landlords, redistribution of land through peasants' committees, and organization and arming of the peasants in order to destroy the resistance of landlords and rural reactionaries.[8] The conference further cautioned the landless to be prepared for a protracted armed struggle. Eviction of Bigul Kisan by a jotedar in spite of a court order in his favour acted as a spark for the melee. Naxalbari quickly came to enjoy an iconic status among Indian revolutionaries.[9]. 'Naxalite' became shorthand for 'revolutionary', a term which evoked romance and enchantment at one end of the political spectrum and distaste and derision at the other.[10]

As Sumanta Banerjee informs, Charu Mazumdar was a frail heart patient. However, he emulated the likes of Mao, Guevara, Castro or may be the monstrous Cambodian dictator Pol Pot in unleashing the 'Eight Documents.' He attempted to substantiate the use of violence against the Indian state by positing his Theory of Annihilation of class enemies. While building the theoretical framework of the movement; partly Marxist-Leninist, else anarcho-communist and verily fanning the sentiments of the youth and the dispossessed by glorifying violence; Mazumdar blew the trumpet: 'Make the 1970s the decade of liberation.'

The students of Presidency College and Jadavpur University spilled out into the rural backyards of Bengal to 'spread' the revolution—with an apparent Cuban-styled 'foco-ism' without however, explicitly and unequivocally accepting the modus operandi. Nonetheless, violence was the fuel—driving the engine of revolution. The class enemy was not clearly defined, but the 'annihilation' campaign was on—which was sometimes grotesquely evidenced in the form of 'police-wallahs' being murdered in broad daylight, often while not on duty and unarmed. Rag-pickers being branded as informers were also not spared the 'fasces' in the name of the revolution—or may be at the altar of Rousseau's ever misconstrued General Will or the new-found Maoism, which over enthusiastically claimed 'Chairman Mao as Our Chairman;' a term strongly objected to and refuted by the Chinese.

Along with the tumultuous demonstration in Calcutta though, the countryside remained the main arena of the movement. Annihilation of usurious landlords through small squad actions, operations which were bloated to be guerrilla warfare, were carried out with impunity—with the fervent hope that such numerous gory actions would definitely raise the revolutionary consciousness of the masses. Rather, to the contrary, such dissolute actions by the Naxalites only hastened their loss of connectivity with the people and paved the way for their eventual defeat in the first phase of the movement and triggered the dismemberment of the party—along the pro-mass line and the pro-annihilation line. The chief architect of the Annihilation Theory, Mazumdar was finally arrested by the Calcutta police on 16 July 1972 and lived only 12 days after his arrest.[11] Was indiscriminate use of violence the fundamental cause of the demise of the romantic revolutionary vision? Indubitably, it was one among others, if not the primary reason.

Violence was ruling the roost—inter-party murders, assassinations of police personnel, and torture of the Naxalites in the physical realm while an ambience of fear, feeling of being in a war-zone; in the psychological sphere. The debacle of the Naxalites, however, was critically dependent on the lack of armed preparedness and the imperfect development of the People's Liberation Guerrilla Army (PLGA). Military affairs were given secondary weightage vis-a-vis political indoctrination by the Bengalee *bhadralok* revolutionary—again a gross misunderstanding of the Maoist souvenir. Kanu Sanyal differed ideologically with Mazumdar's line in as far as developing the mass organizations were concerned. Interestingly, this dichotomy would turn out to be the seeds for the next level synthesis of the Naxalite/Maoist programme in India, though after considerable bloodshed and energies sapped and time consumed.[12] And as Banerjee described, the movement fizzled away with a 'farrango of factions' and gradually the scene as well as the leadership rotated outwards to Bihar and Andhra Pradesh. The baton of the race which was left unattended was picked up by two disconnected groups—the Kanhai Chatterjee-Amulya Sen faction giving rise to the Maoist Communist Centre (MCC) in Bihar whereas the three Andhra groups—led by Nagi Reddy, Chandra Pulla Reddy and Kondapalli Seetharamayyiah (KS, in short) finally in the 1980s reflecting the KS-bred People's War ([CPI (M-L) (PW)] as the major faction.

Maoists

From the spreading of the movement in Andhra during 1978-85 to coming under heavy state repression in 1985-90 and again resurgence in 1990-92, and culminating in a ban in 1992; the Naxalite movement was not only given a fresh life but also a new direction. On 22 April 1980, the CPI (M-L) (P-W) was proclaimed on a formal basis. Among other things, around 1982, the group formulated an important document called the 'Guerrilla Zone Perspective' and attempted to enter Dandakaranya.[13] Former BBC journalist,

Shubhrangshu Choudhary, tells that a Bengali from Hyderabad, Tushar Kanti Bhattacharyya was sent by the group to form the first squad in the strategic junction of Karimnagar district—a tri-junction where the borders of Andhra, Maharashtra and Madhya Pradesh meet.[14] Actually, the document was an imperative in order to launch guerrilla warfare against the state—something which was lacking during the early days of the movement. In fact, presently too, though the Maoists are under heavy doses of police and paramilitary vigilance, if mainstream media reports are to be believed, they are trying to create similar guerrilla bases in the Sahayadri mountains and in the Malabar.[15] Interestingly, the Maoists of late, especially in the last couple of years, have time and again in various forums acknowledged that they are under severe constraints.

The choice of *Dandakaranya* was strategically obvious—a geographical area which sprawls across Odisha, Madhya Pradesh, Andhra (now Telangana) and Chhattisgarh. To 'create' the bases, KS sent seven teams of seven members each towards the region. Incidentally, one team was led by Ramji *aka* Koteshwar Rao alias Kishenji. The guerrilla zone was to be realized through an undeclared, yet implicitly evident foco-theory popularised by Che.[16]

Foco-ism [Spanish: foquismo]

To quote Che from Guerrilla Warfare, 'In my opinion, considering the normal desertion and weakness in spite of the rigorous process of selection, there should be a nucleus of 30–50 men...'

The vanguard 'foco', however, does not solely radicalise the peasantry; in addition, the peasants serve to politicise the guerrilla fighters and vice-versa in a symbiotic revolutionary relationship. Although the proletariat does not play the primary role in the insurrectionary stage, its participation will be fundamental in the post-revolutionary period.[17] It is also a demand by Che that foco theory discovers Marxism naturally and it accords primacy to military actions over political ones. However, Guevara's increasing theoretical rigidity is seen in the prologue he wrote to Vo Nguyen Giap's 'People's War, People's Army'—wherein he claimed that in Vietnam too, the liberation struggle began with a mobile guerrilla foco.

Did KS and his seven squads create the revolution in *Dandakaranya* through an insurrectional foco? It is not unlikely, at least on the theoretical plane. But on the ground, it had to be a combination of mass organizations, squad-level operations and consequent formation of local militia, under the banner of a vanguard party—a theoretical merger of Leninism, Maoism and Guevaraism—and in the process re-discovering Marxism in their own way. The guerrilla zone has been established though and a protracted people's war against the state is on in *Dandakaranya* at present. The passing of the leadership to Ganapathy in 1991 and the merger of the PW with MCC in 2004, just at the commencement of the Andhra Peace Talks, surely provided fresh turns to the movement. The Naxalites started to be called as Maoists and the movement turned more organized and hence hierarchical and more militarized. Incidents of Jehanabad in Bihar (2005), Nayagarh in Odisha (2008), and Dantewada ambush of the 75 security personnel (2010), along with scores of others, pointed to the new-found vigour of the Maoists inasmuch as undertaking massive operations were concerned. And they were bolstered by the unity of the Bihar and Andhra groups—accepting the role of a vanguard party (Leninism) and the need for a Protracted People's War (PPW) through guerrilla warfare as tutored by Mao Zedong (Maoism).[18]

Regular ambushes entrapping the security forces at Dantewada (Chhattisgarh) or Gadchiroli (Maharashtra) or Jharkhand evinced their capabilities in guerrilla warfare techniques and moreover gave a clear expression to the fact that the guerrilla zone had been established—and this couldn't have been done without a thorough knowledge of the topography and without winning the 'hearts and minds' of the local populace. The lack of governance as a historical factor in these backward, yet resource rich regions, was the prime factor for the Maoists to intrude. Furthermore, it is germane to mention that whether pre or post-independence, government officials *aka* state was reportedly notorious in dealing with the tribal population; whether it was alleged sexual exploitation of tribal women or open abetment of the oppression by the local non-tribal gentry. The success of the tendu-leaf movement of the tribals against the contractors is a case in point. The irony of the situation though is now the Maoists themselves demand revolutionary tax from the tribals—once emancipators, turned exploiters. The post-2004 Maoists did face violent repression both from the state, which was desperate to station its infrastructure and other democratic moorings in the region, and also from non-state actors like the erstwhile vigilante group and now banned (according to a verdict of India's Apex Court) *Salwa Judum* or 'Purification Hunt' (in Gondi language).[19] If recent media reports are to be given any weightage, the Maoists are lamenting the non-existence of *Salwa Judum*—since due to lack of oppression, a steady stream of recruits into the Maoist camp has been clogged. It's again to re-iterate that violence sustains the movement and the movement further augments violence—a spiral energizing itself. Needless to mention that perpetrators of violence in this theatre have vested interests to continue it, foment it, nurture it—after all it's a protracted war, a war of attrition, and the endgame is clearly unclear; it's certainly being fought by the people, a tribal, a policeman or a *jawan* of the Central Reserve forces; whether it's being fought for the people is, however, a matter of intense debate.

Peace

Periods of peace are to be treated as punctuation marks in the path of the Protracted People's War (PPW), suitably adjusted, keeping in view the relative power exercised by the state and the insurgents. Talking with/to the state authorities is a viable option, rather a tactical choice when the period is a downslide for them or if they plan to re-group/re-orient/re-configure. Peace is definitely an asset in times of distress or more technically speaking, Strategic Defence. At other situations, when the Maoists claim to push the ground towards a Strategic Offence, peace is a liability. However, during the middle phase of a guerrilla war—Strategic Stalemate, choice of peace is decided by several factors. The Andhra Talks of 2004 and the Bengal Talks of 2011 need to be viewed in this backdrop.

A straight lift from Gautam Navlakha's paper is essential here:

> '*If holding talks in Andhra was wrong, then did the CPI-Maoist approach the talks in Bengal along the majority line at the Unity Congress 2007 on the issue of talks in Andhra Pradesh, that is, 'to utilise the relaxation [emphasis added] in the enemy's repression in order to complete the preparation for confronting future offensive'....?*'[20]

However, there are 'scholarly' arguments regarding peace which put forth the perspective of the insurgents:

> '*Every time the authorities say they want to initiate a peace process, they want their armed adversaries to 'abjure violence'. Clearly the state policy all along have been to liquidate illegally its Maoist opponents in the name of peace talk....Peace talks with the Maoists have become a ploy for trapping and killing them in cold blood.*'[21]

Intriguingly, such rhetoric fails to appreciate the fact that for a compact modern state to flourish, the 'monopoly' of using force lawfully must be with the state itself and allowing armed groups to loiter around is a clear signal of the failure of the state apparatus. Furthermore, it's strange to expect peace negotiations to commence while a parallel war is going on. A mutual ceasefire is a pre-requisite to any 'talks' with the adversary.[22]

Kunal Chattopadhyay seems sceptical and to a large extent cynical about the fertility of the peace talks. He argues that the Indian state uses the pretext/ bogey of the Maoist insurgent to unleash violence on the Adivasis. Naturally, as per Chattopadhyay's analysis, the Indian state would be reluctant to engage in 'true' talks.[23] On the other hand, the Maoists too, are not serious about talks since they are built on the solid platform of Stalinism-Maoism—which hardly believes in the precepts of socialist democracy. In this regard, the international scenario also needs to be re-viewed. In August 2012, Colombian President Juan Manuel Santos announced that the government was engaged in exploratory peace talks with the violent leftist insurgent group, the Revolutionary Armed Forces of Colombia (FARC), in a bid to resolve a nearly 50-year internal armed conflict. The secret, initial dialogue between the Santos government and the FARC's leadership led to the opening of formal peace talks with the FARC—the oldest, largest, and best financed guerrilla organization in Latin America.[24] These talks began in Oslo, Norway, in October 2012 and thereafter moved to Havana, Cuba. But violence has continued in the country as both sides agreed not to hold a cease-fire during the negotiations. Such peace talks could be peculiar in the Colombian scenario but one thing comes out unscathed—even after 2 years of dialogues, that too being brokered by third parties, peace may not be conclusive in Colombia.

Another glaring example comes from the Filipino case. The International Crisis Group reports that talks between the Philippine government and the National Democratic Front of the Philippines (NDFP), which negotiates on behalf of the Communist Party of Philippines—New People's Army [CPP-NPA], have been intermittent and inconclusive since they began under the Cory Aquino government in 1986. Even decades later, they have scarcely touched on substantive issues. Indeed, the civil war is still on in the interiors of Philippines. And if the Nepal phenomenon is something to cheer about, then it could be seen more of an aberration than linearity or something which the Indian Maoists could disdainfully castigate as 'armed revisionism.' Further, after watching the manner in which the democratic process has unfolded in Kathmandu and the way the Unified Communist Party of Nepal (Maoists) [UCPN (M)] have held onto their positions, serious questions could be raised regarding the intent of the Maoists to resolve the political stalemate.

However, on a rather positive note, Peter Sederberg comes up with the war model and the rational actor model through which he shows that these models actually incorporate conciliatory strategies while the state negotiates with the terrorists; though the researcher acknowledges that conventional wisdom suggests that regimes should never bargain with terrorists.[25] Speaking from an American perspective, Daniel Byman asserts that talking with the insurgents is often a necessary first step toward defeating them or reaching an acceptable compromise. Moreover, along the lines of what the Colombian government and the FARC rebels had been doing, Byman further states that these talks must often be done even as insurgents shoot at US soldiers, and they in turn, shoot at them.[26]

Are the Indian Maoists interested in peace? As highlighted in this chapter already, they are more concerned in 'hoisting their Red flag of revolution over the historic Red Fort.' They are far more interested in materializing their New Democratic Revolution (NDR) within the periphery of Marx's historical materialism. They are obdurate in donning the combat role against the Indian state. They are eager to push forward, sometimes trudge as a tactical move, in this asymmetric yet long war. They might have the vested interest in prolonging the violence, pinching the state structures so as to initiate a reaction which could so speciously be termed as 'state repression.' However, in this carefully engineered process, the Maoists—specifically the leadership, intellectuals or no-intellectuals or even the pseudo, are cautious in winning the hearts and minds of the *Adivasis* and other native inhabitants of the Red Corridor, keenly adhering to Mao's maxim: 'The Guerrilla must move amongst the people as a fish....' The moment the guerrilla loses the safe havens, the movement fizzles out; after all, it's a war for the people and has necessarily to be fought by the people. This is exactly where the fundamentals reside. The Indian state needs to and is knowledgeable enough to target the real stakeholders in this war—a rather 'bad war.' The *Adivasis* in Chhattisgarh or the deprived lower-castes in Bihar-Jharkhand or the malnourished in Amlasole and Lalgarh in West Bengal; they are the real stakeholders and need to be targeted as far as proper governance and developmental schemes are concerned. In parallel, the leadership of the Left-wing ultras could be pruned, systematically, as a strategy. However, extreme caution is to be ensured in not unleashing a spectrum of violence, at least on a scale which affects the population and, in turn, depletes intelligence gathering by the security forces. Violence or power, as the interpretation may go, could be skilfully used by the state to diminish the movement without however indulging in humanitarian excesses and rights violation so as to lose the war of propaganda in a mammoth scale, both in the national as well as in the international arena.

For the Indian state, it is important to contain the insurgency—but far more important is to win the war in the media, print or otherwise. And for that, an unrestrained use of violence devoid of rationale could be catastrophic. At the same time, sitting mum would be scoring a duck in the cricket field—which the state can ill afford. In this context, it will add to the wisdom what India's Home Minister categorically expressed:

> *'There is no question of any talks now. We will take a balanced approach. But the forces will give a befitting reply if the Naxals launch attacks.'* [27]

The same reportage further referred to a Union Home Ministry official/officer that talks with the Maoists will be held only when the rebels shun violence and come forward for dialogue. A rather old position held by the state. However, such admission remains unofficial at this juncture. In fact, the Union Home Minister exhibited his seriousness on the issue by saying that the Home Ministry will fully fund formation of Special Forces on the lines of the elite anti-Naxal Greyhounds of Andhra Pradesh and initially such squads will come up in the four states of Chhattisgarh, Odisha, Jharkhand and Bihar. It is hardly too old to trigger a lapse of memory that Greyhounds succeeded in flushing out the insurgents from Andhra. And it's probably no wonder why the freshly recruited IPS officers are being given a gruelling training of counterinsurgency warfare as an attachment with the Greyhounds unit. They are enduring a few days [seemingly months to the officers] in the jungle and living the life of a guerrilla so as to fight the guerrilla. A snake-soup is not uncommon to the guerrillas in the thickly forested areas of *Dandakaranya*. To get conditioned in such adverse situations is a pre-requisite to win the war.

In Sum

To drive home the point, peace is desirable by both the warring parties the state as well as the insurgents. The violence by the insurgents is justified by the radicals within the realm of the construct of 'state repression'—when a bus is blown away in Dantewada by the ultras, the Maoists expect to be morally exonerated by raking up the fact that it was boarded by Special Police Officers of the *Salwa Judum* variety. Borooah after meticulous research finds that there is a direct correlation between Maoist activity in a district and the level of violent crimes in it.[28]

The Maoists envisage peace in the environs of a successful New Democratic Revolution and the state persistently experiments with the development-cum-democracy model. A mutually agreeable peace is elusive, scrupulously sequestered from the 'round table' of strategic discourse, the lexicon of the insurgent and a coerced counterinsurgent gearing up to the requirement—and miserably failing to achieve the workable concordance which could have streamlined the functioning of the democracy. Finally, another indiscriminate Chhoto Pelia of November 2008, a frail, 55-year old Chintamani Murmu and her lost eyesight, some more inflexibility—are what the state understands would be detrimental for establishing the contours of democracy in the 'fragile islands,' and Lalgarhs, Nayagarhs and more such 'garhs' could be the rigid fortresses for the Maoists. Invariably, no one likes to eat soup with a knife!

NOTES

1. Friedrich Carl J. and Brzezinski, Z. (1965), "Totalitarian Dictatorship and Autocracy", Cambridge university press [as quoted in Fukuyama ibid, p. 4]
2. Francis Fukuyama (2005), "State Building", Profile Books.
3. Partha Chatterjee (2010), "The State", in "The Oxford Companion to Politics in India", edited by Jayal, N G., and Mehta, P.B., Oxford Publication.
4. Ramachandra Guha (2007), "India After Gandhi", Picador India,New Delhi.
5. Sumanta Banerjee (2008), "In the Wake of Naxalbari", Sahitya Samsad, Kolkata.
6. Peter Reed (1985), "Latin America: The Move to the Cities", in "Guerrilla Warfare", edited by John Pimlott, Bison Books, Nebraska.
7. Ibid.
8. Sumanta Banerjee (2008), "In the Wake of Naxalbari", Sahitya Samsad, Kolkata.
9. Ramachandra Guha (2007), "India After Gandhi",Picador India.
10. Rabindra Ray (1987), "The Naxalites and their Ideology", Oxford, New Delhi.
11. Sumanta Banerjee (2008), "In the Wake of Naxalbari", Sahitya Samsad, Kolkata.
12. Rabindra Ray (1987), "The Naxalites and their Ideology", Oxford, New Delhi.
13. N. Venugopal (2013), "Understanding Maoists", Setu Prakashani, and Shubhranshu Choudhary(2012), "Let's Call Him Vasu", Penguin, New Delhi.
14. Shubhranshu Choudhary (2012), "Let's Call Him Vasu", Penguin, New Delhi.
15. Biju Govind (2014), "Maoists plan new war front in Sahyadri", *The Hindu*, October 1, 2014 [Online: web] Accessed 7 Oct 2014, URL: http://www.thehindu.com/news/national/kerala/maoists-plan-new-war-front-in-sahyadri/article6462926.ece.
16. Santhosh Christy (2014), "Maoist Presence Spreading in Malabar, Says Intelligence", The New Indian Express, October 2, 2014, http://www.newindianexpress.com/states/kerala/Maoist-Presence-Spreading-in-Malabar-Says-Intelligence/2014/10/02/article2459013.ece
17. Regis Debray (1967), "Castroism: The Long march in Latin America".
18. Amit Bhaduri (2012), "Peace That is More Dangerous Than War", and "People's War as Strategy and Peace Talks as Tactics", edited by Biswajit Roy in "War and Peace in Junglemahal", Setu Prakashani.
19. Ibid
20. Gautam Navlakha (2012), "People's War as Strategy and Peace Talks as Tactics", in "War and Peace in Junglemahal", edited by Biswajit Roy, Setu Prakashani.

21. Amit Bhaduri (2012), "Peace That is More Dangerous Than War", and "People's War as Strategy and Peace Talks as Tactics", edited by Biswajit Roy in "War and Peace in Junglemahal", Setu Prakashani.
22. Sujato Bhadro (2012), "Peace-talk Process in Junglemahal: A Brief Review", and "People's War as Strategy and Peace Talks as Tactics", edited by Biswajit Roy in "War and Peace in Junglemahal", Setu Prakashani.
23. Kunal Chattopadhyay (2012), "Maoists and the Indian State: Is Peace Possible?" and and "People's War as Strategy and Peace Talks as Tactics", edited by Biswajit Roy in "War and Peace in Junglemahal", Setu Prakashani.
24. June S Beittel (2014), "Peace Talks in Colombia", CRS Papers.
25. Peter C. Sederberg (1995), "Conciliation as Counter-Terrorist Strategy", *Journal of Peace Research*, Vol. 32, No. 3: 295-312
26. Daniel Byman (2009), "Talking with Insurgents: A Guide for the Perplexed", *The Washington Quarterly* 32:2:125-137.
27. Vijaita Singh (2014), "Rajnath Draws Hard Line on Maoists", the *Indian Express*, June 27 2014, [Online: web] Accessed 7 Oct 2014 URL: http://indianexpress.com/article/india/politics/rajnath-draws-hard-line-on-maoists-no-talks-attacks-will-get-befitting-reply/
28. Vani K Borooah (2008), "Deprivation, Violence, and Conflict: An Analysis of Naxalite Activity in the Districts of India", *International Journal of Conflict and Violence.*

18

India's Cyber Security System: Threat and Challenges

T.K. Singh

Background

Cyberspace for India can historically be connected with the famous Indian epic *Mahabaratha* (Great India) written by sage Vyas where he explained about concepts of virtual reality, transportation through a matrix and web conferencing on the medium of space. In the Great Mahabaratha War, a warrior (archer) chants a password on a unique bow (of arrow) and converts it into a hundreds bows. This can be assumed simply as the early concept of using a password to unlock certain hidden elements. The introduction of electronic network in India began in the 19th Century when the telecommunication system was introduced during British Rule. The first experimental electric telegraph line was developed between Kolkata and Diamond Harbour, West Bengal, in 1850. This was later improvised by British East India Company by connecting with Chennai and Bombay (Mumbai). Thereafter a series of revolutions took place and internet came into existence in India on 15 August 1995 with its distribution in Calcutta, Chennai, Bombay, Delhi and Pune. The service was provided by Indian international telephone private company, erstwhile Videsh Sanchar Nigam Limited (VSNL) now called Tata Communications Limited (TCL). However, before VSNL provided the service, Gateway Internet Access Service (GIAS) had existed in the country for years in the form of Educational Research Network (ERNET).

However, it was not accessible by the general people as it was meant only for educational and research communities, as per policy laid down by the American Internet Manager of National Science Foundation Network (NSFNET), United States (US).

Such developments on Information Technology (IT) have been considered to be some of the most important inventions of the 20th century. Its applications are today widely used in economic, security, political and social spheres for relevant benefits. On the contrary, exposing the failure of its protection, multiple threats are increasing day by day through this electronic medium. So much so that it is useful, as much as it is vulnerable in several aspects. As India is in the process of becoming a digital nation, safeguarding of cyberspace has turned out to be one of the biggest challenges of the 21st Century. Concerning the vulnerability in cyber space, modernization of cyber technology has become a critical component of digital India too.

The Indian utilization of cyberspace is primarily for enhancement of economic growth and prosperity of the nation with a defensive mechanism. However, it should not also be ruled out that the cyber network has been used by defence and security agencies in the interest of the nation (collection of intelligence/information about threats and potential attacks). India considers it as a fifth dimension of warfare after land, air, oceans and space. The dedicated government department or Ministry that is involved in safeguarding the information systems is the Department of Electronic and Information Technology (DeitY or commonly known as DIT), Ministry of Communications and Information Technology (MC&IT). DIT's main objective is to set up National e-Governance, e-Industry, e-Innovation, e-Education and e-Security. The Computer Emergency Response Team-India (CERT-In), under DIT has been the India's nodal agency for responding and preventing any computer related (security) incidents. Apart from MC&IT, the Ministry of Defence (MoD), Ministry of Home Affairs (MHA), Prime Minister Office (PMO) and Ministry of Finance (MoF) take part in securing India's cyberspace.

The function of securing electronic and information systems is governed by the DIT introduced Information Technology Amendment Act-2008 (first introduced in the year 2000) or ITAA-2008 and National Cyber Security Policy (NCSP) drafted in March 2011 and publicly revealed in 2013. This Act mainly deals with data protection and justice dispensation systems for cyber misuses. Understanding the current scenario of India's ad-hoc and belittle approach to cyber security, the NCSP was framed to secure the computer environment and maintain adequate thrust confidence in electronic transaction. The policy addresses several areas related to cyber security, particularly incident response, vulnerability management and infrastructure security. While the nation is facing multiple threats from cyber-attack, cyber espionage, cyber terrorism, cyber warfare and cybercrime, the implementation of NCSP may hopefully lead to enhanced information security system in India. The policy is yet to be executed in the nation.

Consequently, DIT identified five Critical Information Infrastructures (CIIs) sectors, viz, Defence, Finance, Energy, Transportation and Telecommunications to take extra safety precautions for their electronic and information assets. These sectors are in fact the economic and security backbone of the country owned by both public and private enterprises. Sectoral-CERTs were subsequently established in these five sectors and their cyber security officers are regularly interacting with CERT-In. CERT-In plays the mother role for the Sectoral-CERTs. To obtain a comprehensive cyber security system in India, both the public and private enterprises have been mulling over to associate closely. Sharing of data, information exchange and frequent interactions between the two are practiced on a regular basis through common conferences and selective meetings. At the same time, establishment of a coordinated government body, where the private sectors can also cooperate, has been initiated by raising National Cyber Coordination Centre (NCCC).

Indian and Cyber Threats

While there is no doubt that IT has brought significant changes in the nation, its dangers need to be addressed cautiously. To protect Indian cyber space from any hostile incursion, India has identified four varieties of threat perceptions, cyber warfare, cyber espionage, cyber terrorism and cybercrime.

Cyber Warfare

Cyber Warfare is a conflict on Internet with politically motivated attacks on information and information systems that disable official websites and networks, disrupt or disable essential services, steal or alter classified data, and cripple financial systems among many other possibilities.[1] It has become a new generation threat to national security and considered to be the fifth domain of warfare. In one of the classic incidents, in August 2012 a 'cyber-attack' was allegedly launched by suspected terror groups, Harkat ul Jihad al

Islami (HuJI) and Jamiat-e-Islami (JeI) against India.[2] Meanwhile, in another incident, protest flares up in parts of India when an anti-Islamic movie, 'Innocence of Muslim' went viral on internet. Such intentional or unintentional misuse of the cyber domain created panic and induce communal apprehensions and ethnic violence in the country. Many, including government officials in India, considered them to be a cyber war against the nation.

On 12 July 2011, the PMO and MHA were under a significant strategic attack when a substantial e-mails with attachment, *cms,ntro:dailyelec. mediareport (2011)* were forwarded to the inboxes of top officials including Ministers, NSA, Secretaries and Para Military Forces' key personals. As they have been considered to be the main opponents in cyber conflict, finger of suspicion pointed towards China and Pakistan for the invasion. There are other reported or unreported instances where these two nations have breached Indian cyber space. Out of others, the best instance would be the attempt to attack information systems during the Commonwealth Games in 2010 where CERT-In had timely detected and effectively protected. Not only in India, Chinese hackers have also reached to Indian missions at Kabul, Moscow, Dubai, Abuja, US, Serbia, Belgium, Germany, Cyprus, the United Kingdom (UK) and Zimbabwe.[3] The other countries where cyber threats originated or were routed from are US, China, Russia, a few east European countries and Iran.

While the concept of cyber warfare is still under discussion, some countries like China and US have established cyber commands under their Defence Ministry. In fact, cyber conflict is not a real war and does not follow any rules of war. And, hence, the laws of armed conflict (LoAC) have not been applied to cyber warfare. However, the shadow behind its reality is quite severe as it was witnessed by the classic attacks of websites of Estonia in 2007 and Georgia in 2008. While no country is responsible for such attacks, usage of non-state actors (e.g., hackers) by state actors was widely discussed. Nevertheless, such incidents made developed nation like the US to set up a cyber command within its Strategic Forces Command and was persuaded to revisit the US military doctrine.

Cyber Espionage

Cyber espionage is a discrete way of collecting intelligence or stealing data from an enemy or adversary (individual, enterprises, state, etc.) through cyber penetration. This phenomenon has become quite common and it entirely depends on the technical capability of the operative (state or non-state). It may not leave the signature of the intruder to the opponent's computer and prevents the victim from awareness about the intruder. No act of physical sabotage will be revealed by the rival group during spying. It should be admitted that cyber espionage is not overtly evident in nature until the victims realize it. The affected state/organization remains silent when their critical information is under attack as they remain unaware. This is mainly because the victim nation has no technology to cope with or defend/detect such spying activity.

Before the 12 July 2011 PMO cyber attack incident, in April and May 2011, National Technical Research Organisation or NTRO (India's premiere technical intelligence organization) identified that computers of key-security affiliated ministers and other apex offices had been silently compromised for months by unknown intruders. These included National Security Council Secretariat (NSCS) computers where intelligence inputs from the country's intelligence agencies such as NTRO, Intelligence Bureau (IB) and Research and Analyses Wing (R&AW) are compiled and stored. Data were also silently accessed from computer of one Rear Admiral in the Directorate of Integrated Head Quarters, a joint Armed Forces setup.[4] These were all a planned reconnaissance (spying) that meant to steal strategic information without leaving any physical damage to the accessed computers. There are possibilities of such similar spying cases which remain undetected due to poor technology.

Besides spying in cyber space by enemy states, stealing of secret information by own agents (black sheep) from computer assets are also familiar in India. Out of various examples, considerable incident would be the infamous 'Naval war rooms scandal' of 2005 in which a Lt Commander named Ravi Shankaran (later arrest in UK in 2010) leaked a number of confidential documents to Thales, a technical security company, which also made Scorpene submarines, amongst other defence infrastructure.

Cyber Terrorism

Cyber terrorism is an act of terror related violence in which cyberspace is being used by terrorist individuals or organisations to plan terrorist attacks, communicate associates, recruit (indoctrinate) sympathizers, make lethal weapons (assembling of bombs) in pursuit of political, ideological and social objectives. Also, it can be described as the deliberate use of computer, networks and public internet to cause destruction and damage for individual or group objectives. Terrorists feel safer to create mayhem through cyber space than a physical attack that includes bombs or guns which is more risky to be carried out at any secure or unsecure environment. Considering a tight security system, a bomb attack may not be launched on a military headquarter, but a cyber malware-bomb can sneak in to such secured institutions. The only difference between the two is that one takes human lives or sabotages physical infrastructure, and the other jeopardizes information and networks, but both equally subject a secure environment to loss (e.g., a military Headquarter). However, both disruptions create an impact on the economy, society, along with political and security scenario at the state and national level.

India being a terrorist infested nation, cyberspace has been a force multiplier for terror target. Terrorists operating against India are not as structured or potent as the cyber command force that a nation has and, consequently, their capability is limited. They normally use cyberspace for propaganda, spreading hate messages, communications, geographic mapping, recruitment, fund-raising and intelligence gathering. With increasing vigilance on the traditional channels of communication (such as tracking of e-mails) terrorists use different tactics of sharing passwords amongst their associates and access from anywhere. They logically collect information from the internet and plan accordingly before an attack. For instance, Maoist terrorists, before targeting a heavy security convoy, gather online information available on the website of the vehicle's capability that how much lethality the truck can bear.[5]

In a different practice, terrorist groups like the Indian Mujahideen (IM) used the internet to send emails before (threatening) and after (claiming responsibility) a terror attack took place.[6] Involvement of tech savvy people in terror modules multiplies the complexities of securing the cyber domain. In the meanwhile, arrest of a perpetrator, Asad Khan, who was involved in the Pune blast committed on 1 August 2012, admitted that he was indoctrinated by Jihadi websites. Similarly, one Mehdi Masroor Biswas from Bangalore was arrested on 13 December 2014 for allegedly operating pro-Islamic State in Iraq and Syria (ISIS) *Twitter* handle *@shamiwitness*. In July 2014, reports have revealed that 18 young Indians from Kerala, Maharashtra and Tamil Nadu were recruited by ISIS through the internet.[7]

Understanding the current trend of increasing usage of cyberspace by terrorists, the challenge of non-state actors to national security is extremely worrisome. Nevertheless, the government has taken a number of measures to counter the use of cyberspace for terrorist-related activities, especially in the aftermath of the Mumbai attack in November 2008 (26/11). The amended IT Act that was passed after 26/11 added provisions on cyber terrorism and cybercrime. Further, the IT (Guidelines for Cyber Cafe) Rules, 2011 have also been enacted under the umbrella of the IT Act.

Cybercrime

Cybercrime, in simple terms, is a punishable act of violence against cyber laws at the local, national or international level. It is a criminal activity committed on the internet and IT enabled services. Cybercrime are committed mainly on three basic components, against persons, property and government. Basic features of cybercrimes that commonly happen in India are hacking, child pornography, cyber stalking, Distributed Denial of Service (DDOS), virus dissemination, software piracy, internet relay chat (IRC), credit card fraud, net exhortation and phishing.

With the increase of internet users in India (through computers or mobile phones), commitment of crime on or through cyberspace has increased. Based on the available data in the National Crime Record Bureau (NCRB), the following table indicates the increasing figure of registered cyber crimes and persons arrested.

These, in fact, are the records registered with the NCBR, however, there are many instances or cyber crimes that remained unreported due to lack of acknowledgement or detection. As cybercrimes expand and crosses borders from one state to another, it has been difficult for police to crack down on the criminals without support from their counterparts in states in which the crime originated. However, to support their investigation process, soon after the amendment of ITAA-2008, the Indian Government has introduced a new initiative, Crime and Criminal Tracking Network & Systems (CCTNS) in 2009. This will connect all the police fraternities at the local, district, state and national level through a common computer network. The primary perspective of this system is to facilitate collection, storage, retrieval, analysis, transfer and sharing of data and information at the police station, State Headquarters and the Central Police Organizations.

Government Role on Cyber Security

The role of the Indian Government in safeguarding cyber space is comprehensive, elaborative, critical and laborious. It is not only the MC&IT (CERT-In or DIT) that ensures the safety and security of cyberspace in India.

Figure I: Cyber crimes/cases registered and person arrested under IT Act during 2010-2013

SL. No.	Crime heads	Cases Registered				% Variation in 2013 over 2012	Persons Arrested				% Variation in 2013 over 2012
		2010	2011	2012	2013		2010	2011	2012	2013	
1	Tampering computer source documents	64	94	161	137	-14.9	79	66	104	59	-43.3
2	Hacking with computer system										
	i) Loss/damage to computer resource/utility	346	826	1,440	1,966	36.5	233	487	612	818	33.7
	ii)Hacking	164	157	435	550	26.4	61	65	137	193	40.9
3	Obscene publication/transmission in electronic form	328	496	589	1203	104.2	361	443	497	737	48.3
4	Failure										
	i) Of compliance/orders of certifying authority	2	6	6	13	116.7	5	4	4	3	-25.0
	ii) To assist in decrypting the information intercepted by govt. agency	0	3	3	6	100.0	0	0	3	7	133.3
5	Un-authorised access/attempt to access to protected computer system	3	5	3	27	800.0	6	15	1	17	1600.0
6	Obtaining licence or digital signature certificate by misrepresentation/suppression of fact	9	6	6	12	100.0	4	0	5	14	180.0
7	Publishing false digital signature certificate	2	3	1	4	300.0	2	1	0	8	@
8	Fraud digital signature certificate	3	12	10	71	610.0	4	8	3	51	1600.0
9	Breach of confidentiality/privacy	15	26	46	93	102.2	27	27	22	30	36.4
10	Other	30	157	176	274	55.7	17	68	134	161	20.1
	Total	966	1,791	2,876	4,356	51.5	799	1,184	1,522	2,098	37.8

Note: @ indicates zero value in previous year

Source: National Crime Bureau Record, Government of India,2014

Directly or indirectly, the role of the PMO, MoD, MHA and Ministry of Finance (MoF) should not be ruled out. While the character of other Ministries are defensive in nature, the use of cyber domain by MoD and MHA are likely to be offensive. Subsequently, while PMO's approach is of a strategic based security system, MoF is more associated with computer based illegal financial transaction. Current Government bodies that are participating in cyber security challenges are as follows:-

Ministry of Communication and Information Technology (MC&IT)

The MC&IT is mainly endorsed by its brainchild, the DIT, which secures India's cyberspace (e-security as its main mandate). The other objective of the department is to implement e-Government (to provide e-infrastructure for delivery of e-services); e-Industry (to promote of electronics hardware manufacturing and IT industry); e-Innovation/Research & Development (to provide support for creation of CIIs in emerging areas of technology); and e-Education (to provide support for development of e-skills and knowledge network). Every electronics and computer related function comes under the DIT adopted rules and regulations.

The IT-Act was passed by the Indian Parliament in June 2000 to provide a legal framework to regulate cyber security on usages of internet and commerce, including digital signatures, securities and hacking. However, it was amended as Information Technology Amendment Act (ITAA) in 2008 and approved by the President of India on 5 February 2009. Prior to 2008, censorship of internet content by authorities was rare and sporadic. Nevertheless, with the new amendment act several changes have been collaborated in the provisions to make the laws more stringent. As a result of this alleged unfriendly nature, it was criticized by some human right groups including 'Reporters Without Borders.' Apart from the ITAA, on 26 March 2011, DIT has issued a discussion draft on National Cyber Security Policy (NCSP) and invited suggestions for recommendations from various Government and non-Government departments/institutions. The policy was an initiative taken up by the Government to address areas related to cyber security, particularly incident response, vulnerability management and CIIs safeguard. Nevertheless, the final draft was further publicly revealed in 2013 but is yet to be implemented. On the other hand, this security policy is considered to be an orphan policy as the country has no formal Grand

National Security Policy/Strategy. The agenda of NCSP would not be complete without a comprehensive national security policy.

Computer Emergency Response Team (CERT-In)

CERT-In was established in January 2004 to enhance the security of India's communications and information infrastructure through proactive action and effective collaboration. Functioning by its 75 technical members, CERT-In is the national nodal agency for responding to computer security incidents as and when they occur. It plays the role of collecting, analysing and disseminating information on cyber incidents. It also forecasts and issues alerts on cyber security incidents. Its Annual Reports of 2014 stated that it has handled 1,30,338 security incidents, issued 13 security alerts, published 69 advisories, published 290 vulnerability notes, organized 22 trainings, traced 25,037 defaced Indian websites, tracked 2,408 open proxy servers and identified 77,28,408 bot infected systems.[8] Most of these attacks were facilitated through attack tool kits such as Techno XPACK, Phoenix Exploit Kit, Neo spolit, Eleonre and Blackhole. It has also handled various types of incidents as indicated below.

Figure II: Summary of CERT-In Handled Incidents

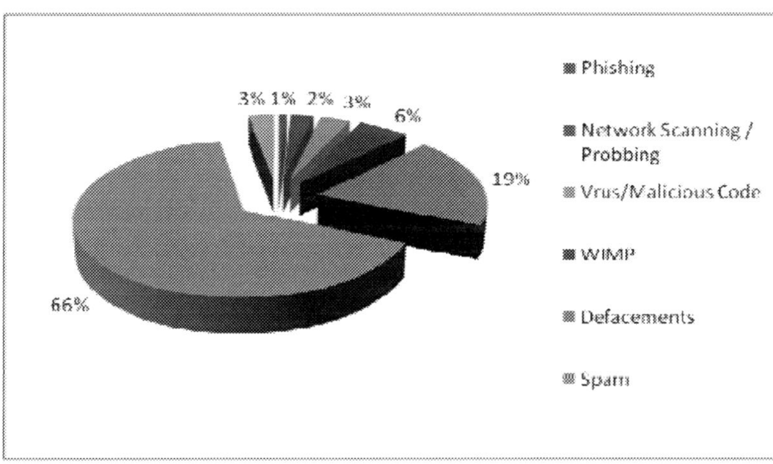

Source: CERT-In Annual Report, 2014.

CERT-In has set up a facility for computer forensics to support investigation of cybercrimes and extends help on training to the law enforcement agencies and the judiciary. It also cooperates with defence, banks, judiciary and law enforcement agencies in giving official training in the cyber domain. CERT-In initiatives include establishing the National Information Security Assurance Programme (NISAP) to create awareness in government and critical sector organizations; to develop and implement information security policy; and information security for protection of their infrastructure.

National Informatics Centre (NIC)

Though the NIC that was established in 1976 does not work as a security or monitoring agency of cyberspace, however, it acts as a premier organization, backbone and e-governance support to central government, state governments, union territory administrations, districts and other government bodies. It provides critical solutions for information management and decision support in the public and private sectors. It also provides essential security for network, servers, applications and client systems by introducing security appliances at the critical network segments of NIC Network (NICNET), the Pan India computer communication network of NIC, using network firewalls, intrusion detection systems/intrusion prevention systems, application firewalls, etc.[9]

NICNET was designed and implemented by the NIC using state-of-the-satellite-based computer-communication technology. Considering the vast geographic spread of India, ranging from islands in Indian Ocean to the highest Himalayan ranges, it has been designed as one of the largest Very Small Aperture Terminal (VSAT) networks of its kind in the world which ensures exceptionally cost effective and reliable implementation. NICNET is also an integral part of various public and private sectors that provide information exchange services. These services include file transfer, electronic mail, remote database access, data broadcast and electronic data interchange (EDI). During natural calamities like cyclones, NICNET served as the basic message communication facility in the affected areas.

Prime Minister's Office

Besides the bodies associated with technical cyber aspects, the Prime Minister's Office, with its apex security body, NSCS plays a strategic role in safeguarding and protecting critical national information infrastructures. As a significant approach to the strategic front of cyber security issues, the National Cyber Security Agency (NCSA) under NSCS was likely to be formed in November 2012 headed by a National Cyber Security Coordinator (NCSC). Mr Gulsan Rai, who is the Chief of CERT-In, was supposed to be the NCSC and his task would primarily be to coordinate among various agencies involved in cyber security.[10] However NCSA was later renamed as National Cyber Coordination Center (NCCC) and mandated to function under DIT (not under NSCS as decided earlier). In June 2015, Minister of MC&IT Ravi Shankar Prashad announced the government approval for the NCCC with initial investment of Rs 770 crore.[11]

Earlier on 15 October 2012, the NSA in New Delhi, also announced the establishment of an 'Institute of Cyber Security Professionals of India.' The declaration was made when he released the recommendation of a Joint Working Group (JWG) report, 'Engagement with Private Sector on Cyber Security' headed by Deputy NSA Latha Redy. Apart from deeper engagement with the private sector in safeguarding cyber security, the report talks about creation of Information Sharing & Analysis Centres (ISACs) in various industry verticals which would coordinate with CERT-In; provide training to law enforcement agencies in cybercrime investigation and cyber forensics; and promotion and dissemination of cyber security awareness among general public.

In the first half of 2011, the computers of the top level Ministers and officers in the PMO, MoD, MEA and MHA were attacked by unconfirmed perpetrators. Thereafter, understanding the impact of growing cyber invasion, NSCS formulated a new comprehensive cyber security policy (not the NCSP of DIT) in April 2012 to enhance the cyber network system and protect from malware attacks, and intrusion by hostile entities. The policy also covers aspect for cyber defence of CIIs that are vulnerable to hostile foreign elements. However, this policy was not relevant enough to challenge the existing cyber threats and find its provisions no different from that of NCSP (DIT). Like NCSP, it was considered to be an orphan policy as NSCS has no Grand National Security Policy (GNSP). Otherwise, NSCS is the apex council in which a grand strategy on India's national security should be produced.

The Prime Minister's Office with Indian top intelligence organizations such as NTRO and R&AW (both functions under it) play a strategic role in securing CIIs of the nation. These agencies not only take preventive action, but apparently take offensive actions accordingly. Though the offensive mechanism was not highlighted in India's NCSP in the interest of national security, the country has been allegedly involved in penetrating the cyberspace of hostile nations. Consequently, the Indian cyber command which is likely to be established in the near future will address the aspect of offensive strikes.

Ministry of Defence (MoD)

The role of MoD in the whole cyber domain is to respond to any cyber security incident related to defence sector. At the same time, when the situation demands, it acts or reacts against hostile nations in the interest of national security. Defence Information Assurance and Research Agency (DIARA) established under the Headquarters of Integrated Defence Staff (IDS) is the nodal tri-Services agency at the national level to effectively deal with all aspects of Information Assurance and operations. It has also formed the Defence-CERT whose primary function is to coordinate the activities of CERTs in three different services (Army, Navy and Air Force). It associates with CERT-In to ensure perpetual availability of Defence networks.

CIIs of Indian defence have been facing threats from China, which possibly has a strong cyber battalion of more than 10,000 soldiers. There were detailed instances where Indian defence assets have been attacked by this battalion. In November 2011, Indian intelligence agencies alerted that the security network at the Eastern Naval Command at Vishakapatanam was likely to be attacked by Chinese hackers. The Defence Minister A.K. Anthony in August 2012 brought up Chinese cyber incursion in Lok Sabha (Lower House) and assured to strengthen the Indian cyber networks which contains sensitive information. There was also a report that Military Engineering Service (MES) was hacked by the PCA in May 2011.

Amidst the increase of using cyberspace as a weapon to target other nations, strategic cyber-attack has been considered as a fifth domain of warfare. Though India's approach to this aspect has been defensive/responsive, it can use its ability for self-defence and deterrence, as other nation like US or China do (with development of CYBERCOM or Cyber Command). The working draft of NSPC also lacks to mention offensive measures of Indian cyber systems. However, the National Security Council (NSC) headed by Prime Minister Manmohan Singh in June 2012 highlighted concerns about his desire to designate the Defence Intelligence Agency (DIA) and NTRO as agencies for carrying out offensive cyber operations, if necessary.

Understanding the precarious trend of cyber warfare, a CYBERCOM supported by DIARA (IDS), Defence Intelligence Agencies (DIA) and its allied intelligence units from the three Armed Force services is likely to be established to command and control strategic action for military related cyber issues. Its activity can be empowered by other intelligence agencies such as NTRO, R&AW and IB. The command force should also be taking assistance from India's premier scientific organisation Department of Defence and Research Organisation (DRDO) and Centre for Development and Advance Computing (C-DAC) to enhance technical parameters.

Ministry of Home Affairs (MHA)

As early as on 5 May 2012, in the Chief Ministers meeting on developing National Counter Terrorism Centre (NCTC) in New Delhi, the then Home Minister P. Chindambaram stated that cyber terrorism has been a growing threat and a 'fifth domain of warfare after land, sea, air and space.' Subsequently, he stated that cybercrimes such as hacking, financial fraud, data theft, espionage in certain circumstances, amount to terrorist acts. Citing unlimited nature of boundaries in cyberspace, he further highlighted the need for the central and state governments to share the responsibility and augment capacities to be able to meet the threats in cyber terrorism.

Responsibility of MHA in the cyber domain is mainly to issue security guidelines from time to time with respect to the protection of physical infrastructure by using security agencies/forces. In the meanwhile, it monitors suspicious terror related issues through cyberspace as a counter terrorism measures. Key concerns of security agencies/forces under MHA are to defend terrorist from using cyber networks, at the same time to chase them by using it. Being the forefront security agency of MHA, Intelligence Bureau plays a fundamental role in providing terror alerts to security forces and other concern departments. IT (cyber unit as such is apparently not set up in police forces) units in central and state police forces monitors and investigate cyber related crimes, including forensic examination of confiscated computer or telecom devices. However, due to lack of dedicated technical resource in sub offices, for further detailed and critical scrutiny, confiscated devices from criminals are delivered to the Central Forensic Science Laboratory or CFSL (Chandigarh and Hyderabad which has cyber division) and Directorate of Forensic Science (DFS), MHA. DIT has also set up cyber forensic labs at CBI and Kerala police for enhancement in skills of cybercrime investigation.

Currently, above 1000 e-mails and almost 10,000 phones have been legally intercepted by security agencies. While IB does the highest interceptions with 1,043 email IDs, the state intelligence units monitors 136.[12] MHA has authorized nine organizations including IB, DIA, Directorate of Revenue Intelligence (DRI), National Investigation Agency (NIA), Enforcement Directorate (ED), Narcotics Control Bureau (NCB) and state police for phone interceptions in India. However, monitoring calls has its limitations and agencies have to approach service provider for certain non-target (calls which are not monitored by agencies) calls. To avoid this dependency on service providers, under DoT, in January 2011, the Central Monitoring System (CMS) was introduced to legally authorize the nine mandated agencies to conduct lawful interception and monitoring of telephones and email communications all over India from one centre.[13]

National Critical Information Infrastructure Protection Centre (NCIIPC)

The National Critical Information Infrastructure Protection Centre (NCIIPC) which was earlier known as National Information Infrastructure Protection Centre (NIIPC, in draft paper of NCSP) was approved by the NSC headed by the Prime Minister of India. It will gather intelligence and keep a watch on emerging and imminent cyber threats in strategic sectors including national defence. It will share information among members of the intelligence, defence and law enforcement agencies with a view to protecting these agencies' ability to collect, analyse and disseminate intelligence.

NCIIPC has been assigned to operate under NTRO, and it would be a command-and-control centre for monitoring the critical infrastructure.[14] The formation of such a nodal agency to protect national CIIs was intimated in ITAA-2008. NTRO along with IB would primarily be responsible for security of various government networks. While NTRO would operate through NIIPC, IB would watch physical security of networks. State polices, CBI, National Investigation Agency (NIA), etc., would be tasked to do follow up action, if any intrusions are detected.

Department of Telecommunications (DoT)

Department of Telecommunications (DoT) which functions under the MC&IT coordinates with all Internet Service Providers (ISPs) and service providers with respect to cyber security incidents. The department is responsible to provide and respond with action whenever demanded by CERT-In and other government agencies. DoT issues guidelines, rules, regulations and responsibilities to all private service providers and ensures that these service providers are able to track the critical optical fibre networks for uninterrupted availability and have arrangements of alternate routing in case of physical attacks on these networks.

Conclusion

Undoubtedly every nation including India is a victim of cyber attacks. Consequently, vulnerability in cyberspace has to be addressed seriously using effective laws with relevant ministries, institutions and industries. As cyber networks are not limited to a particular territory and threats emanating from any part of the globe, without international cooperation, India alone cannot handle its cyber threats. Hence, there are requirements for setting up an international cyber regime that can deal with cross border cyber incursions. This regime must not be a post incident review organization, but should also be a body that ensures nations not to commit cybercrimes against other. On the same approach, a bilateral and multilateral body may also be instituted.

While safeguard of CIIs would be imperfect without a comprehensive support from regional or international organizations, cooperation between public and private sectors within the nation can enhance its protective capability and reduce the menace of cyber attacks. Actionable data and valuable common inputs which one needs from another should be shared through regular interactions. A regular platform or a dedicated body may be set up where both the segments can join and work together. NSCP has also suggested for stronger cooperation between both. At the same time, there is an impression that private companies are reluctant and shy away from working together with the government, and cover up attacks of their CIIs. This is mainly to cover up their shortcoming and to protect themselves from losing their important clients and bad impression of the company.

Apart from state actors, penetration of the cyber domain by potential terror groups should not be ruled out. The arrest of Asad Khan and ISIS indoctrination of Indians disclosed how terrorist used cyber networks in various disciplines. MHA with support from its associates, public and private departments can strengthened its infrastructure for investigation, training of law enforcement and cyber forensic labs. Without the support of private industry, MHA alone cannot ensure the safety of India's domestic cyber challenges. Firms like the National Association of Software and Services Companies' (NASSCOM) involvement in the spectrum of national security should be considered. Government's undertaking initiatives on deputing a senior police officer to NASSCOM to work on cyber security issues should be continued.

As far as cyber warfare (mainly state sponsored espionage) for India is concerned, though there are no formal rules or guidelines at the multilateral or international level, it would be appropriate for the MoD to initiate a cyber war framework in the interest of the nation. Concerning the rising cyber threat from China, Pakistan and other countries, the NSCS, should bring a strategic vision to challenge any future cyber menace. Understanding the threat perceived, cyber security should be put in the top national security agenda and the process of raising cyber command in defence department should be accelerated. While the country has capable research and development ability in the public sector, having persistent partnership with private enterprises shall help in India becoming a secured digital nation.

NOTES

1. http://www.cycron.in/cycron2/Cycron-is-a-business-event-on-cyber-warfare.php
2. These outfits have uploaded dangerous manipulated photographs of fake Muslim victims killed in Assam in Northeast-India and Myanmar on a Pakistani website and propagated threats to attack North-easterners (people from Northeast India) who are working in Indian main cities. Content of the video carries messages that warned the North-easterners to leave the cities immediately and return to their home town. As a result of the propaganda, thousands of Northeast workers and students in Bangalore, Chennai, Hyderabad, Pune and Mumbai flee their home states, and created a socio-political chaos in the nation.
3. "5 lakh cyber warriors to bolster India's e-defence" (2012), *Times of India,* 16 October 2012.
4. Saikat Datta (2012), "*DNA* investigation: PMO faces largest strategically targeted cyber attack", [Online: web] Accessed 21December 2012, http://www.dnaindia.com/india/report_pmo-faces-largest-strategically-targeted-cyber-attack_1578051.
5. At several instances, Maoist operatives in India used such tactic to attack Central Reserve Police Forces (CRPF) convoys. Though they do not have powerful explosives, large quantities of explosives (landmines bomb) were used for such strike.
6. The blasts in Delhi (September 2008), Ahmedabad and Bangalore (August 2008), Jaipur (May 2008), Varanasi (March 2006), Hyderabad (August 2007), and the serial blasts in Uttar Pradesh (November 2007) were some incidents in which internet was utilised/involved.
7. "The Internet: ISIS's favourite playground" (2015), [Online: web] Accessed 28 November 2015, http://www.rediff.com/news/slide-show/slide-show-1-iraq-isis-internet-is-isis-favourite-playground/20140717.htm.
8. Annual Report, 2014 available at: http://www.cert-in.org.in/
9. http://www.nic.in/sites/upload_files/nichome-files-dcouments/annual_rep_10.pdf
10. "Gulsan Rai tipped to be 1st head of national cyber security agency" (2012), *Times of India,* 4 November 2012.
11. "Government to set up National Cyber Coordination Centre" (2015), *Times of India,* 3 June 2015.
12. http://www.thehindu.com/news/national/10000-phones-1000-email-ids-under-the -scanner/article3992185.ece
13. "Staff crunch delays monitoring system to track mobile phones" (2013), *Indian Express,* 28 January 2013
14. Josy Joseph (2012), "Hackers may bring down India's power grids", *Times of India,* 2 August 2012; also see Josy Joseph, "India to add muscle to its cyber arsenal", *Times of India,* 11 June 2012.

19

Perspectives on India's National Security Challenges in South Asia

Nanda Kishor MS

> *If you know the enemy and know yourself, you need not fear the result of a hundred battles. If you know yourself but not the enemy, for every victory gained you will also suffer a defeat. If you know neither the enemy nor yourself, you will succumb in every battle.*
>
> —Sun Tzu, *The Art of War*

The question of security is one of the most debated topics in International Relations (IR) and often people are accused for an obsession with it. The concept of security undoubtedly has continued to remain a State centric subject, though many scholars have observed that as traditional security. As the demarcation between traditional and non-traditional security seems to be fading, still the reference point for the concept of security continues to revolve around the State. Whether it is military oriented security, environmental security or food security, the decision making authority still continues to remain with the State. It is under this pretext that we assume that security is still a State centric approach and without the State the discussion on security would be incomplete in IR. An interesting paradigm often observed in the post-cold war era has been the broad definition of security and adaptability of IR scholars to the new multifaceted concept of security conceiving both traditional and non-traditional concepts of security equally. It is also important to note that there is nothing called security of the Western World or the Third World, as far as security is concerned, security is common in all nations but it varies only in degrees.

Many a times, the word security is very difficult to explain as there is no single definition of it. This does not mean that it is vague, but it is certainly in-depth that many a time's people try amalgamating several notions to it. A question that often arises in the debates on security is whether defining what insecurity is the best way to explain security? One would hesitate to agree with this question but the reality would make us to ponder upon it and we eventually accept it so. It is this concept of insecurity that evokes what security is and often what it has to be. No country in the world would say that security is not important to them, rather would probably like to define it in a different way. The world in the twenty first century, though not prone to the type of wars the twentieth century witnessed, unfortunately is not free of fear and insecurity. It is this nature of insecurity that makes the states and the scholars working on security in International Relations to work and asses the nature of security in the world and in their respective States.

The tectonic geopolitical shifts after the Cold War era and post 9/11 have given new dimensions to the concept of security in the world. The States have become conscious of their sovereignty, existence and also their stature often being tested due to insecurity. India is no exception to this problem and with the change of political leadership in 2014 general elections the new government has been posed with many national security challenges by the South Asian neighbours. Though India's national security challenges encompass the South Asian region, Southern Asia, Indian Ocean region and beyond, this paper is limited to exploring India' national security challenges in South Asia. There are certain geopolitical characters associated with India which are of the colonial construct. The very idea of creating Pakistan, the first seed of geopolitical rivalry has pushed India to militarize itself heavily. It is also an issue which India has not come to terms with even today. Off late, India has learnt to live with these geopolitical realities though she is blamed on several occasions due to the geographical size and demographic diversity on which it has no control nor has the ability to alter. There are few questions which are essential to be considered in the discourse before debating Security Challenges in South Asia. What is the role of perception, power and politics in the South Asian region with regard to India? Are Indian priorities in conflict with other States of the region? Is India constructing a hyper national security sense within the region? Are India's apprehensions towards its security justified?

Each of these questions would form part of this paper, though they might not essentially be dealt in the mentioned order.

Perceptions have a direct bearing on discussing India's national security challenges in South Asia. The most interesting part of the nature of perception is the striking contrast in understanding of different states within South Asia on a similar action of India. As Madhavi Bhasin puts it, 'advice is viewed as interference; assistance is viewed as instigation; guidance is viewed as domination. The manner in which policies are projected and interpreted by the South Asian states clearly demonstrates a lack of understanding of the concepts of power, leadership, hegemony and formation of perceptions. Issues like relativity of power, perceptual biases, responsibilities of leadership and challenges to hegemonism need to be examined for a better understanding of the South Asian affairs.' This statement speaks against the popular notion of similarity in culture and connection through civilizational roots. Scholars have assessed that perception and threat go hand in hand. India has been a victim of misperceptions by its South Asian neighbours most of the time. There are several historical anecdotes to prove it but at the same time there are well founded fear perceptions on some occasions such as India going nuclear. It was one occasion that had escalated the threat perception of South Asia to a large extent as having a nuclear neighbour is certainly not normal. India termed it as a prerequisite for its national security by quite blatantly expressing its realist tendencies. A few years ago, Subrata Mitra argued that 'India's preponderant size relative to its neighbours which does not translate into overwhelming power over them is one of the main causes of the stalemate in South Asia. A quintessential successor state, India is keen to retain the status quo which its leaders understand in terms of its relative power and territorial boundaries that it was privy to prior to the end of colonial rule. India's neighbours (prominently China) contest this status quo, which they see as tainted by imperial rule.' What Mitra seems to have missed out or what would have made him to asses India as status quo power in South Asia would have been his limited imagination of India's rise over the years and not assessing a single party gaining power at the centre. Both these concepts were treated as distant dreams to India. The question of perception is central to understanding security challenges as Pakistan has a fixed perception of India as a hegemon and would try to unsettle India even at the cost of domestic unrest and getting branded as a safe haven for terrorists and violence. One striking example of change in perception leading to change in relationship is that of Bangladesh. Bangladesh started from the point of gratitude towards

India for help it received in its creation as a state, moved towards turbulence and a skewed view during the military regime, furthered the same sentiment and helped in building anti-India elements during the Zia regime and, finally, it is back to the beginning sentiment of gratitude under Hasina's regime. The case of Sri Lanka also strengthens this argument. Under Rajiv Gandhi, a section of Sri Lankan population thought of India as an enemy supporting the Sinhalese government but simultaneously India was the home to thousands of Sri Lankan refugees without signing the 1951 convention. Though on several occasions India and Nepal are seen as the closest among South Asians due to the commonality of a particular religion, Nepal has always perceived India as a power that is interested in Nepal's domestic politics and has been resisting India in international forums. India was never seen capable of becoming part of development of a war torn Afghanistan till the war on terror took place and India played a positive role in building Afghanistan rather than just fight terror. Bhutan and Maldives have been a bit exceptional as India's relationship with them has been predominantly peaceful.

Power is one of the most central and yet problematic concepts in International Relations. Baldwin opines that 'from Niccolò Machiavelli and David Hume to E.H. Carr and Hans Morgenthau, power has been an important (some would say too important) variable in international political theorizing. Although some may regard power analysis as old-fashioned and outdated, recent refinements in social science thinking about power suggest the possibility of revitalizing this approach to understanding international relations'.[1] Robert Gilpin defines power as an actor's ability to impose his or her will despite resistance. There are other scholars who express that 'power always depends on the context in which the relationship exists.'[2] If these are general ways of terming what power is, the realist school of thought much more upfront and has been brutally honest in accepting what power is in International Relations. Morgenthau declared that 'international politics, like all politics, is a struggle for power.' He further argued that 'whatever the ultimate aims of international politics, power is always the immediate aim.'[3] Echoing the same Carr argued that 'politics are, then, in one sense always power politics.'[4] Carr argued that power was indivisible, yet he claimed that for purposes of discussion it could be divided into three categories: military power, economic power, and power over opinion. Taking this argument further and contextualizing would lead us to a predominantly accepted notion of power. India is successful in two aspects mentioned above, but it is still grappling with the third aspect of 'power over opinion.' Morgenthau's assumption of man's inherent lust for power to describing the behaviour of states in the twenty first century may not give us the real picture of the present scenario in South Asia as geopolitical realities would not allow such use of power among states, but it is not far from realization in the domestic context of some countries in South Asia. The context of India's 'power' in the region is shaped by a mix of historical experiences, national priorities, regional compulsions and ingrained perceptions.[5] It is a fact that India due to her size or because of her military might has not imposed any of her values on the neighbours. Though India has been attributed with the credentials of largest practicing democracy, till date there have been no instances of India pushing the democracy agenda with any of the countries, in general, and South Asian neighbours, in particular. This is a fine example of historical experiences coupled with regional compulsions. Whereas citing examples of being reluctant on water sharing, boundary disputes and securitizing human movement across the border have been her national priorities and partially due to her own ingrained perceptions. India's role in creating Bangladesh in 1971 is often cited by many scholars as an example of her willingness to take up challenges during necessity but one would hardly see such behaviour beyond an example or two. This also essentially draws ones attention to the founding principles of the state and core values. India's power is more often expressed by the neighbours than herself. It is the neighbours who talk about power of India with its military might, its ability to remain democratic in character, handle huge institutions and to a large extent maintain its diverse culture and character. This point only proves to us the relation between power and perception forming the bedrock for politics.

The notion of politics is extremely diverse in South Asia. Though, ideally, all the nations aspire to be democratic, quite often they have failed to be so. A few of them have just come out of the clutches of monarchy and have introduced themselves to the new institutions of democracy and are yet to consolidate. Three other countries started off with democracy as their aspiration but very soon fell in to the trap of military rule which was ultimately instrumental in changing their perception, power and politics. One country was even ruled by a party which is also often called as a violent non-state actor. The threat to democratic politics is generally emphasized by such regimes as they would seek help from non-state actors to sustain in power and later struggle to mend ties with them and finally become victims of their own policy. Detailed account of how politics is leading to the threat perception of India in the South Asian neighbourhood would be discussed. After gaining a certain amount of ground on what perception, power and politics is, the inquiry would move further to take some empirical evidences to reiterate what these three concepts are to India in terms of its national security in South Asia.

The early part of the twenty first century started off with terrorist organizations making their mark in the world politics by attacking the United States of America. Soon, India also had to bear the brunt of it through an attack on its Parliament. With India acquiring nuclear weapons and declaring herself as a full-fledged nuclear weapon state did not deter its adversaries the way it was anticipated. Rather, it led to asymmetric conflicts taking place at regular intervals as wars between nations have been largely ruled out. The use of terror to attain political objectives is essentially visible in every action so far and they seem to be growing transnational in character. If the state has intelligence, the terrorist organizations have counter intelligence. The use of technology has grown equally among terrorist organizations. India has been a victim of terrorism ever since its birth as a modern nation in different ways. Terrorism has been the most important security concern for India since 15 years. Time and again Prime Ministers of the country have been reiterating their stand at different forums. In fact, one can even say that India visualizes terrorism as the major hindrance in maintaining its sovereignty and social fabric. Terrorism in any form leads to tensions within India due to its multicultural character. Addressing the 68th UN General Assembly session at the United Nations headquarters in New York, the former Prime Minister of India, Manmohan Singh, declared in UN that 'terrorism remains a grave threat to security and stability everywhere and extracts a heavy toll of innocent lives around the world. From Africa to Asia, we have seen several manifestations of this menace in the last few days alone. State-sponsored cross-border terrorism is of particular concern to India, also on account of the fact that the epicentre of terrorism in our region is located in our neighbourhood in Pakistan.'[6] He also reiterated and called for zero tolerance towards states sheltering, arming, training or financing terrorists. The present Prime Minister of India, Narendra Modi, very recently pointed out that 'every now and then Pakistan keeps disturbing India, creates nuisance, promotes terrorism and such incidents keep recurring. Terrorism has no boundaries. India has been troubled by it for the last 40 years. So many innocent people have died and what did those associated with terrorism gain and what have they given to the world. Terrorism has no values, no principles, no traditions and it has only one motive and that is enmity against humanity.'[7] The rationale behind quoting the Prime

Ministers is to highlight the utmost importance they have been giving to end the menace of terrorism on Indian soil. Unfortunately, Pakistan uses it almost like a state policy. Pakistan sponsors terrorism for subversion, sabotage, destabilization and fragmentation of India in order to achieve its foreign policy or political objectives. This action includes providing logistics, training, weapons, camps and financial assistance to terrorist groups that amounts to almost a full protection to terrorist outfits and individuals. For many years Indian leaders even convinced themselves that terrorism is a law and order issue. Pakistan provides safe havens on the basis of mutual interest. Pakistan categorically denies its soil being used by terrorist organizations but gets trapped in a contradiction when a leader of a terrorist organization listed as wanted by the United States gives a public speech from the country's capital. It is about time for the whole world to understand Pakistan's role in international terrorism and stand up against it. State sponsored terrorism is a form of war that cannot be countered by conventional war.[8] Needless to say that Pakistan always invokes the Kashmir issue and reiterates its stance on the issue at regular intervals. It essentially believes that Kashmir should be part of Pakistan and not of India. In the verge of realizing this objective, it has cultivated and deployed numerous so-called Kashmiri *tanzeems* (organizations) to pressure India to resolve the ongoing Kashmir dispute in Pakistan's favour.[9] Pakistan's implacable hostility towards India and its unwillingness to rein in cross border terrorism has made India militarize Kashmir and protect herself. India wants Pakistan to realize the damage terrorism has done to its own society but Pakistan seems to ignoring any such suggestions and continues with inflicting aggression on Indian soil in one or the other way.

Since the earliest years of the conflict, Pakistan has used Islamist militant groups to conduct a variety of low-intensity operations in India in an effort to coerce India to concede to Pakistan's territorial claims. The two most active groups in Indian-administered Kashmir are Lashkar-e-Taiba and Hizb-ul-Mujahideen.[10] Lashkar-e-Taiba and Hizb-ul-Mujahideen both have the distinction of spewing venom at India on every occasion they get. The Pakistani military undertook operations against groups that conducted attacks within Pakistan such as TTP (Tehrik-e-Taliban Pakistan), but did not take action against other groups such as Lashkar-e-Taiba, which continued to operate, train, rally, propagandize and fundraise in Pakistan. Recently on 26 May LeT (Now called as Jamaat-ud Dawa) carried out an attack on the Indian Consulate in Herat, Afghanistan. The most problematic area of Pakistan's involvement is its inability to understand India's efforts and help to Afghanistan.[11] Though the security forces were successful in killing the terrorists, the problem will continue to haunt India as its footprints in Afghanistan are firm and it has the willingness to engage with Pakistan, partially for the welfare of the region and neighbourhood but also self interest of using Afghan soil to reach to Central Asia for its energy requirements. The enormity and brazen nature of Lashkar's November 2008 Mumbai terror attacks focused international attention on the group. The Mumbai attacks brought the LeT to global prominence among militant Islamist groups, with its capabilities, intentions, and international linkages attracting worldwide attention.

One important development in recent times and a big relief for India is the political regime of Sheik Hasina in Bangladesh. Though the problem of terrorism towards India is not completely rooted out from Bangladesh, still the magnitude of the problem has drastically come down. Harakat ul-Jihad-i-Islami/Bangladesh (HUJI-B) was formed in April 1992 by a group of former Bangladeshi Afghan veterans to establish Islamic rule in Bangladesh. According to the database of South Asia Terrorism Portal (SATP), 2010, by December '26, the government had arrested some 958 cadres and leaders of the Islami Chhatra Shibir (ICS), the student front of the JeI and the JeI in 2010. Along with these cadres the Security Forces also arrested 43 JMB and nine Harkat-ul-Jihad-al-Islami-Bangladesh (HuJI-B) militants.[12] Though the Islamist extremists have not carried out any major strikes in the last few years, it will be not be right to say that they have been completely wiped out. One should keep in mind that the militant outfits like JMB and HuJI-B have the capacity to undertake major attacks since reports suggest that the JMB has gone for a major recruitment drive in the year 2010. Moreover, foreign funding for militant outfits has not been drastically checked and this continues to be a matter for worry. While dealing with the JMB militants, the Sheikh Hasina government should not forget the serial bomb blasts by the JMB and JMJB in August 2005. Similarly, HuJI-B continues to maintain close links with a number of Pakistani militant outfits determined to expand their base in the country.[13] On 2 October 2014, an improvised explosive device (IED) explosion killed two men, alleged to be terrorist conspirators in the process of handling the device, in the town of Burdwan in West Bengal, about 70 miles northwest of Kolkata. Subsequent investigations by the Indian and Bangladeshi governments alleged the involvement in the blast of an interstate terrorist network believed to have been run by Jamaat-ul-Mujahideen

Bangladesh (JMB). Police arrested two females and a male from the blast site who were found destroying evidence, and seized IED components and violent extremist literature. India is aware if this problem and continues to rate the menace of terrorism as the highest security threat in South Asia.

Apart from terrorism, there are threats emanating due to a variety of reasons for India in the South Asian region. The issue of water sharing, illegal migrants, support to Maoist movements, illicit human and drug trafficking, border disputes, environmental security are few among many security threats India faces.

The issue of water sharing has been taken to the level of war between India and Pakistan. There is growing feeling in Pakistan that while India is increasingly building dams on its western rivers, it is simultaneously engaged in activities aimed at stopping Pakistan, the lower riparian, from building storage dams on Pakistani rivers. The water dispute between India and Pakistan is serious not only because of water, but also due to the political rivalry between the two countries.[14] Their rivalry has made things more complicated than they really are. Islamabad has been attempting to include water as a core issue and to internationalize this bilateral matter.[15] One can even say that there might be a day when some of the Pakistani radicals may call for destroying some of the dams and other hydroelectric projects of India to vent out their frustration and inflict pain on India. Unfortunately, over the years the IWT, too, has failed to pacify the water conflict. Hindu right-wing groups in India call on [the government] to stop flow of water to Pakistan or flood it. In the meantime, Islamic radicals in Pakistan call for water jihad against India. Moreover, the water dispute between the two countries is embedded in their political relationship.[16] There are other scholars within Pakistan who are of the opinion that the problem is not exactly due to India but due to the bad management of available water within Pakistan. Aziz Nayani, an independent consultant, advising businesses on South Asian social trends observed that Pakistan's water woes are exacerbated by other factors as well, including the government's erratic water management policies, poor infrastructure and wasteful farming practices. India was one of the first to respond when floods hit Pakistan and this gesture only reiterates that India is aware of the lower riparian status of Pakistan as India is also a victim of such situation being a middle riparian state. The security threat one can anticipate in the water issue is: what if Pakistan equates its land dispute with India and uses its sponsored terrorist groups to attack water installations?

The second important case in water dispute between India and Bangladesh is that of Teesta being the fourth major trans-boundary river in Bangladesh. According to the Bangladesh Water Development Board, the country is dependent on the Teesta for its pressure irrigation projects covering 750,000 hectares of land and has accordingly built a barrage (1st Phase) on the Teesta. Any water shortage in the Teesta very often disrupts irrigation in the vast tracts of land and undermines Bangladesh's agriculture. As a lower riparian under pressure from the fluctuating flows on the Teesta, Bangladesh is keen to reach a deal.[17] Water sharing of Teesta River is one of the thorny issues between New Delhi and Dhaka. In this respect, a water sharing agreement was supposed to be inked in 2011, but due to the West Bengal Chief Minister Mamata Banerjee, it could not be implemented. Ms Benerjee's apprehensions in regards to Teesta are well-founded as the Northern region of West Bengal also faces major issue of water scarcity and it is the only source of water to agricultural crops. With the reduced flow it would further inhibit the prevailing hydro deficit situation of the northern region which may lead to domestic tensions and may create major problem for governance itself. The creation of an artificial canal at the Teesta (Gajoldoba) Barrage in Jalpaiguri to irrigate Northern Bengal was the only option left before the West Bengal Government. Bangladesh calls this as unilateral as its share of water has been reduced largely due to the Gajoldoba canal. Though one can locate larger politics associated in the issue by West Bengal government in keeping pressure on the Union Government in India, one cannot completely ignore the problems faced by the north Bengal region. Some recent statements by West Bengal Chief Minister Mamata Banerjee on her visit to Dhaka were positive with regard to finding amicable solution to the Teesta issue.[18]

It is also equally important to take note of the water crisis India is going through in recent years. As a middle riparian state even India is struggling to meet the expectation of the agriculture sector. The water demand projection is quite alarming and India is making efforts to manage it and failure to do so would lead to domestic unrest. The World Bank in its 1999 report indicates that the overall water demand will increase from 552 BCM (Billion Cubic Metres) to 1050 BCM by 2025, which will require the use of all available water resources in the country.[19] According to the World Bank, India is the largest user of ground water in the world, after China. If something is not done soon, an estimated 114 million Indians will soon face desperate domestic, agricultural and industrial shortages.[20] There are real pertinent issues which are directly linked to India's economic progress. Lack of water resources has taken it towards facing food crisis and failing to act on water conservation and innovative methods would very soon make it a food importer. Government agencies say that by 2050 India must nearly double grain production, to over 450 million tons a year, to meet the demands of prosperity and population growth.[21] India being a middle riparian state faces tremendous pressure from the upper riparian states such as China. India's dependency on the rivers originating from the Tibetan plateau is a well-known fact and China is pursuing major inter-basin and inter-river water transfer projects in the region which has evoked a very negative response in India. As an alternative, the Indian policy makers came up with a plan to link major rivers of the country. The plan has not seen the light of the day as there are several issues between several states within India. Bangladesh needs to understand these dynamics India has been facing for a long time. Bangladesh, instead of being only emotional the need of the hour is being realistic in terms of India's problems. As India is developing better relationship with Bangladesh in recent times and giving adequate importance, there is hope that the issue would be resolved very soon like that of the land issue which got resolved recently during the Prime Minister's visit to Bangladesh in June 2015.

The issue of flow of illegal migrants into India from Bangladesh has been an irritant in the relationship between India and Bangladesh. It has been a burning issue in the North East of India, especially in Assam, and has serious socio-political implications. India's plans of constructing 4000 km border fence to seal India-Bangladesh international border is essentially to break the movement of the militants and curb infiltration. Apart from these issues, there is also a major problem of smuggling and circulation of fake currency notes, human trafficking, cattle trafficking and illegal arms. One can always understand the sentiments of the people from Bangladesh on more cooperative behaviour from India but it poses serious threat to India's national security. According to an affidavit submitted by the Ministry of Home Affairs in the Supreme Court in 2014, out of the 3326 km of fences along the India-Bangladesh border (including reconstruction of damaged fences) that has been sanctioned, construction of 2828 km has been completed and another 78.8 km will be completed by May 2016. Widespread illegal immigration into India's north-eastern states comes from Bangladesh and it has even lead to communal tensions in the state of Assam. The Supreme Court of India in the month of April 2015 observed that both the Centre and Assam government should stop 'dragging their feet' on the illegal migrants issue and rejected their affidavits on steps taken to check influx of illegal Bangladesh nationals into the north-eastern states through the porous Indo-Bangla border. The issue of illegal migrants does not essentially come up for discussion in summits except the issue of stopping fake currency and human trafficking to India. India is generous enough to extend its help to Bangladesh but equally sensitive to the issue of illegal migrants as it directly affects its national security.

The porous border between India and Nepal has created problems that have adversely affected the relations between the two neighbouring countries. India faces major issue of smuggling, women trafficking, crime and easy transition for terrorists. A tight-knit network of informal traders is exploiting a vacuum of law enforcement in southern Nepal to generate significant operating capital for the Pakistani militant group Lashkar-e-Taiba.[22] The arrest of Yasin Bhatkal, the brain behind the Indian Mujahideen, has alerted the Indian Government of the primacy of national security in the India-Nepal border. Often, the porous border between India-Nepal with the absence of an extradition treaty with has complicated the issue further. There are serious concerns on Nepal in India as it works as a source of drugs, counterfeit currency, and many a times used as a transition by the jihadi elements who perpetrate acts of terrorism. Reportedly, the Pakistan intelligence agency, the ISI is exploiting the vulnerability of the India-Nepal border to pump in fake currency, arms, drugs and terrorist elements into India. A stable Nepal with a government and constitution is of utmost importance for India as it poses a major threat to India's national security.

The geopolitical location of Afghanistan is very crucial to India for its economic growth and stability but at the same time it also poses serious security problems for India. President Ghani's interest in engaging Pakistan to provide political space for the Taliban in the existing framework has come as a big surprise to India and India would not want to see a extremist group like Taliban in power sharing or in any other capacity in the mainstream politics as it only aggravates its security concerns in Kashmir. Apart from this, India also has speculation of what would be the political condition of Afghanistan after the planned withdrawal of the United States. Even though India wants to play a very positive role in Afghanistan, Pakistan would virtually become uneasy and start inflicting India through asymmetric ways. A *Talibanized* Afghanistan is certainly not in the interest of India. India would rather want to engage with Afghanistan and realize its energy requirements by utilizing Afghan territory with cooperation. There are always possibilities of Pakistan influencing the radical elements in Afghanistan to fight against India and this is a grave national security issue for India.

In the present scenario, Sri Lanka seems to be in transition as the new regime of Maithripala Sirisena has taken the centre stage. The major concern in the post-LTTE era has been the rising influence of China in Sri Lanka and its adverse effects on India. There are scholarly works stating that going too close to China was the detrimental factor in the defeat of Rajapaksa. It is due to this particular factor, the new government seems to be guarded in embracing China compared to what it was in 2014. There are some real concerns of fishermen from Tamil Nadu but there is a hope that it would be solved in the course of time. Sri Lanka has shown signs of interest in better cooperation with India in recent times. The issue of Tamils in Sri Lanka is also an important factor for India, but it is sagacious for India not to interfere in the internal matter of Sri Lanka. The gravest security concern for India continues to be China's presence in Sri Lanka and India is certainly looking to balance it by going closer to Sri Lanka.

Bhutan and Maldives do not pose a major security threat to India but India would only wish that both of them grow in democratic path. Maldives is going through political instability and it has major issues to handle such as rising sea water level and safety of its citizens. Maldives also needs to check the radicalization of its society as not acting at the appropriate time would probably turn it into a grave situation and there would not be an option to return to normalcy.

Conclusion

It is certainly not an easy issue for India to govern herself in the geopolitical conditions of South Asia. The national security of India concerns need to be prioritized. The case of Land Border Agreement between Bangladesh and India can be taken as a good example of how to resolve issues of grave concern with bold decisions. What one never saw as a possibility could happen with the political will in a span of one year of the new government in office. This proves time and again that with the ability to influence the others positively and take the counterparts into confidence, most of the national security issues can be resolved. There would be certain irritants in every scheme of things like that of Pakistan, but the best way to deal with Pakistan is to ignore it and take the other South Asian neighbours into confidence. India seems to be also learning to treat countries with different size of geography, resources and political conditions equally with that of bigger nations or great powers. This in itself is a positive move in terms of addressing some of the core national security problems. One would also be reminded that after finding relative or permanent solutions to external threats to national security, there is no guarantee that internal security issue would not haunt India. A fine balance of managing national security concerns considering both internal and external conditions would allow India to grow geopolitically, geo-economically and geo-strategically. Remembering Leon Megginsons quote that 'it is not the strongest or the most intelligent who will survive but those who can best manage change.' India needs to constantly remind herself and behave appropriately to take South Asia along with it in growth, peace and prosperity.

NOTES

1. A. Baldwin (1979), "Power Analysis and World Politics: New Trends versus Old Tendencies," *World Politics*, 31(2).
2. R. Bernstein (2003), "Foreign Views of US Darken after September 11", [Online: web] Accessed 12 June, 2015, [Online: web] Accessed 19 September 2015 URL: http://www.nytimes.com/2003/09/11/world/two-years-later-world-opinion-foreign-views-of-us-darken-after-sept-11.html
3. J.H. Morgenthau (1954), *Politics among Nations: The Struggle for Power and Peace*, University of Chicago Press, Chicago.
4. H.E. Carr (1946), *The Twenty Years' Crisis, 1919-1939: An introduction to the Study of International Relations*, Harper and Row, New York.
5. M. Bhasin (2008), "India's Role in South Asia: Perceived Hegemony or Reluctant Leadership?" *Indian Foreign Affairs Journal*, 3: 2.
6. E. Roche (2013), "Manmohan Singh at UN: Pakistan should dismantle terror machinery", [Online: web] Accessed 10 March 2015,URL: http://www.livemint.com/Politics/7yL41ezE4OSUhp4gAMKJZN/Manmohan-Singh-says-Pakistan-must-not-aid-terrorism-agains.html
7. J. Jacob (2015), "In Bangladesh, PM Modi accuses Pakistan of promoting terrorism", [Online: web] Accessed 20 June 2015, URL:http://www.hindustantimes.com/india-news/in-dhaka-pm-modi-accuses-pakistan-of-creating-nuisance-promoting-terrorism/article1-1356202.aspx
8. A.S. Narang, and Parimila Srivastava (2001), *Terrorism: The Global Perspective*, Kanishka Publishing, New Delhi.
9. C. Fair (2011), "The Militant Challenge in Pakistan," *Asia Policy*, 11:121-122.
10. C. Fair (2013), "Insights from a Database of Lashkar-e-Taiba and Hizb-ul-Mujahideen Militants", *The Journal of Strategic Studies*, 37:2:259–290.
11. Country Reports on Terrorism, United States Department of State Publication Bureau of Counterterrorism, (2014), [Online: web] Accessed 12 June 2015,URL: http://www.state.gov/documents/organization/239631.pdf
12. Bangladesh Assessment in South Asia Terrorism Portal (SATP), [Online: web] Accessed12 June 2015,UURL: http://www.satp.org/satporgtp/countries/bangladesh/index.htm
13. A. Behera (2011), "Deradicalisation in Bangladesh: Challenges Ahead," *Journal of Defence Studies*, 5:2:138.146.
14. M. Notezai (2014), "Interview: The India-Pakistan Water Dispute, Can the decades-long tensions over access to diminishing water resources ever be solved?", [Online: web] Accessed

10 June 2015, URL:http://thediplomat.com/2014/11/interview-the-india-pakistan-water-dispute/

15. P. Grover (2014), "Water: new 'core issue' in India-Pak ties?", [Online: web] Accessed 22 June 2015, URL:http://www.hindustantimes.com/chandigarh/water-new-core-issue-in-india-pak-ties/article1-1222917.aspx
16. M. Notezai (2014), "Interview: The India-Pakistan Water Dispute, Can the decades-long tensions over access to diminishing water resources ever be solved?", [Online: web] Accessed 22 December 2015, URL:http://thediplomat.com/2014/11/interview-the-india-pakistan-water-dispute/
17. Water Security for India: The External Dynamics" (2010), IDSA Task force report, IDSA, New Delhi.
18. H. Habib (2015), "Mamata relents on Teesta deal, LBA,", [Online: web] Accessed 10 March 2015, URL:http://www.thehindu.com/news/international/mamata-assures-hasina-of-resolving-teesta-issue/article6919815.ece
19. "Water Security for India: The External Dynamics" (2010), IDSA Task force report, IDSA, New Delhi.
20. Ram Mashru (2014), "India's Worsening Water Crisis", [Online: web] Accessed 12 June 2015, URL:http://thediplomat.com/2014/04/indias-worsening-water-crisis/
21. B. Chellaney (2013), "Neighbours leave India high and dry for its water supply,", [Online: web] Accessed 12 June 2015,URL: http://www.thenational.ae/thenationalconversation/comment/neighbours-leave-india-high-and-dry-for-its-water-supply
22. J. Miklian (2009), "Illicit Trading in Nepal: Fueling South Asian Terrorism," International Peace Research Institute.

20

Phenomenon of ISIS and Threat to India

Narender Kumar

Introduction

The ideological roots of Islamic State of Iraq and Syria emerge from Doctrine of Wahhabism that states that "One Ruler, One Authority, One Mosque". This is being interpreted as one Caliphate for all Muslim of the word. Therefore, to achieve Caliphate conquer the people and force them to submission. Those who resist be killed. Wahhabism argue that all Muslims must individually pledge their allegiance to a single Muslim leader (Caliph). Those who would not conform to this view should be killed, their wives and daughters violated, and their possessions confiscated. The list of detractors meriting death include the Shiite, Sufis, other Muslim denominations, and all those whom Abd al-Wahhab did not consider to be Muslim at all.[1] ISIS believe strict return to the purity of first ancestors known as Salafist (*Salaf al-Salih*). It was Sayyid Qutb an Egyptian thinker who was responsible to provide a direct bridge from the thought and heritage of Abd al-Wahhab and his predecessors to a new generation of jihadist militants, leading up to al-Qaeda and ISIS.[2]

The landmark events that changed the geopolitics of the world were Soviet occupation of Afghanistan, Iraq's Invasion by US and 9/11 attack by Al-Qaeda on World Trade Centre. Since then the world has not been the same again. Ray of hope was brought by Arab Spring that was perceived as an opportunity for ushering in an era of democratization of West Asia and liberation from autocratic regimes. Instead of creating smooth transition from autocratic regimes to a self-rule, Arab Spring threw up more instability and experiment seems to have gone horribly wrong. It created more instability that led to vacuum of governance and anarchy. Non-state actors thrive in an unstable environment. That marked the beginning of power struggle between states and non-state actors.

In the Arab world the extremists got massive support since it was perceived that so called soldiers of Islam are fighting infidels and especially Shias. The war that unfolded was considered a war between Sunni Arab versus Shiite Iran. But no one knew that this war ultimately will bring global powers on opposing sides. The conflict is now between Western Allies led by US against Iran, Syria and Russia. On other side it is a war between Sunni Arab countries led by Saudi Arabia versus Shite Iran and Bashar Al Assad of Syria.

Geopolitical Twist

Rise of ISIS as a state in Syria and Iraq is not an accident but a fact born out of instability and vacuum of governance in West Asia. Post Saddam Hussein the Ba'ath Party was reduced to splinter groups with sphere of influence restricted to Northern Iraq. The political divide between Shias and Sunnis in Iraq was so deep that led to Sunni insurgency but was quickly subdued by Iraqi forces with the help of US in 2008. Russian and Iranian backed Bashar Al Assad's autocratic regime where 12% Alawite (Shia) were ruling the majority Sunni population through an iron fist. In the same strategic space, there are multiple conflicts taking place. There is conventional war between states, sub conventional war being fought by non-state actors and state sponsored non-state actors and regulars fighting irregulars. Nature of warfare ranges from hybrid, electronic, proxy, air campaign, net centric, information and even psychological warfare. At the other end of the spectrum there is a war for survival by close to 12 million people displaced from their ancestral land.

Each stakeholder is fighting its own war to pursue their respective strategic objectives. US is in the war to ensure that Russians are evicted from their last two bases in Mediterranean (Tartus and Latakia) and at the same time to ensure that Iranian proxies are defeated. Saudi Arabia, Qatar and Jordan are fighting to defeat Shias and establishment of Sunni state in Syria and Iraq. Turkey has issues with Assad and ethnic Kurdish inhabitants of Iraq, Syria and Turkey. Creation of Kurdistan would ultimately impact territorial integrity of Turkey as well as Iran. On Kurdish issue even Shite Iran and Sunni Turkey are on the same page. Turkey and US are NATO allies but when it comes to the issue of Kurdistan they both are on different page. US and Russia both support Kurdistan, US support Kurdistan as leverage against Iran and Syria. Russia support Kurds as leverage against Turkey. Looking at the twisted geopolitical landscape, one thing is evident that most of the stakeholders are in it to capitalize the chaos. More than the fight against the ISIS the war is now to increase and expand their sphere of influence and territory. That is resulting into one of the biggest human tragedy after the holocaust.

Phenomenon of ISIS

ISIS burst on the world stage in 2014 when it swept towns after towns in Syria and Iraq. It had passive support from Sunni world and thrived on sale of oil through oil mafia. ISIS found willing business partners from Turkey and Europe and oil was smuggled through Turkey and even through Syria and Kurdish held territory. ISIS established Islamic state with its capital at Raqqa and controlled territory equal to Great Britain with a population of approximately 9 million. In Iraq, ISIS controlled almost 40% territory but has now shrank to 17%. Three major cities have been reclaimed from ISIS (Tikrit, Ramadi and Fallujah). In Syria ISIS has already lost almost 20% territories. Syrian Democratic Forces (SDF) with the support of Turkey and US are closing on to Raqqa to retake it. Loss of so called capital of ISIS will practically mark beginning of an end of ISIS rule in Syria and Iraq. Chances of ISIS consolidating its positions in Iraq and Syria are slim given the exodus of its cadres and economic strangulation by US led alliance and Russia. Islamic State has been forced to cut salaries of its fighters by 50% in Syria due to "exceptional circumstances" as air strikes continue to target its revenue streams. There are signs of revolt within the rank and file and exodus of cadres from the frontline is a regular affair.[3]

It is estimated that ISIS has 27,000 foreign jihadists from 86 countries, more than half of them from the Middle East and North Africa.[4] The reach of ISIS and its appeal is in its extraordinary skill in using the internet and social media[5] as a propaganda to attract the youth world over. It has created a facade that Caliphate will usher in golden era of ancestral period.

ISIS has its foot prints in North Africa. Tunisia and Libya are emerging as the epicentre of ISIS activities. Sirte is Raqqa of Africa and Adjabiyah oil fields in Sirte are now under the control of ISIS. Objective is to spread the Caliphate to North Africa known as Maghreb Wilayet. ISIS has sold the dreams that it will erase the artificial boundaries created by Western power during 100 years of colonization of Arab where they carved out nations based on their sphere of influence. Thus Syria and Iraq as separate nations do not exist and were created to divide the Muslim and subjugate them for centuries. Creation of Israel in Arab heartland is an injustice to the Arab and is being portrayed as insult of Arab pride. Western powers have appointed un-Islamic regimes that are corrupt tyrannical and needs to be removed. The invasion of Afghanistan and Iraq was being seen as an aggression on Islam. Therefore ISIS has sold the ideology that it will establish a pure Islamic state with Pan Arab nationality.

ISIS has two separate identities, Islamic State a symbol of rise of Caliphate as central authority and ISIS as terror organization. Collectively Global community may be able to eliminate or destroy the Islamic State, but what is more dangerous is ISIS as a terror organization. It has global reach, autonomous and can act and is mostly self-radicalized. The ISIS militants chose their targets, create autonomous terror modules and acquire subversive material from the host countries itself. That is proving a bit of problem, because they are educated, techno savvy and home grown. The radicals thrive on creation of false sense of duty to Islam and an idealism of being in service to God/*Allah*.

ISIS has proved that no nation is beyond their reach. Attacks in Paris, Bangladesh, Iraq, Medina, Istanbul, Belgium, Orlando, Kazakhstan, Egypt, Tunisia, Yemen list is endless. The attack ranges from suicide bombings to shooting of innocent citizens. It has created sense of insecurity and an environment that appears to be a clash of civilizations. The terrorists have exploited Islamic sentiments and have created hatred among the various faiths. The world seems to be divided vertically. The biggest threat is to the millions of refugees who are stateless and stand abandoned by the world community. Unfortunately Arab nations led by Saudi Arabia and Turkey who extended support to ISIS initially, have refused to accept refugees from Iraq and Syria. The threat is not only from terrorists but from mass relocation of population and destruction of life support system that would make rehabilitation much bigger challenge.

Threat to India

India faces prospects of instability due to threat from ISIS. It will be a costly mistake to assume that Indian Muslim youth is unlikely to be radicalized by

ISIS ideology. It may manifest in multiple manner be it demand for a Muslim state within Indian state, terror attacks by home grown or by proxies, forced mass relocation of minority community from Bangladesh, Pakistan or even from Afghanistan. Attack on Indian Diaspora in West Asia and North Africa, disruption of oil supply by attacking oil shipment, targeting of Indian strategic and economic interests across Africa and West Asia. Any of the above scenarios are detrimental to the fragile secular fabric of India. The impact will be on national security, economic empowerment, social and cultural harmony, security of life and property, political stability and India's position in comity of nations.

Corridors of Peril. ISIS and Al-Qaeda have made it known that Ghazwa-e-Hind (Battle for India) is their objective as part of expansion of Caliphate. ISIS and Al-Qaeda refer Hind and Khurasan to India, Pakistan, Afghanistan, and Bangladesh.[6] Corridors of peril that could threaten national security can resonate through multiple corridors. Therefore, it is important to examine some of these issues to come to a plausible response measures.

(a) **Radicalization of youth through social media and internet**: Today almost every youth has access to social media and internet. This is the most vulnerable corridor of peril to India. Because the impact is known when the problem mutates and reaches critical stage.

(b) **Maritime Corridor**: West Asia, African coast and Maldives are maritime neighbours of India. There are large numbers of youth from Maldives those who have joined ISIS. The onset of Wahhabism in the country can be linked to a rise of the ultraconservative ideology in the region. It has maritime security predicament, threat to island territories and the coastal areas such as Kerala that has one of the largest percentage of Muslim population in Indian peninsula. India's main stay of economy rest on maritime transportation and thus SLOCs are definitely threatened by the Jihadi terrorists. The Maldives is heading towards becoming a Wahhabist country, a puritanical interpretation of Islam only seen in Saudi Arabia and Qatar.[7] It certainly is not a good news for India.

(c) **Intrusion by ISIS through Pakistan**: Pakistan is an internal security challenge to India. Proxy war is not only limited to J&K but Pakistan has targeted entire India from Mumbai to Pathankot. It is obvious to assume that Pakistan would like other terror organisation to target India to initiate instability and uncontrolled chaos. Therefore, will it also give access to ISIS and Al-Qaeda to target India? The opinion of the author is that Pakistan is known to be irrational but not stupid enough to give launch pad to ISIS and Al-Qaeda to operate in a similar manner as LeT and other terror organisations from Pakistani soil. Because Pakistan is aware that allowing ISIS to establish foot hold in POK or Punjab would be suicidal and whatever is left of Pakistan will also go up in flames. Thus possibility of ISIS operating from Pakistan is a remote. But Inter-Services Intelligence would like ISIS and Al-Qaeda or their proxies to cause instability in India through other corridors such as Bangladesh, Nepal or even maritime route.

(d) **Corridor of Peril from Bangladesh**: Bangladesh lends itself to be a pivot for ISIS and Al-Qaeda to gain access to South Asia and India in particular. Jamaat-e-Islami has deep roots in Bangladesh and has Jihadi tilt. Bangladesh is known to have the foot prints ISIS sympathisers, Al-Qaeda, Hizb-ut-Tahrir, Lashkar-e-Taiba and JMB (Jamaatul Mujahideen Bangladesh).[8] ISIS is aware that Bangladesh is a soft state with huge vulnerable population that can be radicalised and used as a frontline foot soldiers for pursuance of objectives of expanding the foot prints in South Asia. Even the role of ISI of Pakistan in past was established to destabilise Bangladesh and also use Bangladesh as a launch pad to initiate terror attacks and spread of fake currency in India. Such a move does not directly affect Pakistan and blow back of ISIS/Al-Qaeda impact will be on Bangladesh for which Pakistan has scanty respect. It is a corridor that has support and sympathizers on both sides of the borders and is poorly managed by state and Central government agencies. Another significant aspect is that as per MHA reports, approximately 5.2 million persons from Bangladesh have legally settled in India, 3.1 million of which in West Bengal. There are also roughly 20 million illegal immigrants in India, many registered as voters, facilitating uninterrupted inflow of militants and clamouring for a lenient approach towards Bangladeshi militants.

(e) **Poverty and Unemployment**: There is a sense of deprivation and subjugation among the Muslim youth. Lack of education, poverty and unemployment is attributed by some subversive elements as a deliberate act of discrimination that in reality is completely untrue. The conflict between moderate and hardliner is causing divide among the youth, as a result radicals have managed to draw huge following. Wahhabism is spreading fast in Kerala, West Bengal, parts of Uttar Pradesh and J&K. At the same time sphere of influence of Sufi Islam is shrinking and that is not a good sign for India. Since Sufi Islam is adaptation of religion with the Indian culture.

Impact on Internal Security of India

Threat to Internal Security. ISIS will not march through the international borders like Alexander's Army and attack India. The tool it has used till now is to attack the minds of vulnerable population and create a psychological space among the potential cadres. Second is to occupy public space by articulation and initiating the debate of creation of "One Ruler, One Authority, One Mosque". And lastly to use terror and violence as a tool to make their presence felt. The threat from ISIS or radicals is real and it will be a costly mistake to live in denial. The impacts on Internal Security are as under:-

(a) Threat to secular, democratic and pluralistic culture of India.

(b) **Threat to Indian Diaspora in West Asia**: India has close to 6 million Indians working in West Asia and North Africa. They remit close to $75 billion per year. Inimical forces and anti-immigration groups would be keen to manipulate and trigger exodus in collusion with ISIS and Al-Qaeda to compromise long term interests of India. There is a need to carefully deliberate and analyse how and who will get benefited by such a move. The enormity of the crisis will have bearing on future prospects for employment and investment in Gulf region and North Africa since India's dependence on energy requirement from GCC is irreplaceable and West Asia and North Africa continue to remain the largest source of employment of skilled and unskilled work force.[9]

(c) Polarisation and internal instability. Terror can lead to polarisation, persecution and communal tension. People will become prisoner in their own home.

(d) Terrorism will impact security of life and property.

(e) States with larger Muslim population could see major turbulence.

(f) Insecure environment will cause economic meltdown and economic growth can be stunted.

(g) It will also divert focus from preparation to deal with the conventional threat, since security forces will get sucked in to deal with internal security predicament.

Response Mechanism

There is a need to build consensus among all nations to collectively fight against ISIS and its proxies across the globe. But at the same time regional cooperation also needs to be created so as to have a sacrosanct policy. Use of radical organisations as strategic assets is a mistake and the nations those who lend support, sanction be imposed under the aegis of UN. Coming closer home following measure needs to be taken:

(a) **Oppose and not appease:** The tendency to appease the radicals for vote bank for political gain must be stopped. A message be sent that those who do not respect the law of the land or go against the law will be brought to book. So far India has succumbed to the aspiration of regional state parties and unfortunately subversive elements have gone scot free including Kashmiri separatists and scholars such as Dr Zakir Naik.

(b) **Jihadis are not invincible:** Therefore, a diligent strategy is must. Security Forces and intelligence agencies should enhance their operational capabilities to prevent acts of terror and subversion.

(c) **Collective and Inclusive Response Regionally:** Fight ISIS state by encircling it economically, politically, ideologically and militarily. India, Sri Lanka, Bangladesh, Nepal and Maldives should develop a common understanding and mechanism to share intelligence and operational details to curb and track the suspects regionally. Collective efforts can also ensure drying up of flow of money and regional network.

(d) Unhinge ISIS from their pivots and areas of influence.

(e) Curb drug trafficking and flow of black money.

(f) Prevent smuggling of weapons and war like stores within the nation and across trans-border.

(g) Awareness campaign to expose the real motive of ISIS and their leadership and the hardship being faced by millions of innocent civilian across Asia and refugees in Europe.

(h) Censorship of Jihadi propaganda on social media and internet.

(j) Monitoring of suspects technologically.

Conclusion

John Gray writes that though ISIS claims to be reviving a traditional Islamic system of government, but the jihadist group is a very modern proposition.

When you see the leader of ISIS, Abu Bakr Al-Baghdadi, in Mosul announcing the creation of a caliphate—an Islamic state ruled by a religious leader—it's easy to think that what you're watching is a march back into the past.[10] But the dichotomy is that ISIS is modern in many ways, it shares more with this modern revolutionary tradition than any ancient form of Islamic rule. The tools used by ISIS to expand its sphere of influence are very modern that includes social media, internet, state of the art of weapon system psychological and information warfare. Thus it is a façade to lure foot soldiers and gain legitimacy of rule by self-serving caliph and leaders.

India is very much a potential target of ISIS and Al-Qaeda. Most vulnerable corridor of peril is through Bangladesh. But threat from the homegrown terror organizations such as SIMI a well-known sympathizer cannot be discounted. The threat does exist as much from the Indian radical youth as much as from those who have illegally migrated from outside. The threat from the ISIS is far more potent since it is stateless, it can infiltrate through virtual world and it has no borders.

The role of intelligence agencies has assumed significance. India needs to build capabilities to monitor cyber space and remain ahead of radicals by employment of technology. Special Forces need to be highly trained and mobile to reach and neutralize threat if it manifest in any manner with speed. Regional states also need to train and equip their own state police to handle crisis till Special Forces arrive on the scene. Delay in responding by security forces in Bangladesh allowed terrorists to do bloodshed for almost 12 hours. They had time to kill selectively each individual by slitting their throats. Whereas the massacre was being done in one of the most secure area of the Capital city Dhaka. Delay in response will embolden the terrorist to undertake more such attacks. Thus a rapid response and rapid neutralization is must.

There is a need to also strengthen legal provision. Today the law is ambiguous with regard to how to deal with those who joins ISIS and then return back to India? Should they be made persona non-grata and not allowed entry or should they be charged for waging war and act of terror in a foreign land? Thus the response required is not only military but even nonmilitary.

NOTES

1. Alastair Crooke, You Can't Understand ISIS If You Don't Know the History of Wahhabism in Saudi Arabia, Huffington Post, August 27, 2014.
2. Jim Muir, Islamic State group: The full story, BBC News, March 11, 2016.

3. Narender Kumar, Defeat of ISIS Will Not Mark The Death of Violent Salafist Extremism, CLAWS Web, June 08, 2016.
4. Jim Muir, Islamic State group: The full story, *BBC News*, 11 March 2016.
5. Jim, N
6. Narender Kumar, Is Terror Attack In Dhaka Part of Ghazwa-E-Hind? *Indian Defence Review*, Jul 05, 2016.
7. Paul Antonopoulos, The Next Wahhabist State? Maldives and Saudi Arabia Sign Religious Deal, https://www.almasdarnews.com/article/19201/ Nov, 19, 2015.
8. Narender n vi.
9. Narender Kumar, Indian Diaspora In The Middle East An Exposed Flank: Need Response Mechanism, Geopolitics.
10. "A Point of View: Isis and what it means to be modern," *BBC News*, July 11, 2014.

Index